Co-preaching

Dissertationes Theologicae Holmienses

Dissertations from Stockholm School of Theology

www.ehs.se/dth

Editors:

Joel Halldorf

Jonas Ideström

Thomas Kazen

Samuel Rubenson

Susanne Wigorts Yngvesson

No. 2

Frida Mannerfelt

Co-preaching

The Practice of Preaching in Digital Culture
and Spaces

Enskilda Högskolan Stockholm
2023

Co-preaching: The Practice of Preaching in Digital Culture and Spaces

Dissertation presented at Stockholm School of Theology, University College Stockholm, to be publicly examined in Room 219/220 at Åkeshovsvägen 29, Bromma, June 16 2023, at 13:00, for the degree of Doctor of Philosophy in Theology (Practical Theology with Church History: Practical Theology). The examination will be held in English.

Faculty examiner: Theo Pleizier, Assistant professor of Practical Theology, Protestant Theological University in Groningen.

Supervisor: Sune Fahlgren, Associate Professor of Practical theology, University College Stockholm.

Assistant supervisor: Peter M. Phillips, Director of the Centre for Digital Theology, Spurgeons College, London.

Abstract

The purposes of this article-based thesis are to explore and understand preaching as a practice in general, and the practice of preaching in digital culture and spaces in particular. Informed by the practice theory of Theodore Schatzki, it presents the results of a cross-case analysis of four different case studies of the practice of preaching in digital culture and spaces in Swedish protestant churches. Based on the analysis, I argue that the deep relationality of the practice of preaching involves not just humans and texts but also material arrangements and that this feature often is amplified in digital culture and spaces. While there were examples of a decrease, overall, there was an increase in interaction, negotiation, and interdependency. In light of this, I contend that the practice of preaching in digital culture and spaces is characterized by co-preaching. Moreover, I argue that some of the implications of co-preaching are the enabling and encouragement of dialogue, imagination, and the priestly function of the priesthood of all believers, but also an increased vulnerability for the co-preachers involved.

Med-predikan: Predikans praktik i digital kultur och digitala rum

Akademisk avhandling presenterad vid Teologiska högskolan Stockholm, Enskilda Högskolan Stockholm, för disputation i sal 219/220, Åkeshovsvägen 29, Bromma, 16 juni kl. 13.00, för graden teologie doktor i praktisk teologi med kyrkohistoria med inriktning mot praktisk teologi. Disputationen kommer att äga rum på engelska.

Opponent: Theo Pleizier, biträdande professor i praktisk teologi, protestantiska teologiska universitetet i Groningen, Holland.

Handledare: Sune Fahlgren, docent i kyrkovetenskap, Enskilda högskolan Stockholm.

Bitr. handledare: Peter M. Phillips, direktor vid centret för digital teologi, Spurgeons College, London.

Sammanfattning

Syftena med den här sammanläggningsavhandlingen är att utforska och förstå predikan som praktik, med särskilt avseende på predikans praktik i digital kultur och digitala rum. Med utgångspunkt i Theodore Schatzkis praxisteori analyseras resultaten från fyra fallstudier av predikans praktik i digital kultur och digitala rum i svenska protestantiska kyrkor. På grundval av analysen argumenterar jag för att den relationella kvalitet som utmärker predikan som praktik, och som inbegriper inte bara människor och texter utan även materiella arrangemang av olika slag, ofta förstärks i digital kultur och digitala rum. Överlag ökade interaktion, förhandling och ömsesidigt beroende, även om det under vissa förutsättningar också kunde leda till det motsatta. I ljuset av detta hävdar jag att predikans praktik i digital kultur och digitala rum präglas av med-predikan. Vidare argumenterar jag för att med-predikan möjliggör och uppmuntrar dialog, uppfinningsförmåga och det allmänna prästadömets prästerliga funktion samtidigt som den leder till ökad utsatthet för med-predikanterna.

Enskilda Högskolan Stockholm

Enskilda Högskolan Stockholm erbjuder utbildningsprogram i mänskliga rättigheter och demokrati, samt i teologi/religionsvetenskap. Högskolan grundades 1993 genom en sammanslagning av utbildningsinstitutioner med rötter från 1866. Teologiska högskolan Stockholm är den samlade benämningen på högskolans båda teologiska avdelningar, Religionsvetenskap och teologi, samt Östkyrkliga studier. Högskolan för mänskliga rättigheter och demokrati är benämningen på utbildningarna i mänskliga rättigheter och demokrati. Forskarutbildningen i Praktisk teologi med kyrkohistoria bedrivs inom inriktningarna Praktisk teologi respektive Kyrkohistoria. Utbildningen fokuserar på den kristna kyrkans utveckling och den kristna trons praktiska gestaltning, i ett konstruktivt samspel mellan empiriska metoder och teori. Utbildningen innefattar bland annat historiska, hermeneutiska, filosofiska, teologiska, sociologiska och etnologiska perspektiv.

University College Stockholm

University College Stockholm offers programmes in Human Rights and Democracy and in Theology / Religious Studies. The university college was founded in 1993 through a merger of educational institutions with roots dating back to 1866. Stockholm School of Theology is the common designation for the two theological departments: Religious Studies and Theology, and Eastern Christian Studies. Stockholm School of Human Rights and Democracy is the designation for the programmes in Human Rights and Democracy. The doctoral programme in Practical Theology with Church History provides specialisations in Practical Theology and Church History respectively. It focuses on the development of the Christian church and practical expressions of Christian faith, in a constructive interplay between empirical methods and theory. The programme includes historical, hermeneutical, philosophical, theological, sociological, and ethnological perspectives.

ISBN: 978-91-88906-21-2

Page and cover design by Carl Johan Berglund. Typeset in EB Garamond. Printed by BoD – Books on Demand, Norderstedt, Germany.

Stockholm School of Theology
University College Stockholm
Åkeshovsvägen 29, 168 39 Bromma, Sweden
www.ehs.se

List of Articles

This thesis is based on the following papers, which are referred to in the text with letters A–D.

A. Mannerfelt, Frida, "From the Amphitheatre to Twitter: Cultivating Secondary Orality in Dialogue with Female Preachers," *Studies in World Christianity* 28:1 (2022), 6–27. DOI: 10.3366/swc.2022.0368.
B. Mannerfelt, Frida, "Closer Away from Us: Theologizing in the Intersection Between Ascension Theology and Experiences of a Pandemic and Digital Space." Accepted for publication in *Words in a Time of Crisis. Conference Proceedings Societas Homiletica 2020* (Berlin: LIT Verlag, forthcoming).
C. Mannerfelt, Frida, "Listening to Listeners in a Digital Culture: The Practice of Listening to Digitally-mediated Sermons." Accepted for publication in *Homiletic* 48:1 (2023).
D. Mannerfelt, Frida, "Co-Preaching: The Effects of Religious Digital Creatives' Engagement in the Preaching Event," *Religions* 13: 1135. DOI: 10.3390/rel13121135.

Acknowledgments

In this thesis, I argue that the practice of preaching is characterized by cooperation, interdependency, interaction, and deep relationality. If I were to describe the thesis writing process, I would probably use the same words. The text that the reader will encounter in the following pages is the result of my interaction with generous and brilliant people that have acted as *co-authors* in the true Bakhtinian sense of the word—as Others with distinct voices of their own who, in texts, conversations, and comments, contributed to the version of the text printed on these pages. I delight in having the opportunity to express my profound gratitude to you.

First and foremost, my supervisor, Sune Fahlgren. I could not have wished for a wiser, kinder, and more supportive Doktorvater to guide me through the Ph.D. process. Second, my assistant supervisor Pete Phillips whose generosity with time, knowledge, and space has been tremendous. Thank you, Pete, for continuously challenging me to make my own voice heard.

In addition, several brilliant scholars have critically and constructively engaged with various parts of the text in different stages of the process. Anna Minara Ciardi, Clara Nystrand, Daniel Strömner, Joel Halldorf, Jonas Ideström, Linn Sæbø Rystad, Magdalena Dziaczkowska, Mia Lövheim, Simon Hallonsten, Tone Stangeland Kaufman, the members of the research school *Church and Society* at University College Stockholm, and the members of the Higher Seminar for Church and Mission Studies at Lund University—thank you all for helping me to straighten out my arguments, thoughts, and texts. I also gratefully acknowledge my amazing line editors, Josh Mackin and David Michaels, who ensured these arguments and thoughts were expressed in impeccable English. Any remaining issues are my own fault and responsibility.

I would also like to extend my gratitude to the people involved in the *Congregational Change in Times of Crisis* project: the diocese of Växjö and Stiftelsen Berndt Gustafssons minnesfond för kyrko- och religionssociologi for financing parts of the project, and to the senior scholars Erik Sidenvall, Jonas Ideström, and

Ulrik Josefsson. I have learned so much from our conversations and your approaches to research.

Likewise, I am deeply grateful to the persons involved in the *Church in Digital Space* project. It was indeed a pleasure to work with you, Sara Garpe, Jonas Ideström, Simon Hallonsten, Tone Stangeland Kaufman, and in particular, my excellent and ever-so-humorous co-researcher Rikard Roitto.

I am also forever indebted to all the preachers and co-preachers who trusted me enough to let me into your everyday preaching and listening practices. I hope I have done your reflections and practices justice.

Throughout my Ph.D. years, I have been blessed with the opportunity to collaborate with skilled and knowledgeable scholars who have traveled the academic road before me. Alexander Maurits, Hege Irene Markussen, Johanna Gustafsson Lundberg, Jonas Kurlberg, Karin Rubenson, Ryszard Bobrowicz, Sara Fransson, Stephan Borgehammar, and Teresia Derlén—thank you! Your advice and encouragement have been invaluable.

I have also been graced with Ph.D. sisters and brothers in Stockholm and Lund: Anki Falk, Björn Asserhed, Clara Nystrand, Daniel Strömner, Ellen Vingren, Elin Lockneus, Erik Bergman, Hanna Alenius, Joel Appelfeldt, Katharina Hallqvist Pernilla Myrelid, Simon Hallonsten, and Torbjörn Toll—we have rejoiced in each other's achievements, shared frustrations and memes, and I am so thankful that I got to share this experience with you.

Furthermore, I gladly acknowledge the scholarly communities that have been critical conversation partners for this thesis: the *Nordic Network for Theology and Practice*, *Societas Homiletica,* the *Nordic homiletical network* (Nordiska homiletiska nätverket), and the *Global Network for Digital Theology* community. The vibrant conversations in these networks have been inspiring and helpful as I developed the arguments for this thesis.

There have also been three church communities that have been vital throughout the Ph.D.: The congregation in Barkåkra who, over the ten years I served as their pastor, taught me the practice of co-preaching; The congregations in Kvistofta parish, where I have received spiritual nourishment as a sermon listener and, occasionally, been allowed to preach when the longing for the pulpit grew too big; The congregation in Rosengårdskyrkan who welcomed me and showed me the strength and beauty of what it means to be part of a Uniting Church in Sweden.

Finally, I would like to thank my family and friends for all your support and patience. In particular, my dear friends Hedvig Krona and Katarina Drott, whose abilities to listen and discern are unparalleled.

And last, but in no way least: Petter, my husband and the co-author to the story of my life. Your gift to me is courage, and without your unwavering faith in my ability to do anything (as long as I get coffee), this thesis would never have made it to the printing press. I dedicate this book to you.

Rydebäck in April 2023

Frida Mannerfelt

Contents

1. Introduction: Problem Statement and Disposition of the Thesis

[Interviewer]: What about preaching, then? Is it the same kind of difference?

[Interviewee 1]: No, I do not think so. Because—well, how do I say this [laughs]—it might be for better or worse, but I mean—in reality, the sermon is one-way communication, at least in our church. Not like a conversation in a cell group when you can twist and turn different angles, like in a Bible study. But it is one person who is preaching, and the others sit quietly, no matter if it is digital or not. That is why I do not think that there is a difference.

[Interviewee 2]: No, I can't entirely agree. The difference is definitely smaller, but I would not say it is insignificant. Actually, in my experience, there has been a difference. And that is probably connected to singing because the element of worship songs that comes after the sermon is often when you reflect on the sermon and respond in singing or prayer.

During the spring of 2021—one year into the COVID-19 pandemic and many churches' transition to digital worship—I interviewed twenty-nine active members and twenty-one employees of Swedish Protestant congregations about their experiences of congregational life during the pandemic. These church members' narratives were similar to results from other inquiries. Generally, members thought there were major differences between online and onsite worship. When asked about these differences, they frequently mentioned that changes in practices like singing hymns and worship songs, prayers of intercession, and the Eucharist caused them to feel a loss of community and a decreased sense of participation.[1] Some of them even cried at the thought of what was being lost.

---

[1] See the overview of research on digitally-mediated worship during the pandemic in Frida Mannerfelt, "Old and New Habits: The Transition to Digitally-Mediated Worship in Four Swedish Free Church Denominations during COVID-19," in *Svensk frikyrklighet i pandemin: En studie av församlingen i corona och corona i församlingen*, eds. Ulrik Josefsson and Magnus Wahlström (Forskningsrapporter från Institutet för Pentekostala Studier, No. 9, 2022), 90–92.

But the element of the sermon was never mentioned. When I asked about the sermon specifically, the interviewees often laughed and answered along similar lines to the opening quote above from group F3. First, those I interviewed would state that, unlike all the other elements of the worship service, the practice of listening to a sermon remained the same in the digitally-mediated worship experience. Then someone would add that perhaps there was a slight difference after all, and try to describe what the difference might consist of. In the case of group F3 above, the interviewee was unsure of what the difference was but figured that it "probably" had something to do with being able to respond to the sermon afterward through worship songs.

The struggles of the interviewees were reflected in the homiletical discussions occurring at the time among pastors and academics. Some homileticians claimed that digitally-mediated preaching was nothing new since "the components that constitute a sermon are unaffected by the medium."[2] Others found that it is "different from conventional preaching [...] and has its own techno-theological reasoning and unique ways."[3] Among the homileticians who thought there was a difference, there were varied opinions on what these differences consisted of and what the proper response to these differences should be. Was digitally-mediated preaching something problematic that "preachers have a responsibility to stir up a kind of holy discontent with"[4]—or an opportunity that "aids the spreading of the gospel by providing us the conduit to preach beyond the walls of our confined sanctuary"?[5] Was there even "something to be learned from this for 'analog' services as well"?[6]

These were also my questions as I set out on this research project. What does it mean for the practice of preaching when it takes place in a culture saturated by digital technology, or when it is mediated through digital media? Or, posed as the

---

[2] Lisa S. Kraske Cressman, "B.C. and A.C: Preaching and Worship Before COVID and After COVID," *Journal for Preachers* 44:2 (2021), 46–47.

[3] Sunggu A. Yang, "The Word Digitized: A Techno-Theological Reflection on Online Preaching and Its Types," *Homiletic* 46:1 (2021), 75.

[4] Michael P. Knowles, "E-word? McLuhan, Baudrillard, and Verisimilitude in Preaching," *Religions* 13:1131 (2022), 13.

[5] Rob O'Lynn, "Digital Jazz, Man: The Intersection of Preaching and Media in the Era of COVID (and After)," in *Academy of Homiletics 2021 Workgroup Papers and Abstracts* (2021), 5–15.

[6] Katrin Kusmiertz, *Predigt als Unterhaltung 2.0*, 2020, https://www.liturgik.unibe.ch [Accessed 1 September 2022]. (My translation.)

overarching research question that guides the inquiry of this thesis: *What charac-terizes the practice of preaching in digital culture and spaces?*

In a sense, the answer to this question depends on the stance one takes on an-other question: How do digital technologies and media relate to the church? As I have shown elsewhere, many homileticians have tended to take the view that digi-tal culture is something that resides *outside* of the church: a feature of contempo-rary society, akin to secularization or pluralism, that the preacher has to address, yes, but not something the preachers and their listeners make use of (or perhaps *should* make use of) in their everyday life or as part of their religious practices.[7]

However, the conclusion that grew out of the theological and empirical work in the various projects that contributed to this thesis is that digital technologies and media are not just *outside* the church. On the contrary, they are *inside* the church in the most profound way; they are an indissoluble part of everyday life and, thus, the practice of preaching, too—both online and onsite.

My conclusion is in no way unique. Scholars who engage in empirical studies of digital culture and spaces tend towards a view of interconnection and interac-tion, frequently describing the relationship between humans and digital technol-ogy with words that designate an intimate and indissoluble connection: "embed-ded," "intertwined," "entangled," and "ingrafted."[8] They point out that digital media has become so integrated with everyday life that it has become almost invis-ible to us—that is, unless the technology stops working.

These scholars also often underline that because of this embeddedness, you cannot understand social life unless you take media into account. For example, the

---

[7] Frida Mannerfelt, "Preaching Online: Developing Homiletics for a Digital Culture," in *Ox-ford Handbook of Digital Theology*, eds. Alexander Chow, Jonas Kurlberg, and Peter M. Phillips (Oxford: Oxford University Publications, forthcoming).

[8] Nicholas Couldry, *Listening Beyond the Echoes: Media Ethics, and Agency in an Uncertain World* (London: Paradigm, 2006), 47; Heidi Campbell and Ruth Tsuria, "Introduction to the Study of Digital Religion," in *Digital Religion: Understanding Religious Practice in Digital Me-dia*, eds. Heidi Campbell and Ruth Tsuria, 2nd ed. (London & New York: Routledge), 7; Chris-tine Hine, *Ethnography for the Internet: Embedded, Embodied and Everyday* (London: Blooms-bury, 2015), Helene Snee et al., "Digital Methods as Mainstream Methodology: An Introduc-tion," in *Digital Methods for Social Science: An Interdisciplinary Guide to Research Innovation*, eds. Helene Snee et al. (London: Palgrave Macmillan, 2016), 3; Eve Stirling, "'I'm Always on Fa-cebook!': Exploring Facebook as a Mainstream Research Tool and Ethnographic Site," in *Digital Methods for Social Science: An Interdisciplinary Guide to Research Innovation*, eds. Helene Snee et al. (London: Palgrave Macmillan, 2016), 62; Sarah Pink et al., *Digital Ethnography: Principles and Practice* (London: Sage, 2016), 10. Nick Couldry and Andreas Hepp, *The Mediated Con-struction of Reality* (Cambridge: Polity Press, 2017), 19.

communication and media theorists Nick Couldry and Andreas Hepp argue in their *The Mediated Construction of Reality* for the importance of including media theory in social theory. According to Couldry and Hepp, social worlds are created and recreated through practices, particularly communicative ones, and media plays an increasingly prominent part in institutionalizing and materializing these communicative practices. We now live in a stage of "deep mediatization," where "the role of 'media' in the social construction of reality becomes not just partial, or even pervasive, but 'deep': that is, crucial to the elements and processes *out of which* the social world and its everyday reality are formed and sustained."[9] Similarly, the sociologist Mia Lövheim has pointed out that we cannot understand contemporary religion without studying how it is mediated.[10]

In this thesis, I argue that this is also the case for the practice of preaching. We cannot understand that practice nor the collective social world of the church community—which preaching contributes to shaping and reshaping—unless we pay attention to media. However, this pertains not only to media but *all* kinds of materiality. In fact, one basic argument in this thesis is that material arrangements always function as "co-preachers" in the preaching event, be it onsite or online. So far, this is something that homileticians have paid very little attention to. Digital media serves both as a reminder and an example of how this entanglement of humans and material entities play out. As I have shown in the four case studies presented in the enclosed articles, the materiality of digital media interacts with and thus affects what preachers preach about, how they preach, who gets to preach, how the listeners listen, and what they hear.

There are many methodological and analytical lenses one could use to describe and analyze the nature of the complex entanglement between humans and materiality. In this thesis, I have chosen to lean heavily on the practice theory of the philosopher Theodore Schatzki. According to Schatzki, social life consists of practices bundled together in nexuses. Every practice consists of two components: *human agency* (bundled together in chains of activities) and *material entities* (commonly bundled together in material arrangements). However, a third and crucial component is needed to make a practice a practice: it must be *organized*. Practices are not just random activities with random material arrangements. They are

---

[9] Couldry and Hepp 2017, 15–33. Quotation p. 213.
[10] Mia Lövheim, "Comments by Mia Lövheim," *Religion and Society: Advances in Research* 7 (2016), 97–115.

instead directed toward an end. People act for the sake of desired ways of being and/or the expectation of a certain state of affairs.[11]

This insight leads to another basic argument of this thesis: We cannot understand the practice of preaching—onsite or online—unless we pay attention to its organization. In the case of the practice of preaching, this organization reflects to a large extent the theology and, in particular, the ecclesiology of the preacher and the church community. However, as I will show in Chapters 2 and 3, this organizational dimension, and its attendant theological and ecclesiological commitments, tends to slip into the background in both homiletical research and research on digitally-mediated religious practices. My work will attempt to hold all this in view, using the example of digitally-mediated preaching to also highlight what these overlooked dimensions might say about the practice of preaching *itself*—and to suggest what we might discover when we allow these dimensions into our analysis.

In this thesis, I will also make claims about the practice of preaching in digital culture and spaces. In the field of homiletics, very little attention has been paid to the influence of digital media on the practice of preaching. While the digital transition during the COVID-19 pandemic increased scholarly interest significantly, studies analyzing the characteristics and consequences of digital mediation of the preaching event, or discussions about the theological meaning of digital culture for preaching, have been scarce.

According to Schatzki, change, broadly defined, occurs when one or more components in a certain bundle of practice changes. Change can grow over time as the interaction between human activity, material arrangements, and organization gradually shifts. Change might also happen abruptly. Such abrupt changes most commonly come about in relation to technological advancement. When new material arrangements are introduced, humans interact with them differently, and new ways of organizing practices arise.[12]

In this thesis, I use Schatzki's theory to analyze four case studies describing the practice of preaching in digital culture and spaces to see how and in what ways the practice of preaching is shaped in relation to the new material arrangements of digital media. The cross-analysis leads to the third basic argument: The digital media

---

[11] Theodore Schatzki, *The Timespace of Human Activity: On Performance, Society, and History as Indeterminate Teleological Events* (Plymouth: Lexington Books, 2010), 111–115;

Theodore Schatzki, *Social Change in a Material World* (London & New York: Routledge 2019), 30–32.

[12] Schatzki 2019, 78–116.

material arrangements, as described in these four examples, tend to amplify the features of collaboration, interaction, deep relationality, and interdependence—and, therefore, the practice of preaching in digital culture and spaces is characterized by *co-preaching*.

In sum, the purpose of this thesis is twofold. First, I aim to use the example of digitally-mediated preaching to explore and understand the characteristics of the practice of preaching generally. Second, my goal is to contribute to basic research on the practice of preaching in digital culture and spaces. These aims converge in the overarching research question about what characterizes the practice of preaching in digital culture and spaces.

The thesis is structured as follows. Chapter 2 introduces the three sub-questions I use to better answer the overarching research question posited above, and outlines the key concepts and theories that undergird my analysis. In Chapter 3, I will present the scholarly conversations this thesis contributes to by reviewing relevant previous research. Chapter 4 engages with methodology and methods. In Chapter 5, I answer the research question through a cross-case analysis of the four case studies presented in the articles and discuss the implications of co-preaching.

And lastly, a word on what I think this text represents. As I have discussed elsewhere, drawing on the work of Paul Ricoeur, meaning is always created *after* we configure events into narratives. As events unfold, their meaning and relation to each other are not clear. Indeed, meaning tends to change over time, as new events give depth and new meaning to past events.[13]

Additionally, as Schatzki would say: activity events are always indeterminate until the very moment they actually take place. Determination is not random, but it does not come beforehand, either. Schatzki rejects the idea that actions are controlled by preconceived goals.[14] It is, for example, not possible to say that I determined exactly beforehand what the precise goal of this thesis was, then mechanically decided on the means to do it (research design), then went out and did it, then wrote everything down, and voilà: the thesis!

Instead, according to Schatzki, the act is only determined when the subject actually performs it—that is, the performance itself is part of the process of determination. I might have an idea of what I want to achieve with a given activity, but what the goal *actually* is, is not determined until I do it. It might be the same goal I consciously set out to achieve, but more often, I discover the goal through the

---

[13] Frida Mannerfelt and Alexander Maurits, *Kallelse och erkännande: Berättelser från de första prästvigda kvinnorna i Svenska kyrkan* (Stockholm & Göteborg: Makadam, 2021), 54–62.
[14] Schatzki 2010, 175–179.

very performance of the activity in question. Parts of the goal may also stay unconscious or unknown to me.[15] I might set out to open my computer to write a section, say, in the chapter on theory—but it is not until I do it that I can say that I opened my computer to write a theory chapter. There is always the chance that the activity of opening the computer instead becomes determined by some other goal, like answering an e-mail or scrolling through my feed.

And so this text, the one you are reading now, represents my understanding of what I have done and how it all holds together meaningfully *at this particular point in time*. It does not mean that this meaning was evident as the events unfolded, or that the meaning of the events is entirely clear even now. On the contrary, my understanding can and will change—not least as readers engage in the practices commonly referred to as "academic conversation." I look forward to it.

---

[15] Schatzki 2010, 181–186.

2. On Theory and Key Concepts

In this chapter, I will present the theoretical framework and research questions this thesis aims to answer. This is done through a presentation of the key concepts that appear throughout these research questions, and which are used throughout the four articles.

In the introduction, I stated that the purpose of the thesis is: 1) to use the example of digitally-mediated preaching to explore and understand the characteristics of the practice of preaching generally; and 2) to contribute to basic research on the practice of preaching in digital culture and spaces. Moreover, I stated that the overarching research question is: *What characterizes the practice of preaching in digital culture and spaces?* Since this is a rather broad question, I have chosen three sub-questions that, taken together, will supply enough of the puzzle pieces needed to provide an answer to the overarching question.

The three sub-questions are: a) *What characterizes the practices in the digitally-mediated preaching event?*; b) *What kinds of authority are practiced by preachers in digital culture and spaces?*; and c) *Which theological features are salient in the practice of preaching in digital culture and spaces?*

In these research questions, six key concepts are introduced: "the practice of preaching" (2.1), "digital culture and spaces" (2.2), "digitally-mediated" (2.3), "the preaching event" (2.4), "authority" (2.5), and "salient theological features" (2.6). In the following, I will discuss them individually while also relating them to the theoretical framework that holds this thesis together: practice theory.

2.1 The Practice of Preaching

The concept of "the practice of preaching" is central to this thesis. It situates the thesis in a research paradigm and provides the theoretical framework and the unit of analysis.

In this section, I will do two things. First (2.1.1), I will describe how and why I chose to situate this study within this research paradigm. Second (2.1.2), I will give a short overview of the characteristics of practice theories and motivate the choice of practice theory developed by Theodore Schatzki.

2.1.1 On Situating the Study in the Paradigm of Practice Theory

The concept of "the practice of preaching" is a crucial part of the subtitle of the thesis. However, this was not always the case. Over time, the subtitle changed several times, a development that illustrates my engagement with various positions in the field of homiletics, and which ultimately helps explain my motivation for ultimately landing on the one I've chosen. Let me explain.

My first attempt at a subtitle was "Preaching in a digital age." I began to write my own version of the section found in almost every Swedish thesis on homiletics: a definition of the concept of "preaching." There is no lack of definitions to choose from. One that is commonly used in teaching is practical theologian Alf Härdelin's definition in the handbook on practical theology *Kyrkans liv* (1993): a sermon is: 1) an orally delivered speech; 2) that occurs as part of a worship service; that is 3) an exegesis of (or at least takes as its starting point) a Bible text; and therefore 4) has a specific content: the proclamation of the Gospel or the Word of God; and 5) is delivered by an ordained person or someone who holds a particular office in a church or congregation.[1]

However, as Härdelin points out, the components of this definition are always questioned as soon as you take a closer look at how preaching has actually been practiced in the history of Christianity. Preaching can also be a text (as with the sermon collections that were mass produced in the 19th century), take place outside of the Sunday service (see the mendicant friars of the Middle Ages, who traveled around to preach in public places), take a starting point in something else other than the Bible text and resemble a lecture (like the catechetical sermons of the church fathers that aimed to explain a specific doctrine), and be held by someone who is not ordained (as in the revival movements of the 19th century).[2]

Furthermore, this deconstruction of definitions seems to be a particularly pressing problem (or possibility) when it came to preaching in a digital age. One of the few other homiletical works to engage with digital mediation, the theologian Casey Thornburgh Sigmon's *Engaging the Gadfly: Homilecclesiology for a Digital Age* (2017), argued convincingly that digital media almost always disrupts everything we take for granted in our usual definitions of a sermon: where, when, and

---

[1] Alf Härdelin, "Homiletik: Ordet och orden," in *Kyrkans liv: Introduktion till kyrkovetenskapen*, ed. Stephan Borgehammar, 2nd revised edition, (Stockholm: Verbum, 1993), 204.

[2] Härdelin 1993, 204–206.

by whom.[3] I realized it would be better to avoid defining preaching as a single, stable phenomenon.

The second attempt at a subtitle included the word practice—"The practice of preaching in a digital age"—by which I intended to make an analogy to the concept of "liturgical practices," in the ordinary sense of the phrase as something that is done. This allowed me to build from the ground up. If preaching is something you do, it follows that you can study and describe how it is done. Instead of coming to the field with a preconceived definition, I could observe and ask preachers what they were doing, and create my own definition based on what they said and what I saw. In addition, "the practice of preaching" was already an established concept in the field of homiletics, used by, for example, the renowned homiletician Paul Scott Wilson in his *The Practice of Preaching* (1995 and revised edition in 2007).[4]

However, as homiletician Linn Sæbø Rystad has pointed out, while the concept "the practice of preaching" is commonly used, it is seldom defined. Furthermore, the practices described are usually the preacher's. Drawing on Marlene Ringgaard Lorensen, Rystad advocates for using the framework of practice theory to more fruitfully explore preaching as a practice.[5]

Rystad is part of a group of Scandinavian homileticians who have begun exploring practice theoretical and socio-material perspectives, pointing out how productive they are in the homiletical conversation and research. Not least, these approaches draw attention to an often overlooked dimension of the preaching event: materiality.[6] Their interest in practice theories reflects the general Scandinavian field of practical theology.

---

[3] Casey T. Sigmon, *Engaging the Gadfly: Homilecclesiology for a Digital Age*, Ph.D. Thesis (Vanderbilt: Vanderbilt University, 2017), 4.

[4] Paul S. Wilson, *The Practice of Preaching* (Nashville, Tennessee: Abingdon, 2007).

[5] Linn S. Rystad, *Overestimated and Underestimated: A Case Study of the Practice of Preaching for Children with an Emphasis on Children's Role as Listeners*, Ph.D. Thesis (Oslo: MF Norwegian School of Theology, 2020), 19.

[6] See, for example, Marlene R. Lorensen, *Dialogical Preaching: Bakhtin, Otherness and Homiletics* (Göttingen: Vanderhoeck & Ruprecht, 2014), 21–40 who argues for a pragmatic and practice-oriented approach to preaching; Tone Stangeland Kaufman and H.O. Mosdøl, "More than Words: A Multimodal and Socio-material Approach to Understanding the Preaching Event," in *Preaching Promises within the Paradoxes of Life,* eds. Johan Cilliers and Len Hansen (Stellenbosch: African Sun Media, 2018), 123–132; Rystad 2020; and, *Forkynnelse for barn og voksne,* ed. Tone Stangeland Kaufman (Oslo: Prismet bok, 2021) that includes sociocultural and practice theoretical perspectives.

Following this turn to practice in Scandinavia, interest in practice theory has increased during the last decade.[7] For example, two of the most recent handbooks in the field testify to the fact that practice theories have come to dominate the methodological discussion. *The Wiley Blackwell Companion to Theology and Qualitative Research* (2022), edited by practical theologians Pete Ward and Knut Tveitereid, gathers a wide range of practical theological scholars and covers a variety of approaches. In her analysis of the contributions written by Scandinavian scholars, practical theologian Tone Stangeland Kaufman points to how practice theory and socio-material and sociocultural sensibilities are dominant within the practical theologians' examples of their research.[8] *Practice, Practice Theory and Theology: Scandinavian and German Perspectives* (2022), edited by practical theologians Kristin Helboe Johansen and Ulla Schmidt, grew out of the Nordic network for theology and practice and presents—as the title suggests—practice theoretical approaches to the field of practical theology. In other words, the choice to situate the study in a practice theory paradigm is to join state-of-the-art practical theology and homiletics as it is currently conceived in Scandinavia.

However, there are additional reasons for situating the thesis in a practice theory paradigm. Method handbooks on digital ethnography repeatedly acknowledge that practice theory and socio-material perspectives benefit empirical studies of digital media and technology. On the one hand, these perspectives draw attention to media and materiality and how human practice is always intertwined with material entities, which play a significant role in how the practices are carried out. On the other hand, they also enable a non-media-centric approach that does not overemphasize the significance of media. Furthermore, they aid in describing and understanding processes of change.[9]

---

[7] Ryszard Bobrowicz and Frida Mannerfelt, "Between *Kuriaké* and *Ekklesia*: Tracing a Shift in Scandinavian Practical Theology Based on Handbooks," *Svensk teologisk kvartalskrift* 97:1 (2021), 47–68; Tone Stangeland Kaufman and Lars Johan Danbolt, "Hva er praktisk teologi?," *Nordic Journal of Practical Theology* 37:1 (2020), 6–18.

[8] Tone Stangeland Kaufman, "The Scandinavian Contribution?," keynote lecture at the symposium and book release of *The Wiley Blackwell Companion to Theology and Qualitative Research*, Oslo, 6 December 2022.

[9] Jeremy Knox, "What's the Matter with MOOCs? Socio-material Methodologies for Educational Research," in *Digital Methods for Social Science: An Interdisciplinary Guide to Research Innovation*, eds. Helene Snee et al. (London: Palgrave Macmillan, 2016), 178–179; Pink et al. 2016, 41–58. See also Alessandro Caliandro, who argues that researchers ought to focus on "the practices through which Internet users and digital devices structure social formations around a focal object." Alessandro Caliandro, "Digital Methods for Ethnography: Analytical Concepts for

In sum, I eventually opted for the subtitle "The Practice of Preaching in a Digital Age"—to situate the thesis in a practice theoretical paradigm using the version of practice theory introduced by Theodore Schatzki.

2.1.2 On Choosing Theodore Schatzki's Practice Theory

As Schatzki points out, practice theory is not a singular approach but rather a family of theoretical approaches that see practices as central to their account of social phenomena and social life.[10] Commonly referred to in introductory chapters to practice theory in various fields of research is Andreas Reckwitz's mapping of social theory,[11] in which he places practice theory under the umbrella of cultural theories. In contrast to social theories of rationalism (that sees the individual as the basic unit of the social) and norm-orientation (which focuses on social relations and intersubjective coordination structures), cultural theories take an interest in social orders as the driving forces behind an actor's actions: what assumptions about how the world is ordered enables them to act?[12]

According to Reckwitz, the core idea of culturalist theorizing is that the patterns that structure action in the world result from common orders of meaning, cues, symbols, and knowledge that together function as rules for action. Culture theories can be sorted into three categories: *mentalism,* which finds this shared order "inside" the human mind and considers culture a cognitive phenomenon; *textualism,* which locates the shared order "outside" in discourses, the structure of meaning, text, and communication; and finally *practice theory,* which claims that shared knowledge is practical knowledge, and thus focuses on situations of everyday life. Reckwitz, who positions himself in the third category, thinks that the other two categories of cultural theory overcomplicate and overintellectualize the social world and tend to forget the importance of everyday actions.[13]

The above list of core contents and preoccupations under the umbrella of practice theory point to slight differences between various approaches in the field.

Ethnographers Exploring Social Media Environments," *Journal of Contemporary Ethnography* 47:5 (2018), 551–578.

[10] Schatzki 2019, 3.

[11] See for example Christian Bueger and Frank Gadinger, *International Practice Theory: New Perspectives* (Basingstoke: Palgrave Pivot, 2014), 14–19; Kristine Helboe Johansen and Ulla Schmidt, *Practice, Practice Theory and Theology. Scandinavian and German Perspectives* (Berlin: De Gruyter, 2022), 4–5.

[12] Andreas Reckwitz, "Toward a Theory of Social Practices: A Development in Culturalist Theorizing," *European Journal of Social Theory* 5:2 (2002), 243–263.

[13] Reckwitz 2002, 243–263.

Still, all accounts see practices as the basic unit of social life and emphasize social life's relational and provisional character, including in the formation of meaning and identity. Social life is composed of streams of practices carried out by multiple individuals, collectively and constantly produced and re-produced. Furthermore, these practices are organized; they are acted out in relation to interests and powers. The practices are also intimately connected to materialities like bodies, objects, artifacts, and technology.[14]

While they share these common traits, specific theories under the practice theory umbrella can still vary greatly. As international relation scholars Christian Bueger and Frank Gadinger point out, the different historiographies of practice theory perfectly illustrate this. Some find their roots in Georg Wilhelm Friedrich Hegel, whose thinking was developed further and given new form by Karl Marx and his concept of object activity, which was then further elaborated on by American pragmatist philosophers like Charles Pierce and John Dewey. Some build on Aristotle's concepts of *techne* and *phronesis* in combination with R.G. Collingwood, Hanna Arendt, Hans Georg Gadamer, and Jürgen Habermas. Others, like Schatzki, draw on Martin Heidegger and Ludwig Wittgenstein.[15]

Yet another historiography is found in Elisabeth Tveito Johnsen and Geir Afdal's overview of different sociocultural and socio-material theories used to study "pools of practices." Tveito Johnsen and Afdal show that Lev Vygotsky was also an important influence on the development of practice theory. Notably, they describe how Vygotsky emphasized the mediated character of reality. According to Vygotsky, reality is always mediated by culturally and socially developed tools and signs that tend to become invisible and taken for granted.[16] This observation points to a feature of practice theory that is not often mentioned in the "lists" of its characteristic features, but which is part-and-parcel of the theory's emphasis on materiality: the idea that *being* itself is mediated.

For this thesis, I have chosen to work within the practice theory of Theodore Schatzki. There are four reasons for that decision. First, Linn S. Rystad has proven how fruitful Schatzki's theories can be in the study of homiletics, not least his concept of "teleoaffective structures."

---

[14] Davide Nicolini, *Practice Theory, Work, and Organization: An Introduction* (Oxford: Oxford University Press, 2012), 1–12; Bueger and Gadinger 2014, 18–20; Schatzki 2019, 3–4.

[15] Bueger and Gadinger 2014, 11–12.

[16] Elisabeth Tveito Johnsen and Geir Afdal, "Practice Theory in Empirical Practical Theological Research: The Scientific Contribution of LETRA," *Nordic Journal of Practical Theology* 37:2 (2020), 58–76.

Second, Schatzki draws on Heidegger, enabling connections to discussions in media theory, since scholars interested in philosophy often build on Heidegger's perspectives on technology.[17] Schatzki's insistence on the indissoluble intertwinement between human activity and material entities is at the core of his understanding of the social as "bundles of practices" and is itself derived from Heidegger. Schatzki also specifically discusses digitally-mediated phenomena in relation to practice theory in his recent book *Social Change in a Material World* (2019).

But what does it mean for Schatzki to say that the social comprises myriads of practices bundled together? For him, a practice generally consists of a sequence of human activity ("chain of events") and material entities grouped together ("material arrangements").[18] Moreover, he defines practices as "open-ended, spatial-temporal sets of organized doings and sayings."[19] The concept of "organized" points to the idea that practices are never just random events; they are always performed to an end. Practices can be organized through "rules" (explicit instructions), "pools of understanding" (for example, the general understanding that footnotes are required in an academic text, as well as the practical understanding of how to make them and which information to include), and "teleoaffective structures" (ways of being and states of affairs).[20] The concept of "spatial-temporal" refers to the fact that practices always "take place in and over time and at particular locations or along particular lines in space," not least because the activity in question is *human* activity and thus involves the materiality of the human body, which is always located.[21] Finally, the concept of "open-ended." As mentioned in my introduction, Schatzki insists that, even if practices are organized, they are never predetermined. No chain of activity is bound to happen, even if given the right conditions. The act is only determined when the person performs it through the performance itself.[22]

The third reason for choosing a Schatzkian framework is his view on the agency of materiality. As, for example, theorist and historian of digital culture, Grant D. Bollmer, points out, one of the inherent problems in a materialist

---

[17] Amanda Lagerkvist, *Existential Media: A Media Theory of the Limit Situation* (Oxford: Oxford University Press, 2022), 65–66.

[18] Schatzki 2019, 26–49. Quotation p. 44.

[19] Schatzki 2019, 28.

[20] Schatzki 2019, 30–32.

[21] Schatzki 2019, 29–30.

[22] Theodore Schatzki, "Sayings, Texts and Discursive Formation," in *The Nexus of Practices: Connections, Constellations, Practitioners*, eds. Allison Hui, Theodore Schatzki, and Elizabeth Shove (London & New York: Routledge, 2017), 175–179; Schatzki 2019, 28–29.

approach to digital media is the tendency to reductive technological determinism.[23] An example is Bible scholar Peter M. Phillips's discussion on the "digital being," in which he criticizes media theorist Amanda Lagerkvist for giving too much
agency to technology in her Heidegger-inspired understanding of media. According to Phillips, such views can lead to analyses in which "human agents of technological change are either ignored or seen as servants or victims of technology."[24] In
Phillips' view, there are several problems with tech determinism: it blames technology for human faults, it "others" technology and turns technology into an
agent separate from human agency, and it creates a separation between human material embodiment and the materiality of technology, which in turn creates an es-
sentialism around human materialism as something unique and non-technologi-
cal. Drawing on practical theologian Elaine Graham's reading of Heidegger, Phillips argues for a view of technology that draws attention to human agency.[25]

Bollmer also argues for such a balanced view. Neither technological nor cultural determinism is productive:

> One cannot understand the world as if it is entirely shaped by one kind of agency—be
> it technological will or human will—even though many popular arguments about the
> effects of technology simply vacillate between these two positions. Our technologies do
> things, and they often do them in ways not intended by humans, with techniques invis-
> ible to human observation or beyond human control. We have to take the objects
> around us on their own terms, not merely as things that perpetuate human will.[26]

Schatzki's reading of Heidegger picks up the same strand of thinking as Graham's.
This reading emphasizes interdependence and thus moves away from the tendency
to give technology too much agency. Through his concept of "bundles of practices," Schatzski acknowledges *both* the intimate entanglement of human agency
with material arrangements *and* emphasizes the precedence and importance of human agency. Due to Schatzki's account of the interaction between human activity
and material arrangements in the process of change, I find him an excellent choice
as a practice theorist who steers clear of the tendency toward technological and
cultural determination, which I wish to avoid in my analysis, as well.

The fourth reason for choosing Schatzki's version of practice theory is his insistence on the role of discourse in practice. As Schatzki points out, practice

---

[23] Grant D. Bollmer, *Theorizing Digital Cultures* (London: Sage, 2018), 25–26.

[24] Peter M. Phillips, "Digital Being," *Crucible: The Journal of Christian Social Ethics* (2023),
22–31.

[25] Phillips 2023, 22–31.

[26] Bollmer 2018, 25–26.

theorists tend to say very little about the role of language in the bundles of practice they analyze.[27] This poses a bit of a problem to homileticians, who study a practice that is supremely dependent on language and words. Schatzki, however, offers a robust understanding of language in his practice theory.

According to Schatzki, practices consist of both discursive and non-discursive components. In Schatzki's view, it is vital to distinguish between these two by refraining to place language and material arrangements in identical categories as the same kind of means of mediation. By making a distinction between them, you can uphold the importance of language—*and* get a more nuanced understanding of what action accomplishes. Furthermore, this distinction facilitates a greater exploration not only of how sayings and doings entangle and converge but, more importantly, how they sometimes diverge.[28] I would argue that Schatzki makes an important point here, not least as it relates to the concept of the "four voices of theology" in analyses of Christian religious practice, which distinguishes between the "espoused theology" of what practitioners say and the "operant theology" of what they do.[29]

Furthermore, Schatzki allows that, since practices are replete with sayings (he includes the act of writing in the concept of sayings since it is the use of language and the saying of things), they might need to be "approached through bodies of investigation and theory that are different from practice theory but compatible with its ontology."[30] Among the phenomena that might need such additional theories are the dissemination of knowledge, power and domination, experience, conversations, and the understanding and interpretation of texts and sayings[31]—in other words, the very phenomena that are crucially important to the practice of preaching. Therefore, the articles' four case studies use supplementary theories that function just as middle-range theories would in a monograph.

Philosopher Nancy Cartwright, drawing on the work of Peter Hedström and Lars Udéhn, defines middle-range theory as

> a clear, precise, and simple type of theory which can be used for partially explaining a range of different phenomena, but which makes no pretense of being able to explain all

---

[27] Schatzki 2017, 128.

[28] Schatzki 2017, 128–129.

[29] Helen Cameron et al., *Talking About God in Practice: Theological Actions Research and Practical Theology* (London: SCM Press, 2010), 39–60; Clare Watkins, *Disclosing Church: An Ecclesiology Learned from Conversations in Practice* (London & New York: Routledge, 2020).

[30] Schatzki 2017, 133.

[31] Schatzki 2017, 133.

social phenomena... It is a vision of sociological theory as a toolbox of semi-general theories, each adequate for explaining a limited range or type of phenomena.[32]

Following Cartwright's definition, I see a particular pragmatic dimension to choosing middle-range theories. Schatzski points out that this is the case for choosing all kinds of theories at all levels. Explanations always have a pragmatic dimension since the explanation doesn't just depend on the event itself but on who is explaining and to whom. The fact that I am a practical theologian and homiletician, discussing with other practical theologians and homileticians, will likely (but not necessarily) lead to a different explanation of a given event than that provided by an economist or sociologist. According to Schatzski, this is "an eradicable condition" of research.[33]

This choice of theories, both the theoretical paradigm and the middle-range theories in each article, has been guided by an equivalent pragmatic attitude: Which theories might be useful in explaining this particular phenomenon? Which theories are relevant, used, and discussed in the field, and how might I contribute to their development?

In sum, by settling for the concept of "the practice of preaching," my research connects to an established research paradigm in homiletics and practical theology. Through the choice of Schatzki's version of practice theory, I found a theory that has proven to be well-suited for studying the practice of preaching in digital culture and spaces.

2.2 Digital Culture and Spaces

Schatzki's version of practice theory calls for the need to consider where the practice in question is situated. In his book *The Site of the Social* (2002), Schatzki explores the ontological implications of practice theories, pointing to how they almost always adhere to "a site ontology" that emphasizes the situatedness of the social. Unlike individualist and contextualist approaches, site ontologies argue that the social is intrinsically and decisively rooted in the site where it takes place. Schatzki defines "social site" as "the site specific to human coexistence: the context, or wider expanse of phenomena, in and as part of which humans coexist."[34]

---

[32] Nancy Cartwright, "Middle-Range Theory: Without It What Could Anyone Do?," *Theoria: Revista de Teoria, Historia y Fundamentos de le Ciencia* 35:3 (2021), 270.

[33] Schatzki 2019, 121.

[34] Theodore Schatzki, *The Site of the Social: A Philosophical Account of the Constitution of Social Life and Change* (University Park, Pennsylvania: The Pennsylvania State University Press, 2002), 146–147.

Schatzki identifies four "forms of coexistence" or "forms of sociality," in which the three components of a bundle of practice—activities, material entities, and order—are woven together into an immense, shifting, and transmogrifying mesh in which they overlap, interweave, cohere, conflict, diverge, scatter, and enable as well as constrain each other."[35] The keyword here for Schatzki is "mesh." Since the social transpires through bundles of practices, and bundles always contain material entities, the social is indissolubly entangled in a particular site.

In this section, I will define how I understand the site where the practice under consideration in this thesis is situated: digital culture and spaces. Notably, the choice to pay particular attention to digital culture and spaces does not mean that I claim that other aspects of situatedness, such as church tradition or region, should be ignored. As, for example, Heidi Campbell has shown, situatedness in a particular religious tradition plays a significant role as communities negotiate their use and understanding of new media.[36] The choice to situate the practice of preaching in digital culture and spaces means that I have chosen to focus on this particular aspect of the situatedness of the practice of preaching.

2.2.1 Digital Culture

In the previous section, I described how the initial wording of my thesis subtitle changed over time to better illustrate positions in the field and account for my choices. The key concept of "Preaching" was not the only concept that changed over time, however. My second attempt at a subtitle, *The Practice of Preaching in a Digital Age*, still needed some tweaking. The concept "digital age" also proved somewhat unrefined. While being a popular expression used by, for example, the aforementioned Sigmon and the anthology *Missio Dei in a Digital Age*, there are two problems with it.

The first problem is whether we are still in a digital age. The project *Efter digitaliseringen* (After digitalization), funded by Riksbankens jubileumsfond, argues that we now live in a *post*-digital age, characterized by the presence of computers everywhere and nowhere, and a critique of digitality.[37] The second problem is that the concept is too imprecise. Historians often point out the difficulty of defining

---

[35] Schatzki 2002, 123–188. Quotation p. 157.

[36] Heidi Campbell, "How Religious Communities Negotiate New Media Religiously," in *Digital Religion, Social Media and Culture: Perspectives, Practices and Futures* eds. Pauline Hope Cheong et al. (New York: Peter Lang, 2012), 81–96.

[37] See, for example, Nina Wormbs, *Det digitalas materialitet* (Göteborg & Stockholm: Makadam, 2022), 9–10.

an era since historical periods are always a construction, in which certain events are bundled together after the fact and labeled as "the Patristic era," "17th century," or "Industrial revolution." If there is a Digital age, when did it start? And why should we define that period as Digital, not as Secular, Anthropocene, Pandemic, the 21st century, or something else?

However, the volume Mission Dei in a Digital Age offers an alternative concept: digital culture. In one of the contributions, theologian Katherine G. Schmidt makes a case for understanding digitality as a culture rather than an instrumentalist understanding of digitality as a tool. Schmidt argues this approach would be especially fruitful in ecclesial contexts since it allows for the use of the concept of "inculturation" ("the intimate transformation of authentic cultural values through their integration in Christianity and the insertion of Christianity in the various human cultures") to understand how churches might relate to digital phenomenon. As Schmidt puts it: "When one comes to understand digital platforms as part of a larger digital culture, one can then begin to analyze and critique the values and meanings being negotiated within it, as one would in any other culture." In addition, according to Schmidt, the concept draws attention to two features of contemporary society: to live in the global north is to live within digital culture, and digitality is not just a tool but entangled in social life.[38]

Furthermore, handbooks on digital ethnography also encourage the concept of culture as an important aspect of understanding digitality. For example, the author of *Ethnography for the Internet: Embedded, Embodied and Everyday*, sociologist Christine Hine emphasizes that the internet is not just part of daily practices; it is also a cultural object, something that we create narratives about that reflect expectations, hopes and fears.[39] Hence, I made a third attempt at a subtitle: "The practice of Preaching in digital culture."

But yet again, objections arose. The aforementioned Couldry and Hepp question the idea that there are waves of different kinds of media in which one medium dominates. They would rather speak of "deep mediatization," a radical increase in the use of different kinds of media.[40] In line with this thinking, would it not be misleading to speak of digital culture? Moreover, as Phillips has pointed out, if you

---

[38] Katherine G. Schmidt, "Digital Inculturation," in *Missio Dei in a Digital Age*, eds. Jonas Kurlberg and Peter M. Phillips (London: SCM Press, 2020), 23–35.

[39] Hine 2015, 11–12.

[40] Couldry and Hepp 2017, 34–56.

collapse technology into culture, you are at risk of interpreting everything in contemporary society as having something to do with media.[41]

A third objection is that talking about a digital culture is problematic. For example, in his Theorizing Digital Cultures, Bollmer argues that since the meaning of "digital culture" has changed over time, and contexts vary across the globe, it would be better to use the plural form "digital cultures."[42] Jonas Kurlberg makes a similar case in his introduction to Missio Dei in a Digital Age. Digital cultures are not static, and therefore it makes much better sense to talk about many cultures, not least because digital technology always interacts with local contexts and cultures and, as a consequence, varies around the globe.[43] In light of these three objections, would not "The practice of preaching in digital cultures," with an emphasis on the plural, be the better option for a subtitle?

Nevertheless, I decided to keep digital culture, singular, for two reasons. Firstly, it is an established concept, used in the same way as oral and textual culture—that is, as an overarching concept. Even Bollmer uses it, despite all his critiques, although he takes care to define it. According to Bollmer, digital culture consists of three elements: narratives about technology, the material infrastructures that shape communication, and human agency in relation to media. These three elements co-evolve over time.[44] This thesis adheres to that definition of digital culture. It sits well within Schatzki's understanding of the social as made up of material arrangements and human activity chains organized through, for example, narratives.

Secondly, a characteristic feature of digital technology is that it is global. Phillips points out that "the omnipresence of digital, its pervasive presence through most global cultures, means that it is affecting everyone at the same time."[45] Kurlberg makes the same argument, saying that while digitality is firmly grounded in the local context, it is at the same time also global, as smartphones shape our communications, identities, and the conditions we find ourselves in, no matter where we are in the world.[46] Or, as Schatzki would put it, the contemporary digital

---

[41] Peter M. Phillips, "Conclusion," in *Missio Dei in a Digital Age*, eds. Jonas Kurlberg and Peter M. Phillips (London: SCM Press, 2020), 263.

[42] Bollmer 2018, 19–20.

[43] Jonas Kurlberg, "Introduction," in *Missio Dei in a Digital Age*, eds. Jonas Kurlberg and Peter M. Phillips (London: SCM Press, 2020), 9–11.

[44] Bollmer 2018, 19–36.

[45] Phillips 2020, 259.

[46] Kurlberg 2020, 9–11.

landscape includes the same material arrangements that humans interact with, the same underlying technologies, no matter where they are across the globe.

Furthermore, digital culture is also global in relation to its cultural content. Andreas Reckwitz also emphasizes the tension between local and global features of digitality. In his book The Society of Singularities, he describes a shift from a society that promotes the general (a feature of Modernity's rationalization) towards a society that values the singular, particular, unique, and extraordinary. This shift is caused by a change in "two of the most powerful social engines": the economy and technology. According to Reckwitz, the technology made possible by the digital revolution promotes the idea of singular and distinct cultures. But at the same time as digitality fosters the cultivation of distinct subcultures, it also makes possible a global hyperculture, in which a person, phenomenon, or object from anywhere in the world might suddenly become valorized everywhere.[47]

In other words: one of the features of the material arrangements of digital technology is that it can create a culture with shared traits. Since digital culture is an established concept, and to acknowledge the feature of "something common" across different contexts, I decided to keep "The Practice of Preaching in Digital Culture" as a subtitle.

2.2.2 Digital Spaces

Almost immediately, yet new objections to the subtitle arose, however. As previously mentioned, Schatzki underscores the ways in which practices are radically situated in specific material arrangements. In other words, in Schatzki's opinion, "digital culture," despite my reasoning above, might nevertheless be a concept still too abstract to account for the multiplicity of situatedness.

This was also something I observed in my own work with article A. The first section of the article discusses how digital culture might be understood in light of developments pertaining to Walter Ong's concept of "secondary orality."[48] In my discussion of the drawbacks and problems with Ong's theory, one key criticism I

---

[47] Andreas Reckwitz, *The Society of Singularities* (Cambridge: Polity Press, 2020), 1–9.

[48] Walter J. Ong, *The Presence of the Word* (New Haven: Yale University Press, 1967) 22–35; Walter J. Ong, *Orality and Literacy: The Technologizing of the Word* (London: Methuen, 1982); 136–144; John Miles Foley, *Oral Tradition and the Internet: Pathways of the Mind* (Urbana, Chicago, and Springfield: University of Illinois Press, 2012); Lars Ole Sauerberg, "The Gutenberg Parenthesis: Print, Book and Cognition," *Orbis Litterarum* 64:2 (2009), 79–80; Tom Pettit "Media Dynamics and the Lessons of History: The Gutenberg Parenthesis as Restoration Topos," in *A Companion to New Media Dynamics*, eds. J. Hartley Burgess and A. Brund (Chichester: Wiley Blackwell, 2013), 53–72.

level is it is too abstract. While it might be a fruitful point of departure for discussion, the theory collapses as soon as it is applied to the complexity of real-life practices.[49] Through an analysis of historical case studies of female preachers' preaching practice throughout the church's history, I found that *if* you want to use the theory of secondary orality in relation to digital culture, it is crucial to pay special attention to the categories of space and bodies—in other words, the materiality and situatedness of the practices in question. I also found that the lens of secondary orality requires careful attention to the genre of communication, which, in the case of digital culture, is complex, to say the least, as there are many different kinds of media represented under the umbrella term "digital."

According to handbooks on digital ethnography, this multiplicity is characteristic of digital technology and media. There are not just multiple digital technology devices; there are multiple digital platforms and environments and multiple ways of interacting with hardware and software.[50] Multiplicity is also evident in the source material generated in my other research projects: digitally-mediated preaching can include anything from watching a pre-recorded short sermon on your mobile phone on your way home from work, to listening to a sermon podcast while driving in your car, or to displaying a livestreamed worship service on the TV in front of the couch—among others.

To account for this multiplicity of situatedness in relation to materiality, I added another concept to the subtitle: "The Practice of Preaching in Digital Culture and Spaces." Making the move to include "spaces" would also allow me to catch the tension between the common, expressed by the concept of "digital culture" in singular, and the diverse, expressed in the plural "digital spaces." Subsequently, the subtitle emerged at last: "The Practice of Preaching in Digital Culture and Spaces."

However, as the sociologist of religion, Tim Hutchings, discusses in his contribution to the anthology *Materiality and the Study of Religion: The stuff of the Sacred* (2017), if you want to argue that digital media is material, you need to be clear on how. In his chapter, Hutchings identifies two common ways of thinking about materiality in religion: "essentialist" (the material is the physical) and "binary" (the material is defined in contrast to something, often "belief"). However,

---

[49] Frida Mannerfelt, "From the Amphitheatre to Twitter: Cultivating Secondary Orality in Dialogue with Female Preachers," *Studies in World Christianity* 28:1 (2022), 7–13.

[50] See, for example, Taina Bucher and Anne Helmond, "The Affordances of Social Media Platforms," in *The SAGE Handbook of Social Media,* eds. Jean Burgess, Alice Marwick and Thomas Poell (Thousand Oaks: Sage Publications, 2017), 233–253.

neither works for someone who wants to study digital media since digital software is neither physical nor conceptual. It does not seem to be made of physical stuff, but it functions as materiality since it has properties and affordances that control what we can do with it. It seems to exist in between the material and immaterial. Because of this, digital media theorists often choose a "functionalist" approach and claim that "material" includes anything that acts like a physical object. But then again, you have to define your functionalist approach.[51]

What kind of spatiality digital environments offer is a much-debated question. For example, Schatzki prefers to speak of digital environments but underscores that "use of the term does not imply the existence [...] of what others have variously called 'cyber space' (e.g., Gibson 1984), 'virtual space,' (e.g., Flusser 2006), or 'digital space' (e.g., Chayko 2017)."[52] Schatzki is critical of both "digital space" and "topological space" concepts: of the first, because it entails an understanding that you enter a space that is its own world; and of the other, because it implies something new opens up where practices occur.

Schatzki thinks that it is enough to define the three categories of *material space* (three-dimensional spaces that are instituted by and occupied by material entities, for example, buildings), *represented space* (maps, globes, and blueprints), and something he—influenced by Heidegger—calls *existential space*, which is the spatiality of being-in-the-world. Existential space comes to be in the intersection between, on the one hand, the places and paths that are anchored in material space and, on the other, the experience of nearness and farness.[53] For example, right now, the coffee cup next to me is part of my existential space. I can interact with it as I write these words. In other words, according to Schatzki, there are no new digital spaces with separate virtual beings. Instead, when people engage in a digitally-mediated practice, it is real flesh and blood humans who use material and existential spaces. However, there is nevertheless a component unique to digital media:

> What is social theoretically noteworthy about this entire situation is simply that material setups have so evolved that relations that once were restricted to face-to-face interactions in single settings or to uncertain circuits of transportation have now been extended to face-to-face interactions that bridge settings at an indefinite range of physical distances from one another. One result, naturally, is that what is present or absent to whom

---

[51] Tim Hutchings, "Augmented Graves and Virtual Bibles: Digital Media and Material Religion," in *Materiality and the Study of Religion: The Stuff of the Sacred*, eds. Tim Hutchings and Joanne McKenzie (London & New York: Routledge, 2017), 85–99.

[52] Schatzki 2019, 20, 75, 185–192.

[53] Schatzki 2019, 75.

changes. But this is an alternation in the topography of power with corresponding changes in the lives of the people involved, not to the institution of topology. The only spaces involved here are material space, existential space, and represented space.[54]

In Schatzki's account, existential space has expanded through digital mediation as we are able to experience nearness over distance. I can interact not just with the coffee cup next to me but also with my Ph.D. supervisor, currently in Jordan, thousands of kilometers away from where I am seated.

I find Schatzki's critique of the concept of "digital space" valid. However, I do not use "digital space" as Schatzki understands it—to designate a world of its own cut off from the situatedness of social life. Rather, I use "digital space" in the sense of "the third space of digital religion."

According to religion and media scholars Giulia Evolvi and Maria Chiara Giorda, people's experiences of digital environments often do not fit into either the category of "space" (a larger environment, socially constructed and reproduced as a result of the interplay of different actors, through different practices, beliefs, and representations) nor the category of "place" (a significant and material portion of "space"). Instead, they find themselves in an environment between the abstract and construed and the concrete and material. According to Evolvi and Giorda, these spaces are increasingly crucial in negotiating religious meaning. Furthermore, since religious practices often involve materiality and "doing something with something," an indeterminate experience of some sort of in-between space often manifests itself as a reality for participants.[55]

Evolvi and Giorda argue that some scholars use the concept of "third space" to describe this notion of in-between, including the media study scholars Stewart Hoover and Nabil Echchaibi. In their recent book, *The Third Space of Digital Religion* (2023), Echchaibi and Hoover discuss the concept in relation to their research in the field of digital religion. They argue for an approach to digital religion akin to the approach in this thesis, which centers on practices instead of structures. Digitally-mediated religious practices must be examined on their own terms in their own locations rather than forced into the "usual" categories of religion, spirituality, media theory, cultural geography, etc. Drawing on sociocultural approaches and scholars like Henri LeFebvre, Judith Butler, and Tim Ingold,

---

[54] Schatzki 2019, 191.
[55] Giulia Evolvi and Maria Chiara Giorda, "Introduction: Islam, Space, and the Internet," *Journal of Religion, Media and Digital Culture* 12 (2021), 5–7.

Echchaibi and Hoover describe practices as tactical and iterative, embedded in meaning and affordances of social spaces negotiated in relation to technology.[56]

When they applied this practice-centered approach in their own research, they found that an "as-if-ness characterized the religious practices." The practitioners acted *as if* they were communities sharing experiences, *as if* they were partaking in public discourse, and *as if* there were a broad spectrum of listeners. The "as-if-ness" deepened and instantiated the significance of the practices and derived from an authentic participation in the practices in question.

The as-if-ness also pertained to space. The practices possessed a "located logic" that Echchaibi and Hoover call "the third spaces of digital religion." In their conceptualization of this third space, the authors draw on Ray Oldenburg, Edward Soja, and Homi Bhabha to describe digital spaces that are "fluid, conceptual, and imagined locations" and "articulated to lived material spaces as well as conceptual iterations of space, but are not constrained by either."[57]

These spaces are characterized by an "in-between-ness" between and beyond polarities like private and public, institutional and individual practice, embodiment and virtuality, and individual and community. To Echchaibi and Hoover, the feature of in-between-ness is particularly interesting since it prompts what they call "reflexivity." Since the third space of digital religion is fluid and operates "in a borderland," there is the need for constant negotiation. Therefore, these spaces are interactive and highly co-generative—"afford[ing] imagined possibilities of what values such as community, authenticity, and civility among others could be in a presumably open terrain of non-linear thinking." In other words, according to Echchaibi and Hoover, practices are conditioned by the "located logic" of digital media, a logic that enables new ways of understanding things like meaning, community, and action.[58]

Echchaibi and Hoover's concept of "the third space of digital religion" thus provides this thesis with a definition of "digital space" and an account of how digital media might be considered material.

However, it is not just from an empirical perspective that one might speak of digital space in this way. A theological viewpoint may find this definition

---

[56] Stewart M. Hoover and Nabil Echchaibi, *The Third Spaces of Digital Religion* (London & New York: Routledge, 2023), 1–8. See also Stewart M. Hoover and Nabil Echchaibi, *Media Theory and the Third Spaces of Digital Religion*, 2014, *https://www.researchgate.net/publication* [Accessed 13 October 2022], 1–35.

[57] Echchaibi and Hoover 2023, 1–13. Quotation p. 4.

[58] Echchaibi and Hoover 2023, 12–13.

salubrious, too. In discussing spatiality in relation to digital worship, practical theologian Miriam Löhr argues that worship services constitute spaces, not the other way around. This means that any space might become a space for worship, even if it was not intended as such from the beginning. Communal worship constitutes the liturgical space, even across distances. There is a spatial connection through the analog room where the liturgical leader is and through the actions of the participants, even if they are distributed. Listening, praying together, and so on creates a virtual space that bridges the distance and pulls the participants together into a virtual center. In this sense, worship services do not just shape a space; they also create spaces. Theologically speaking, we are drawing near to the doctrine of a border-crossing, invisible church that reaches across space and time.

Furthermore, theologically, worship services are tied to a place but do not depend on this place. Worship services are tied to places because they are embodied events wherein bodies together become one body. This happens in digitally-mediated worship services, too, but differently. Digital services are embodied because they involve bodies in a place, even if those bodies are distributed in front of computers and smartphones across the world—with the communal body gathered in a community of experience (*Erfahrungsgemeinschaft*) instead of a church building.[59]

Given these interpretations of "digital space," there are several good sociological and theological arguments for using the concept of "digital space" to denote the digital environments involved in the practice of preaching.

In sum, the concept of "digital culture and spaces" accounts for the very aspects of the situatedness of the practice of preaching this thesis focuses on: a digital culture, consisting of the entanglement of narratives about technology; the material infrastructures that shape communication; and human agency in relation to media. Due to its materiality, digital culture is characterized by certain common traits that traverse specific contexts. Digital culture takes place in digital spaces, or "third spaces of digital religion," that exist in between the material and immaterial, the concrete and the conceptual. These third spaces function "as if" and carry a located logic characterized by in-between-ness and border crossing. Theologically, digital spaces may be understood as the *Erfahrungsgemeinschaft* that comes to be when the border-crossing invisible church, rooted in bodies and locations, gathers through digital mediation. This gathering can happen in a myriad of ways, depending on hardware, software, and how people choose to interact with them.

---

[59]   Miriam   Löhr,   *https://www.liturgik.unibe.ch/GottesdienstimvirtuellenRaum_ger.pdf*
Gottesdienst im digitalen Raum, 2020, *https://www.liturgik.unibe.ch/* [Accessed 26 August 2022]

2.3 Digitally-Mediated

As I mentioned above, the fact that practice theories emphasize materiality and "site ontology" often leads to the principle that being is mediated. This is the case for the Heidegger-inspired Schatzki, who also deploys the concept of mediation in relation to digital technology and media. In Schatzki's analysis of group formation in three digital environments, for instance, he continually uses the word "mediation."[60] Accordingly, a third key concept in this thesis is "digitally-mediated."

While discussed mainly in article C, "digitally-mediated" designates a position that underlies all four articles. As I point out at the beginning of Article C, the concept of "online preaching" is quite common, but it is also problematic because it assumes "online and offline" exist as easily distinguished categories. Sociologists of religion Heidi Campbell and Ruth Tsuria point out in the introduction to *Digital Religion* that it is no longer meaningful to speak of online versus offline since the digital is so intertwined with everyday life.[61] In addition, creating such hard online/offline distinctions can easily terminate in an ontological dead-end, in which "real" and "virtual" are treated as a dichotomy, which in turn leads to normative conclusions about "real preaching" and "online preaching." As, for example, the homiletician Michael P. Knowles, writes:

> The implication of the Incarnation, surely, is that the community in question should be real, substantive, and personal, rather than merely virtual. To state the matter in a more ironic fashion, whereas our communion with the Savior may be to all appearances "virtual"—He is, after all, no longer visible among us—our communion with one another is normally, normatively, in the flesh. Christian community is best lived face-to-face, with real people, rather than virtually or at a distance. In turn, communication and reception of the Christian gospel seem likewise best suited to flesh-and-blood presence on the part of the believers.[62]

Here, Knowles contrasts real and virtual, concluding that "real" flesh-and-blood preaching is better than "merely virtual." Anthropologist Tom Boellstorff has argued that this contrast of real/virtual "appears with alarming frequency" and that this misrepresentation has "devastating consequences for addressing the reality of the digital"—especially since insights from the so-called ontological turn question

---

[60] Schatzki 2019, 19–22; 142–152, 186.
[61] Campbell and Tsuria 2022, 1–22.
[62] Knowles 2022, 10.

the presumptions underpinning such a hard distinction between real, virtual, and digital.[63]

As theologian Katherine G. Schmidt has shown, opposition undergirds most theological accounts of the internet. Theologians commonly do as Knowles does above, building their arguments on the idea that online interaction somehow does not involve the body or materiality, and set against the backdrop of the general assumption that technology draws people away from what is real. This means that to most theologians, social action in digital spaces can never measure up to its offline counterpart, and—even worse—it threatens to lure people away from what is real: God. According to Schmidt, in this tenor of theological discourse, the disembodied realm of the internet is often juxtaposed with its antidote: the embodied, un-mediated, real, local church community. This, in turn, leads to the tendency to compare the best of the local community with the absolute worst of the digital.[64]

During the first two years of the COVID-19 pandemic, when most of the source material for this thesis was created, this debate became more than a trend in theological discourse. Fueled by the grief of the loss of local worship, the theological assessment became emotionally charged and largely colored by nostalgic remembrance, with the oppositional pair "physical and digital" established and entrenched. In light of this, it became even more important to me not to further this prevalent dichotomy by speaking of "online" preaching.

Instead, I have opted for the concept of "digitally-mediated." As the professor of religious studies Birgit Meyer has discussed, it can be hugely productive to conceptualize religion as mediation.[65] Drawing, among others, on the work of Hent de Vries, Meyer approaches religion "as a practice of mediation between humans and the professed transcendent that necessarily requires specific material media, that is, authorized forms through which the transcendent is being generated and becomes somehow tangible." In other words, Meyer is among the scholars who conceptualize media as materiality, just like the above-mentioned Hutchings (and myself!). However, she distinguishes between first- and second-level media, where

---

[63] Tom Boellstorff, "For Whom the Ontology Turns: Theorizing the Digital Real," *Current Anthropology* 57:4 (2016), 387.

[64] Katherine G. Schmidt, *Virtual Communion: Theology of the Internet and the Catholic Sacramental Imagination* (Lanham, Maryland: Lexington Books/Fortress Academic (2020), 15–18.

[65] Notably, Meyer encompasses the same Wittgensteinian idea of concepts and overviews as Schatzki and consequently underlines that she uses religion as a generalizing concept through which certain practices, ideas, and things can be grouped and compared. Birgit Meyer, "Religion as Mediation," *Entangled Religions* 11:3 (2020), 1–15.

the first level is all media taken as a categorical whole, and second-level media are the complex authorized sensational forms employed to connect God and humans.[66]

Used in analysis, mediation as a concept enables comparison, for example, between religions, but also a comparison between religions and cultures. How so? The fundamental idea in theories of mediation is that humans relate to each other and the world through media that shape how they sense, communicate, act, and socially construct reality. This means that both religion and culture are dependent on mediality as a "fundamental aspect of relating to, acting in, knowing, understanding, and (re)making the world" that "places the approach to religion as mediation in a wider frame." To Meyer, this is a productive way to understand world-making, especially in societies characterized by plurality.[67] Moreover, the approach solves the problematic dichotomy identified by Boellstorff, pushing beyond dualisms like visible/invisible, tangible/intangible, and material/spiritual, and pointing instead to how the spiritual is *in* the material, so that the material is experienced to point beyond itself.

According to Meyer, this approach is commonly critiqued on three points. Firstly, other scholars might suspect that you assume the existence of a transcendent divine since religion is seen as a mediation between humans and their professed transcendent being. Meyer claims that it is not necessarily so. Another critique of the religion-as-mediation approach is that it brushes over differences between religious traditions. Meyer does not agree and points to how she has used a mediation-driven analysis multiple times to spot both commonalities and differences between traditions. This is the case in this thesis as well, as shown in Article C, for example. Notably, Meyer also claims that it facilitates diachronic comparison between different points in time, just as I do in article A.

A third critique of this approach might be that it differs too much from how practitioners themselves understand and use media. The example Meyer mentions is interesting in the context of this thesis. According to her, one religious group that might have a problem with the idea of religion as mediated is Lutherans, since they "usually emphasize immediacy." Notably, this did not seem to hold true for my experience in the context of the Lutheran Church of Sweden. There were many things listeners objected to in the almost 60 public lectures I gave during the first two years of the pandemic on being a church in digital culture and spaces. Yet the idea of religion being mediated was never one of them.

---

[66] Meyer 2020, 1–15.
[67] Meyer 2020, 1–15.

This might be because I often anchored the statement theologically. In her book *Virtual Communion*, the previously mentioned Schmidt argues that mediation is at the heart of the doctrine of the incarnation and a constitutive part of sacramental and ecclesial theology. Mediation is not just a function of the internet; it is "the very practice that sustains the sacramental imagination. The church needs a 'virtual logic' to understand both the sacraments and the physical-material entities that participate in the larger sacramentality of creation itself."[68]

Schmidt compares descriptions of incarnation with descriptions of what the internet "does" when it mediates. Drawing on Jay David Bolter and Robert Grusin, and their concept of "remediation," she points to the existence of a double (or simultaneous) logic. On the one hand, the human desire for "immediacy" urges humans to create media as a means to experience presence. On the other—and that is the paradox—there is always the potential for "hypermediacy" when we become aware of the medium, and the illusion of immediacy breaks down. In other words, digital media oscillates between the transparency of immediacy and an obscured hypermediacy. Schmidt points out that this is precisely how sacraments function theologically, except we speak of presence and absence instead. The sacrament is a medium that connects us to the reality we desire; but at the same time, we perpetually experience that we cannot get all the way there. While Christ is really present in, with, and under the bread and wine, it is still a mediated presence that contains an absence.[69] Throughout her book, Schmidt argues this tension between presence and absence has been lost in 20th-century theology's focus on the local community. Digital media may therefore have a pedagogical function as a reminder of profound spiritual and doctrinal truth.

Interestingly, like Schmidt, Schatzki believes digital devices teach us something important about presence and absence. He expresses this so beautifully I cannot help but quote him at length:

> Human life does not embrace only what is physically present: people's bodies, the entities amid which they act, the earth upon which they proceed, the air they breathe [...], the atmosphere through which they move, and the sky and heavens toward which they look. Human life also embraces entities that are present despite being absent. It might seem that digital devices are responsible for this phenomenon, but they only make it more evident. Human life has always embraced what is present in its absence.[70]

---

[68] Schmidt 2020, 19.
[69] Schmidt 2020, 59–70.
[70] Schatzki 2019, 192.

Next to the works of Schatzki, Meyer, and Schmidt, Theresa Berger's @Worship: Liturgical practices in digital worlds (2018) was seminal for my conceptualization of religion as mediated. The book came out almost at the same time as the start of my Ph.D. process, and as an excellent primer for the study of digitally-mediated practices, it exerted a significant impact on my work. Berger states the importance of using the expression "digitally-mediated" to circumvent the notion that liturgical practices can be "im-mediate" as in unmediated: "Christian worship should not be understood as an originally unmediated or pre-mediated world to which (artificial?) media technologies then came to be added."[71] Her book emphasizes the same thing as Schmidt: mediation is not new to the church. Christian faith has always been mediated. For Berger, this insight has two downstream implications.

First, like Meyer, she underlines the importance of diachronic comparison. In the section "Looking back, into liturgy's past," Berger points to several historical sources that might shed light on what constitutes liturgical presence and participation.[72]

Second, it affects terminology. Berger uses the pair "digitally-mediated church" and "brick-and-mortar church" instead of online church/church. However, these concepts do not translate very well into Swedish. It was quite difficult to find equivalent suitable terms in Swedish. At last, I settled for "digital" and "local" to designate the difference, in part because the Swedish word for "local"—"lokal"—has a double meaning and can also mean "premises, room." Therefore, the pair digital/local shows up here and there in the interviews and articles as translations of my translations of Berger's work.

2.4 The Preaching Event

In Schatzki's version of practice theory, the concept of "event" is central. As previously mentioned, the social consists of practices, and practices consist of human agency and material entities. When something happens to either of these two components, that is an event, and a practice is made up of a series of such events.[73] The practice of preaching is created via myriad events, but to facilitate analysis, I have used a fourth key concept: "the preaching event." I discuss this in more detail in article D, connecting Linn Sæbø Rystad's argument for using the concept to my

---

[71] Teresa Berger, @Worship: Liturgical Practices in Digital Worlds (London & New York: Routledge, 2018), 7.

[72] Berger 2018, 23–26.

[73] Schatzki 2019, 6–7, 31–32.

own analysis. Rystad claims that the concept is beneficial since it enables an under-standing of preaching as a practice, which illuminates preaching as "processual, performative and emerging," radically relational, and not least, highlights the im-portance of material entities in the meaning-making process.[74]

Moreover, the concept of "event" is not beneficial just for studying homiletics. According to Pink et al., it is also fruitful in the study of digital ethnography—both the classical, ritual theory-inspired concept of "event" as a structured and symbolically meaningful series of repeated activities, and more recent understand-ings, in which events are conceived as processual and experiential accounts of the world.[75]

Like Rystad, I draw on Wilfried Engemann's conceptualization of the preach-ing event. Engemann states that because it is difficult to discern precisely when the sermon becomes a sermon, it is vital to keep all parts of the preaching event to-gether in the process of analysis. However, the preaching event can be broken down into four phases for clarity of analysis, as shown in the figure below.[76]

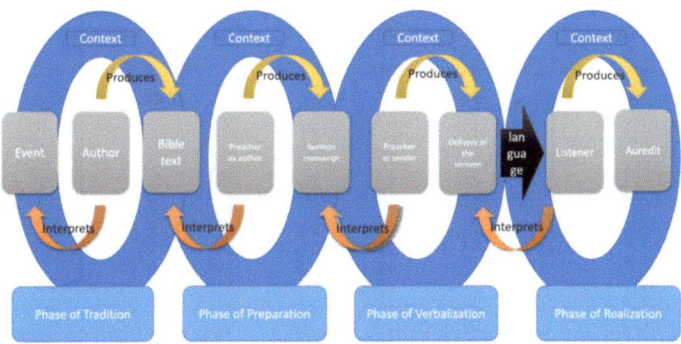

Figure 1: The Preaching Event according to Wilfried Engemann

Each phase contains an element of interpretation and an element of meaning pro-duction. In the first phase of *tradition*, the author(s) of the Bible text interpreted an event related to a revelation of God and produced a text that is now part of the canonized collection of texts we call the Bible. In the next phase, *preparation*, the preacher interprets the Bible text and, as an author, produces a sermon

---

[74] Rystad 2020, 122–123.

[75] Pink et al. 2016, 147–165.

[76] Wilfried Engemann, *Homiletics: Principles and Patterns of Reasoning* (Berlin: Walter De Gruyter, 2019), xix–xx.

manuscript.[77] This manuscript is later, in the phase of *verbalization*, interpreted again—this time, by the preacher as sender, as she delivers the sermon orally. Finally, in the phase of *realization*, the listener interprets the words of the preacher to create an *auredit* (Latin for "what has been heard").

In this thesis, Engemann's understanding of the preaching event is not just part and parcel of the conceptual framework in the articles. It has also inspired the research design, as articles B, C, and D each represent a case study of the preparation, verbalization, and realization phases.[78]

However, there is a difference between my understanding and Engemann's as it pertains to the preaching event. As seen in my reproduction of Engemann's illustration, he states that every phase occurs in relation to a specific situation (the blue circles). Each interpretation and process of meaning production is situated in a context. However, the main three actors involved are the texts, the preacher, and the listener. While material arrangements (other than the Bible) are not entirely forgotten or ignored, they appear as a backdrop. In other words, this is a case of what Schatzki would call "contextualism," a social ontology in which material entities function as context, "a setting or backdrop that envelops and determines phenomena."[79] Material arrangements have a more prominent role in my understanding of the preaching event.

2.5 Authority

In Schatzki's thinking, bundles of practices are never isolated. They are always connected in a "mesh" that he calls "the practice plenum," which is the sum of all bundles of practices that make up the social life as we know it. However, there is a sort of middle level within this larger mesh. Bundles of practices tend to group together in complex bundles of bundles, or "constellations." Bundles connect into constellations in several ways.

Schatzki lists five basic ways these can connect: 1) common and orchestrated teleologies, rules, emotions, or general understandings (for example, the idea that the Holy Spirit works through the Word of God in a sermon); 2) intentional relations (like involving in the bundle of practices of sermon preparation with the

---

[77] Of course, some preachers do not produce a written manuscript. However, as a result of the preparation phase most preachers have a mental equivalent of a manuscript: a planned structure and content.

[78] The phase of tradition is excluded here, because it is the concern of Bible scholars.

[79] Schatzki 2002, xiv.

intention to deliver it later); 3) chains of action (for example, the bundle of practices involved in reading from the lectionary leads to the bundle of practices involved in delivering a sermon, as part of the constellation of practices labeled "worship service"); 4) material connections among arrangements (like infrastructure in telecommunication); and 5) prefiguration (for example, a liturgical handbook that prescribes that the sermon must interpret the designated gospel reading).[80]

In other words, "the practice of preaching" is a constellation of many bundles of practices. Since it is not possible to examine all these different bundles, someone interested in "what characterizes the practice of preaching" needs to strategically choose relevant aspects of the constellation to look at in closer detail. The phases of the preaching event are such aspects. Another aspect is the fifth key concept, "authority."

There were several reasons for focusing on how authority is practiced and performed within the constellation of the practice of preaching. This is discussed in detail in article D, where I argue that authority has been a critical issue in the field of homiletics for decades. This is evident, not least, in the title of the landmark volume by Fred B. Craddock that set off the New Homiletic movement: *As One Without Authority*. It was published in 1971 and quickly became influential, not least in the Swedish context.[81] In the literature review of her thesis, the aforementioned Sigmon argues convincingly how developments in the field of homiletics since the 1960s can be understood as attempts to solve the central problem Craddock identified: the asymmetrical distribution of power, or, as Sigmon prefers to call it: "the pulpit-pew binary."[82]

Authority is a key question not just in the field of homiletics but also in research on the intersection of digital media and religion. Another landmark volume, *Digital Religion*, names authority among the five key questions in the field.[83] This was also confirmed by my findings in article A, in which authority surfaced as one of the aspects in need of consideration.

A third reason for paying attention to how authority is practiced is a consequence of my choice to use practice theory. One of the drawbacks of this

---

[80] Schatzki 2019, 44–47.

[81] For an extensive discussion on the influences of New homiletics on Swedish homiletics, see Frida Mannerfelt, "Kontrast och kontinuitet: Predikoideal i Svenska kyrkans prästutbildning 1903–2017," in *Årsbok för svenskt gudstjänstliv* 93, ed. Stephan Borgehammar (Skellefteå: Artos, 2018), 123–158.

[82] Sigmon 2017, 12–16.

[83] Heidi Campbell, *Digital Religion: Understanding Religious Practice in Digital Worlds* (London & New York: Routledge, 2012).

theoretical paradigm is that power relations tend to become invisible.[84] As media theorist John Durham Peters has argued, practice theory tends to overemphasize relationality and mutual interdependence, which makes it difficult to discern "the great inequality of things" and offer ethical and political critique.[85] Issues of power tend to be elusive in theories and narratives about digital media, too. Couldry and Hepp point to how the dominant narrative about digital media—that it is democratic, sharing, and characterized by relationality—tends to make scholars blind to the fact that these relations often are asymmetrical.[86] Torsten Meireis points out that the internet is part of the general public square "in which asymmetric power plays a vital role."[87]

In sum, among all the aspects of the constellation labeled "the practice of preaching," authority stood out as particularly important to examine in order to better answer the overarching research question.

2.6 Salient Theological Features

There are two additional important components in Schatzki's practice theory that have informed the key concepts and research questions of this thesis. The first is Schatzki's claim that practices are never just random events; they are always organized. Practices can be organized through "rules" (explicit instructions), "pools of understanding" (for example, the general understanding that footnotes are required in a thesis, and the practical understanding of how to make one and which information to include), and "teleoaffective structures."[88]

"Teleoaffective structures" is a central concept in Schatzki's thinking, discussed in depth in his *The Timespace of Human Activity: On Performance, Society, and History as Indeterminate Teleological events* (2010). According to Schatzki, human activity is teleological, directed towards an end. People act for desired, wanted, or sought-after "ways of being" or believed, perceived, imagined, expected, or presumed "states of affairs." Teleoaffective structures are a combination of desired ways of being and the state of affairs prescribed and acceptable in a

---

[84] Tveito Johnsen and Afdahl 2020, 67. See also James Ash, "Flat Ontology and Geography," *Dialogues in Human Geography* 10:3 (2020), 345–361.

[85] John D. Peters, *The Marvellous Clouds: Toward a Philosophy of Elemental Media* (Chicago: University of Chicago Press, 2015), 30.

[86] Couldry and Hepp 2017, 60–63.

[87] Torsten Meireis, "Jesus in the eShop. A Christian Perspective on Power in the Digital World," *Cursor_ Zeitschrift Für Explorative Theologie*, 22 April 2021.

[88] Schatzki 2019, 30–32.

particular context and time. Therefore, what makes sense for a person to do in a given situation relates to both the past and the future.[89]

The second component is his account of social change. According to Schatzki, change occurs when: a) humans engage in *chains of activity*; and/or through b) *material events and processes*. In other words, when there are changes to activities, material arrangements, or in the relations between activities and arrangements, social change necessarily might occur as well. However, to be able to talk of change, there must be significant differences in these constitutive parts.[90]

Schatzki insists that human activity always is the principal generator of social change. A classic example is technological innovation, which comes about foremost through human activity. Still, he is careful to point out that it is not always easy to disentangle the two and determine which elements truly brought about any given change. For example, the vast societal changes of the COVID-19 pandemic were brought about by both material events (a virus) and human activity (lockdown orders, and so on). Change may happen abruptly. The invention of the laptop, for instance, caused significant changes to the practice of writing a thesis, compared to when the practice involved the good old typewriter. More commonly, however, change occurs as "inflection." According to Schatzki, when you perform a practice, you never replicate it the same way. There is always a slight difference. In time, enough difference accumulates to be able to talk about a change.[91]

Organization of practices and social change is discussed in more detail in article C but is also assumed in article B. In both articles, I argue that changes in material arrangements cause changes in the practice as a whole, not least in the part of the practice's organization called theology. Through the third and final sub-question and the key concept of "salient theological features," this thesis pays special attention to this theological dimension.

Such a research question might be considered unnecessary in a practical theological thesis, especially one that uses practice theory. The underlying assumption in such an approach is, after all, that theology is embedded into practice. As practical theologian Ulla Schmidt points out, practical theology's turn to practices has not only affected *what* we study but also highlighted the epistemological significance of practices. Practices are, as she puts it, "not only enactments of religion but

---

[89] Schatzki 2010, 111–115. Schatzki points out that his discussion encompasses cognitively functional human beings, and exclude infants and people with severe mental disease.

[90] Schatzki 2019, 78–104.

[91] Schatzki 2019, 78–104.

are also increasingly recognized as theologically generative."[92] There is theology in
the lived. This means that, in a sense, any research question about the practice of
preaching is theological in its nature. Then why add a specific question that singles
out theology as an aspect of the organization of practices that is particularly important?

First, theology tends to be overlooked in practical theological research projects
that employ qualitative methods. In his contribution to *What Really Matters:
Scandinavian Perspectives on Ecclesiology and Ethnography* (2018), the previously
mentioned Ward argues for the need to ensure the place of theology in the ongoing
conversation. According to Ward, the attention to practices risks leading to the
silencing and marginalization of systematic and doctrinal theology. He mentions
several reasons for this: the wish to reduce the tension between doctrine and empirical research; the fact that it is challenging to include both qualitative research
and systematic theology in one project; the wish to distinguish between faith and
theology; the focus on the human experience as the locus for theology, and doctrine as problematic—or even oppressive—from the perspective of power dynamics. However, to Ward, the omission of doctrinal theology is reductive. Practical
theological projects need to be theological in the sense that they must establish
how the particular understanding of the divine that frames the research (and the
researcher) sits in relation to broader theological conversations.[93]

The tendency for theology to be overlooked seems particularly strong in Scandinavian contributions to practical theology. As Stangeland Kaufman points out
in her analysis of Scandinavian contributions to research at the intersection of theology and qualitative methods, there are two typical features of Scandinavian practical theology. She identifies "an obsession with methodological issues." In the
Scandinavian countries, practical theologians were primarily influenced by sociologists in their use of qualitative methods, which has caused them to emphasize
methodological rigor. The notion that meticulous methods create reliable data has
rendered Scandinavian practical theologians methodologically conservative. This
relates to the second feature, "the missing T-word," or the fact that international
colleagues tend to ask Scandinavian practical theologians: "What is actually

---

[92] Ulla Schmidt, "Practice, Practice Theory and Theology," in *Practice, Practice Theory and
Theology: Scandinavian and German Perspectives*, eds. Kristin Helboe Johansen and Ulla
Schmidt (Berlin: De Gruyter, 2022), 35.

[93] Pete Ward, "Is Theology What Really Matters?," in *What Really Matters: Scandinavian
Perspectives on Ecclesiology and Ethnography*, eds. Jonas Ideström och Tone Stangeland Kaufman
(Eugene, Oregon: Pickwick Publications, 2018), 157–172.

theological with your practical theological research?" As Stangeland Kaufman highlights in her keynote lecture, this is unfair since there is plenty of mentions of "lived theology" in their work. However, engagement with "the formal voice" of academic theology and "the normative voice"[94] of theological tradition tends to retreat into the background or even be lacking altogether.[95]

In the *What Really Matters* volume, Tveitereid discusses some of the reasons for these difficulties in attending to a theological conversation. Qualitative research requires theories to "make the data speak." However, few theories are suited for practical theological analysis. Theologians then turn to social science theories that are tailored to making data speak as social data. However, these theories are not equipped to bring theological potential or theological implications in the data to the forefront. Tveitereid then discusses various options for theologians to over-come this problem. Theological typologies might offer tidy categories, but since they often are too broad and assembled deductively "from above," they tend to obscure the dynamics in the data and overlook the lived complexity of practices. Systematic theology functions more as "metatheory" and underplays the signifi-cance of theology in the data. In light of this, Tveitereid points to the importance of acknowledging these difficulties and contributing to developing theologically-*and* empirically-informed typologies that can be used in analysis.[96]

In sum, practical theology that focuses on practices and uses qualitative meth-ods—that is, the kind of practical theology done in this thesis—runs the risk of overlooking theology, especially in the contexts in which this thesis was written. It runs the risk of possibly underplaying *all* theology, even the lived theology found in practices, and perhaps more likely, underplaying how the lived theology in prac-tices sits in relation to formal and normative theology.

Second, theology tends to be overlooked when theologians deal with digital culture. As Peter Phillips points out, theologians who study digital culture and its

---

[94] "The four voices of theology" is an analytical model created by the ARCS team and fur-ther developed by Clare Watkins to describe different locations in which theology is articulated. Theology is formulated in the *normative* voice (church doctrine and tradition), the *formal* voice (for example, academic theology), the *espoused* voice (disclosed in the sayings of practitioners), and the *operant* voice (disclosed in the doings of practitioners). Cameron et al. 2010, 39–60; Wat-kins 2020.

[95] Tone Stangeland Kaufman 2022.

[96] Knut Tveitereid, "Making Data Speak – The Shortage of Theory for the Analysis of Qual-itative Data in Practical Theology," in *What Really Matters: Scandinavian Perspectives on Eccle-siology and Ethnography*, eds. Jonas Ideström och Tone Stangeland Kaufman (Eugene, Oregon: Pickwick Publications, 2018), 41–57.

attendant phenomena tend to focus on the novelty factor in digitalization—and forget the factor of theology. Discussions tend to focus on topics like an exploration of how to go about digitally-mediated practices or how digital cultures influence religious practices. Furthermore, the theoretical tools used in analysis tend to center on communication theory, cultural theory, mediatization theory, and the like, while theology quietly slips into the background.[97] In a recent lecture about the development of digital theology, Jonas Kurlberg points out that this tendency also has relatively mundane causes: in a secular environment, theologians are pressured "to downplay the theological significance of their research proposals to attain funding." Therefore, it is essential to retain a commitment to theological reflection.[98]

This phenomenon was also something I saw at play in my own context. For example, in the digital transition made by churches during the COVID-19 pandemic, these very topics dominated the Swedish discussion—notably, even in the research project *Church in Digital Space*, which had as one of several stated purposes an engagement in theological analysis! The researchers and practitioners had to remind themselves constantly not to lose sight of theology. As I looked at my own choices pertaining to theoretical approaches in the articles, I realized that I, too, was prone to use non-theological theoretical frameworks.

This was partly connected to a third phenomenon that eventually prompted the inclusion of a research question emphasizing the aspect of theology: in homiletical research, ecclesiology tends to slip into the background.

According to practical theologian Theo Pleizier, sermon reception research has developed over time in relation to communication theories and theories of hermeneutics to result in a bias toward the individual listener. As Pleizier puts it: "in its conceptualization, the listener has become rather lonely—a meaning-making individual in a pluralist universe."[99] He points to several reasons to include a communal perspective in homiletics: "Congregational worship is the natural habitat of preaching; preaching is a social act; contemporary homiletics has stressed the fact that the preacher reads the text 'on behalf of the congregation'; as a communicative event, preaching constructs community." And he asks: "Is it possible to articulate

---

[97] Phillips 2020, 261–262.

[98] Jonas Kurlberg, *Challenges Facing Digital Theology Today*, October 2022, *https://medium.com/@jonas.kurlberg* [Accessed 9 December 2022].

[99] Theo Pleizier, "Studying the Listener? The Paradox of the Individual in Sermon Reception Research and a Reassessment of Preaching as Caring for the Community of Faith," in *Preaching Promise within the Paradoxes of Life*, eds. Johan Cilliers and Len Hansen (Stellenbosch: African Sun Media, 2018), 161.

an understanding of preaching in which not only the individual hearer's faith is shaped, but that also acknowledges how preaching sustains and nurtures the congregation as a community?"[100]

Homiletician Sune Fahlgren has developed such an understanding of preaching. In an analysis of Swedish homiletical handbooks published from 2003 to 2006, Fahlgren observes the same tendencies towards fragmentation and individualization as Pleizier. In light of this, Fahlgren argues that "the practice of preaching needs to be informed and driven by ecclesiological awareness." To this end, Fahlgren developed the practice-based concept of "preachership" to signify how preaching is an expression of the church and a constructive mechanism within the church. The concept grew inductively from his analysis of six historical preaching events, resulting in a theory for ecclesiological reflection on preaching. In his argument, Fahlgren draws on Alasdair McIntyre's concept of practice, including his idea that a social grammar exists that consists of convictions, social practices, and reflections. This enables Fahlgren to conceptualize preachership as a fundamental ecclesial practice that embodies religious convictions. Preaching is a practice that creates and sustains identity and implies the practitioners' understanding of what the church is. Preachership and congregation presuppose and sustain each other. This means a specific preachership relates to a specific understanding of the ecclesial community.[101]

Pleizier and Fahlgren are also supported by the previously mentioned Sigmon, who subtitled her thesis about preaching in a digital culture *a homilecclesiology for a digital age.* To her, homiletics and ecclesiology are intimately tied together. She draws on Craig Dykstra's understanding of practices, who claims that these constitute the common life of the church. This means that the church is the practice of homiletics made visible over time. The practice of preaching creates a church, and the church shapes the understanding of the practice of preaching. Therefore, preachers must "reflect what kind of communities are being formed by the kind of practices, especially preaching, they participate in."[102]

Sigmon's homilecclesiology is discussed by theologian Sunggu Yang, who claims that "one thing is undeniable; digital communication means weak

---

[100] Pleizier 2018, 162–163.

[101] Sune Fahlgren, "Preaching and Preachership as Fundamental Expression of Being Church," *International Journal for the Study of the Christian Church* 6:2 (2006), 180–199.

[102] Sigmon 2017, 37–40. Quotation p. 40. Sigmon criticizes McIntyre's understanding of practice. "If preaching, a practice, is defined by one set of ideals or "internal goods" unique to that one practice, then it may be all too easy to marginalize preaching that may occur on the margins of the hegemonic ideal." Sigmon 2017, 39.

ecclesiality." This, combined with the fact that digitally-mediated preaching can be practiced in many different ways and therefore express a variety of ecclesiologies, calls for further discussion about the ecclesiological and theological implications of online preaching.[103]

The importance of theology, and in particular ecclesiology, for how digitally-mediated practices were enacted was also evident in our findings in the project *Church in Digital Space*, in which we found that the practices in the digitally-mediated worship services were negotiated in relation to presumptions about what church ought to be and do, even when the practitioners did not explicitly express these presumptions.[104] In sum, in an effort to avoid the mistake of overlooking theological and ecclesiological reflection, I included a research question that explicitly required an inquiry into these aspects of the organization of practices.

In sum, theology tends to be elusive in all the fields I relate to in this thesis: Scandinavian practical theology, digital theology, and homiletics. The usage of theories of communication, hermeneutics, and media leans toward the neglect of theological, in particular ecclesiological, dimensions of the practice of preaching. This is problematic because the practice of preaching is intimately connected to ecclesiology. How preaching is practiced discloses different understandings of the church, and contributes to the construction of different understandings of what the church is and ought to do. Therefore, theologians in all fields call for constructive theological and ecclesiological work. In light of this, I chose to include a research question that asks explicitly which theological features are significant in the practice of preaching in digital culture and spaces.

2.7 In Sum

In this chapter, I have discussed six key concepts found in the research questions undergirding the theoretical framework of the thesis. With the concept of

---

[103] Sunggu A. Yang "Preaching / Hermeneutics and Rhetoric / Religious Speech," in *International Handbook of Practical Theology*, eds. Birgit Weyel et al. (Berlin: De Gruyter, 2022), 445–456. Quotation p. 453.

[104] Frida Mannerfelt and Rikard Roitto, "Mellan rit och reklam del 1: Berättelsen om två församlingars utveckling," in *Kyrka i digitala rum: Ett aktionsforskningsprojekt om församlingsliv online*, eds. Sara Garpe and Jonas Ideström (Uppsala: Svenska kyrkan, 2022a), 47–60; Frida Mannerfelt and Rikard Roitto, "Mellan rit och reklam del 2: Interaktion, synkronicitet och integritet i förinspelade digitalt förmedlade andakter," in *Kyrka i digitala rum: Ett aktionsforskningsprojekt om församlingsliv online*, eds. Sara Garpe and Jonas Ideström (Uppsala: Svenska kyrkan, 2022b), 61–79.

"Practice of preaching," I situated my work in a practice theoretical paradigm, an approach that is beneficial in the fields of homiletics, practical theology, the study of digital media, and in cases like the one at hand here: where there is precious little previous research. Due to his views on the relationship between materiality and agency, and his insistence on the role of discourse in practice, I chose to work with the practice theory of Theodore Schatzki.

With the concept of "digital culture and spaces," I accounted for the social site where the preaching practice is situated. I stated that I understand digital culture as consisting of narratives, material arrangements, and human agency that are common across the globe, and digital spaces as context-specific multiplicity. I also stated that I understand the spatiality and materiality of digital spaces as a "third space of digital religion" characterized by in-between-ness.

I then explained how "digitally-mediated" means that I understand religion (and indeed being) as mediated, an understanding that often is part-and-parcel of practice theory. Moreover, I accounted for how conceptualizing the practice as an event is considered fruitful when studying digital media and homiletics, and harmonizes nicely with practice theoretical approaches. Thus, I will use the "preaching event" concept to analyze the practice of preaching in terms of phases in a communicative and interpretive process.

Moreover, I argued that "authority" is a key question in homiletics and the study of digital religion, and thus a crucial aspect in the bundles of practices that form the constellation labeled "the practice of preaching." To answer the overarching research question about what characterizes the practice of preaching in digital culture and spaces, it is essential to examine what kinds of authority preachers practice.

Finally, I pointed to the tendency to overlook theology and ecclesiology in the fields of practical theology, digital theology, and homiletics, and that I wish to adhere to the call within these fields to pay attention to the role theology, and in particular, ecclesiology, plays in the organization of the practice of preaching. I argued that from a practice theoretical point of view, changes in material arrangements and human agency might cause changes in organization, too, which makes it interesting to take a closer look at salient theological and ecclesiological features of this particular, digitally-mediated way to practice preaching.

3. On Scholarly Conversations: Review of Relevant Research

This chapter is devoted to a review of relevant research. In the vast field of homiletics, there are two scholarly conversations that I would like to contribute to: "the practice of preaching" and "preaching in digital culture and spaces." This dual focus mirrors, in a sense, two strands in recent Nordic homiletical research, as identified by practical theologian and homiletician Marlene Ringgaard Lorensen. In her review of homiletical research from the Nordic countries for the last two decades (2000-2020), she identifies two characteristics: on the one hand, an empirical turn toward the interaction between listeners and preachers and, on the other hand, the interaction between preaching and contemporary societal events or currents.[1]

Subsequently, two articles in this thesis discuss the interaction between preacher and listener in the digitally-mediated preaching event (articles C and D), and two others that consider preaching in relation to the contemporary societal current of digital culture (articles A and B).

In the following, I will give an overview of relevant literature, positioning my articles and the overarching research question in relation to other scholarly work. The account is structured in two parts, mirroring the two scholarly conversations I want to engage with: The Practice of Preaching (3.1) and Preaching in Digital Culture and Spaces (3.2).

---

[1] Marlene R. Lorensen, "Nyere nordisk homiletik: Empirisk vending, fremmedhed og resonans," *Nordic Journal of Practical Theology* 37:1 (2020), 42–53.; Marlene R. Lorensen, "Homiletik i den praktiske teologi," in *Den praktiske teologi i Danmark 1973–2018: Festskrift til Hans Raun Iversen*, eds. I. L. Christoffersen, N. H. Gregersen, and K. M. S. Leth-Nissen (København: Anis, 2019), 111–119.

3.1 The Practice of Preaching

As mentioned in Chapter 2, the empirical turn in practical theology and the sub-sequent interest in lived theology and practices has, in the Scandinavian context, sparked an interest in practice theory. In that chapter, I also gave an account of how this turn to practice theory in practical theology (and subsequently, homilet-ics) informed the research design and the choice to focus on practices of preaching in this thesis. Accordingly, this thesis enters into an already established discussion in relation to this topic. What has then been done already in this field?

A landmark volume in the Scandinavian context is Marlene Ringgaard Loren-sen's *Dialogical Preaching: Bakhtin, Otherness and Homiletics* (2014), based on her thesis *Preaching as a Carnivalesque Dialogue: Between the 'Wholly Other' and 'Other-Wise' Listeners* (2012).[2] Lorensen uses Mikhail Bakhtin's philosophy and communication theory to "explore in which ways various 'others,' different from the designated preached, influence contemporary preaching practices and in that sense can be seen as co-authors of homiletic meaning."[3] The discussion centers on two of Bakhtin's key concepts, "dialogue" and "carnivalesque."

In the case of "dialogue," Lorensen points out that, while the concept is pre-valent in homiletical discourse, it "is used in very different, if not incompatible ways."[4] It is often used in pursuit of a communication theory that goes beyond the so-called "transfer model," in which the preacher is thought to "send a message" to a recipient—the listener. However, according to Lorensen, many of the homi-letical solutions that attempt to move beyond this paradigm are insufficient, as they merely complicate the picture by pointing out obstacles to this approach and then posit how to overcome them, which, in effect, means that they paradoxically contribute to upholding the very transfer model they intend to deconstruct.[5] From a Bakhtinian perspective, dialogue is a "two-sided action," a cooperation be-tween a polyphony of voices and an assembly of interacting bodies. Words uttered are always shaped simultaneously by the future (the anticipated answer) and the past (what has been said before, not only in the immediate conversation but also

---

[2] Marlene R. Lorensen, *Preaching as a Carnivalesque Dialogue: Between the 'Wholly Other' and 'Other-Wise' Listeners*, Ph.D. thesis (Copenhagen, Copenhagen University, 2012).

[3] Lorensen 2014, 13.

[4] Lorensen 2014, 14.

[5] Lorensen 2014, 43–44.

"conversations" at large, including cultural discourse and tradition). This means that the reader (or, in the case of a sermon, the listener) is always the "co-author."[6]

Moreover, dialogue—its interaction and re-creation—depends on differences. Conversation must not collapse one voice into the other, neither by dominating the other conversation partner nor by abandoning one's own voice to take the standpoint of the other. Accordingly, Lorensen underlines the importance of upholding a "double otherness."[7]

The concept of "carnivalesque" suggests that preaching cannot be understood with communication theory alone. Carnival can mean two things: the overturning of everyday life and a celebrative elevation of the flesh and the body. Thus, it is a reminder that preaching is embodied and certain aspects of preaching, such as embodiment, tonality, rhythm, time, and place, are essential too, and that a sermon has the potential to transform lives.

Furthermore, genres (like sermons) can be carnivalized, meaning they can re-enact the ritual reversals of public roles and hierarchies, break the lines between actors and audience, and transpose the embodied interaction to literary texts—thus making apparent how incarnated acts live on in literary genres.[8]

Lorensen discusses both methods of practical theology and different homiletical approaches in light of Bakhtin's theories. Concerning methods, Lorensen argues for new frameworks to studying the preacher-listener interaction, advocating for a practice-oriented, situated approach to theology which finds practice theoretical approaches in line with Bakthin's thinking. She pairs Bakthin with Pierre Bourdieu and his work on habits and actions. Because discourse is incarnated, it is, therefore, crucial that "the objects of the field of homiletics are studied as situated practices rather than texts abstracted from their discursive environment."[9] Notably, Lorensen emphasizes physical situatedness and repeatedly underscores the fact that she studies "practice and theory, speech and text, words and bodies."[10] In other words, it is the bodies of the preacher, listener, Bible text, and God—and the interaction between them—that are at the center of her discussion. Other material entities and arrangements merely hover in the background.[11]

---

[6] Lorensen 2014, 22, 58–64.
[7] Lorensen 2014, 38, 161–175.
[8] Lorensen 2014, 15–16.
[9] Lorensen 2014, 36.
[10] Lorensen 2014, 37.
[11] Lorensen 2014, 21–41.

The Bakhtinian concept of co-authorship is recurrent in Lorensen's work, both in relation to practical theological methodology[12] and as a theoretical framework in the analysis and discussion of the practice of preaching. An example of the latter is the article "Listeners as Authors in Preaching: Empirical and Theoretical Perspectives" (2013), co-written with Marianne Gaarden. In their article, Lorensen and Gaarden turn the tables on preacher-centric approaches and discuss the preaching event from the listener's point of view. Recent homiletical studies claim listeners also have agency in the preaching event, but how? Based on the results of Gaarden's empirical study, Lorensen and Gaarden conclude that listeners' involvement in the preaching event is so profound that, from a Bakhtinian perspective, it might be said that listeners should be seen as authors of the sermon. Preachers have the role of co-authors.[13]

Gaarden's book *Prædikenen som det tredje rum* (2015) and the revised English version *The Third Room of Preaching: A New Empirical Approach* (2021) elaborate on these perspectives. Gaarden presents an empirical, grounded theory to study sermon listeners. In the Danish version, she points out that this grounded theory made her realize how much she was influenced by communication theories from The New Homiletic movement and studies in rhetoric, in which listening to a sermon is primarily about understanding a message. In light of her empirical studies, she had to revise that assumption.[14]

Instead, Gaarden found that the preaching event is not about listeners taking over the preachers' message; rather, it is an event in which listeners create their own meaning. Gaarden conceptualizes this as a meeting between the preachers' outer words and the listener's inner experience, in which a "third room of preaching" unfolds where the listeners create meaning. Gaarden summarizes her results in five points. First, the preacher's person is significant for the sermon's reception and the listeners' willingness to engage in listening to it. If the listeners feel sympathy for

---

[12] See, for example, the case study of asylum seekers in the Danish church, in which Lorensen and Gitte Buch-Hansen show how their listening to the voice of the refugee provoked an adjustment of theory, which can be understood as her being a co-author of practical theology. Marlene R. Lorensen and Gitte Buch-Hansen, "Listening to the Voices: Refugees as Co-authors of Practical Theology," *Practical Theology* 11:1 (2018), 29–41.

[13] Marianne Gaarden and Marlene R. Lorensen "Listeners as Authors in Preaching: Empirical and Theoretical Perspectives," *Homiletic* 38:1 (2013), 28–45.

[14] Marianne Gaarden, *Prædikenen som det tredje rum* (Köpenhamn: Anis, 2015), 47–48.

the preacher, they will listen. Sympathy emerges in relation to the preacher's attitude and authenticity.[15]

Second, the relationship between the preacher and the listener is reciprocal and interactive. Notably, she mentions the significance of the church building, but only in passing: "Going into a church Sunday morning sets the mind and shapes the expectation for what is going to happen, and this obviously participates in forming the preaching event."[16] Third, listening to preaching can be understood in Bakhtinian terms as an internal dialogue. Gaarden found three kinds of dialogical interactions with the sermon: associative, critical, and contemplative.[17] Fourth, the listeners create meaning in relation to their own lives, and the preacher cannot control the listener's meaning-making process.[18] Fifth, the listeners' inner sermon is an intersubjective creation of new meaning. In her discussion, Gaarden draws on the communication theory of Barnett Pearce and his concept of "coordinated management of meaning." Meaning-making is a process in which interpretation and understanding are formed through our relationships. For Gaarden, this resonates with the creation story of Genesis 1, in which the world comes into being through words. She also points to similar interdependencies expressed throughout the Bible.[19]

In discussing her findings, Gaarden insists that the preacher does not control meaning. The ownership of meaning is not to be found in the pulpit, as contemporary homiletical theory claims. The preacher is not the builder of "the third room." Instead, "the third room" depends on the preacher's willingness to serve as a tool. Preachers need to surrender to the preaching event and accept that they are part of something bigger than themselves. As Gaarden puts it: "In this way of thinking, preachers are called to give up the idea of being able to transfer their own intentionality to the listener and instead give God the glory."[20]

At the end of her book, Gaarden offers a theology of preaching, or "a communication theology." She writes:

> God is not a substantial and transcendent reality about which we can preach, external to ourselves, but a reality in which we human beings are always and already participating. [...] Participation in God can be seen as a gift of divine grace, and 'in the act of faith

---

[15] Marianne Gaarden, *The Third Room of Preaching: A New Empirical Approach* (Eugene, Oregon: Pickwick publications, 2021), 55–68.

[16] Gaarden 2021, 71.

[17] Gaarden 2021, 74–94.

[18] Gaarden 2021, 94–99.

[19] Gaarden 2021, 55–106

[20] Gaarden 2021, 122–126. Quotation p. 126.

the initiative is reversed: God takes over, leading human beings into in/finite time and space, which is God. Finitude is not infinitude, but open to it.' [...] When human beings participate in God, they are not only to be understood as autonomous and limited individuals but also as relational and related beings embedded in the body of Christ. [...] This understanding is consistent with process-relational theologians, where everything is dynamically interconnected with God, who is the most relational reality of all; and consistent with Scandinavian Creation Theology, believing that we all live in networks of deep interdependence [...] considering humans as living in a web of interdependence with our fellow human beings and with the rest of God's creatures.[21]

In this quote, there are several important points to take note of. God is understood as immanent, a flow of creative life in which humans participate. Here, Gaarden draws on the formal theological voices of Scandinavian Creation Theology and process theology to frame the lived theology of the third room of preaching. Theologically, humans are understood as limited, interdependent, and embedded in the body of Christ. Like Lorensen, Gaarden focuses primarily on the constellation of preacher, listener, word, and God. Still, as seen in this quote and the mention of the church building above, she hints at how non-human agents are part of these "networks of deep interdependence," too.

This thesis takes the next step, expanding Lorensen's and Gaarden's ideas about co-authorship and deep relationality and cooperation by acknowledging even more co-authors. A few other Scandinavian homileticians have recently begun taking first steps along this road with me.

A prominent contribution is the previously mentioned Linn S. Rystad's work, particularly her thesis *Overestimated and Underestimated: A Case Study of the Practice of Preaching for Children with an Emphasis on Children's Role as Listeners* (2020). In her case study of preaching for children, she combines Bakhtinian communication theory with practice theory. Instead of Lorensen's choice of Bourdieu, Rystad pairs Bakhtin with Theodore Schatzki to define preaching as a dialogical practice. Rystad's study highlights the importance of studying not just the chains of actions in a practice but also how practices are organized and what listeners *do* with the preaching event. It also points to the role that materiality and timespace play in the practice of preaching. The role of materiality is discussed in a case study of two preaching events, where she uses yet another theorist from the practice theoretical paradigm—James Wertsch—to show how "mediating means," such as a Bible and a narrative told with theatre props about the Bible text, contribute to the dialogue in the preaching event.[22]

---

[21] Gaarden 2021, 128.

[22] Rystad 2020, 1–12.

In the same discussion, Rystad presents two other ideas significant to this thesis. First, she points to how authority is conceived in Bakhtin's communication theory and draws on Olga Dysthe to add nuance to Bakhtin's understanding of authority. There is an authoritarian discourse (that builds on tradition and power), as well as the authority that Bakhtin himself associated with dialogue: an inner persuasive discourse without authority. But there is also a third kind of authority that preachers often strive for as an ideal: a discourse in which authority is based on trust and respect.[23]

The second point involves Rystad's discussion about "preaching at the thresholds." Rystad refers to Bakhtin's statement that important things happen at thresholds, and shows how Gaarden's description of "the third room of preaching" can be understood as a "liminal space." Rystad continues:

> The terms threshold, liminality, and third room all denote the importance of preaching as something that happens *in between*. Understanding preaching as an event, as dialogical, as something that *happens in between* allows us to describe and research preaching in terms of practice theory. [...] This way of understanding preaching is also radically relational. The preacher no longer has a primary place in describing what happens in the preaching event. Preaching happens in relation to listeners and the church room, and the preacher always preaches with mediational means, including language.[24]

Again, preaching is understood as relational—radically so—but here it includes mediational means/materiality which contribute to the preaching event. The preacher is decentered, and liminality comes to the fore through the concept of "threshold."

Rystad's research is part of a larger project, *Fyrkunnelse for små og stora* ("preaching for young and old"), that has the overarching aim to examine how preaching as practice is performed and experienced in a specific worship service context—namely, those part of a reform of Christian education in the Church of Norway. The results were published in the volume *Fyrkunnelse for barn og voksne: En studie av sju gudstjenester i trosopplaeringen* (2021), edited by Tone Stangeland Kaufman. The introduction states that the project is guided by a sensibility for sociocultural and socio-material theories and the notion that preaching is a practice. Thus, the researchers worked out from the insight that the preaching event is

---

[23] Rystad 2020, 118–122.
[24] Rystad 2020, 122.

not just a matter of words and content, but also embodied, relational, and material.[25]

Apart from the contribution from Rystad, the volume includes a chapter by Stangeland Kaufman and Hallvard Olavson Mosdøl, which use yet another practice theorist, Bruno Latour, to discuss how material entities, artifacts, and art play a significant role in the meaning-making process of the preaching event. In their conclusion, Kaufman and Mosdøl refer to Lorensen and Gaarden's work on "listeners as authors," stating that they want to take a step further and call the preaching event a "trialogic interaction" since it is not only a dialogue between the preacher and the listeners. The preaching event also depends on material objects, also understood as actors, because they, too, contribute significantly to the preaching event. However, in light of this conception of a "trialogue," they would rather speak of "co-authors" than authors.[26]

This thesis continues in this direction and contributes by taking a closer look at *how* materiality and mediational means contribute to the different phases of the preaching event, by focusing on particular kinds of material arrangements—arrangements that are crucial to this kind of preaching practice. This thesis also further explores the consequences of this radical relationality between materiality, mediation, the preacher, and the listener-as-co-author in the preaching event.

Additionally, in the scholarly conversation embodied by this thesis, there have been four other important conversation partners. The first is Sune Fahlgren, who wrote historical case studies on Free church preaching and "preachership." As mentioned in Chapter 2, Fahlgren draws on social theory and Alaisdair McIntyre's concept of practice to describe the preaching event's connection to ecclesiology.[27] In his later developments of his argument, Fahlgren points to the fact that these practices are not just social but also communicative. In other words, while Lorensen and Gaarden argued that communication theories alone are insufficient and call for practice theory as a means to fuller and more fruitful analysis, Fahlgren

---

[25] Tone Stangeland Kaufman, "Forkunnelse for barn og voksne," in *Forkunnelse for barn og voksne*, ed. Tone Stangeland Kaufman (Oslo: Iko-Forlaget, 2021), 7–18.

[26] Tone Stangeland Kaufman and H.O. Mosdøl, "Forskjellen som (ut)gjør en forskjell: En analyse av prekenhendelsen i to gudstjenester med utdeling av fireårsbok med vekt på materialitet," in *Fyrkunnelse for barn og voksne*, ed. Tone Stangeland Kaufman (Oslo: Iko-Forlaget, 2021), 91–112. See also Stangeland Kaufman and Mosdøl 2018, 123–132.

[27] Sune Fahlgren, *Predikantskap och församling: Sex fallstudier av en ecclesial baspraktik inom svensk frikyrklighet fram till 1960-talet* (Örebro: ÖTH rapport, 2006a). See also Fahlgren 2006b, 180–199.

argues that social theory of practices is insufficient and needs to be supplemented by communication theory—or, more pointedly, communication theology.[28]

Along with the methodological considerations in Fahlgren's case studies, this thesis is also in conversation with his analysis of historical preaching events. One of the preaching events Fahlgren analyzed was the Baptist pastor Hjalmar Danielson's radio sermon from 1925. Fahlgren concludes that the radio-mediated sermon constructs the listeners as a congregation of people who reflect critically and seek the truth. In the sermon, Danielson speaks not just about his own Baptist tradition but of a universal church that has existed for 1900 years. The ecclesial model in this preachership thus resembles what Peter M. Phillips (and others) call a *hybrid church*,[29] related to both a local congregation *and* listeners throughout the country. Fahlgren argues that there are two ecclesiological models at work simultaneously here: on the one hand, the model of church as *familia* (pertaining to the local congregation) and, on the other, the model of *universalitas* (church as a community that stretches out through time and space). Both are operant, he insists, for the radio listeners in his case study. According to Fahlgren, both models are drawn together in the heavenly church, *ecclesia triumphans* where the local and the universal are combined.[30]

The second conversation partner was also introduced in Chapter 2: Theo Pleizier. His book *Religious Involvement in Hearing Sermons* (2010), in which Pleizier presents an empirical study of the practice of preaching, uses grounded theory like Gaarden, instead of entering the analytical field with a predetermined theory. In fact, Pleizier is quite critical of such theoretical approaches because the empirical findings that result tend to serve as confirmation of the starting theory, rather than what he believes should be the other way around, where theory is instead informed by empirical findings.[31]

Like the other homileticians mentioned in this section, Pleizier argues that communication theories alone are insufficient for studying the preaching event. One reason is that these theories conceal the event as a religious phenomenon. Pleizier conceptualizes sermon listening as a social-religious process of "getting

---

[28] Sune Fahlgren, "Studying Fundamental Ecclesial Practices," in *Ecclesiology in the Trenches: Theory and Method under Construction*, eds. Sune Fahlgren and Jonas Ideström (Eugene, Oregon: Pickwick Publications, 2015), 102–105.

[29] Peter M. Phillips, *Hybrid Church: Blending Online and Offline Community* (Cambridge: Groove Books Limited, 2020).

[30] Fahlgren 2006a, 201–236.

[31] Theo Pleizier, *Religious Involvement in Hearing Sermons* (Delft: Eburon Academic Publisher, 2010), 13.

religiously involved in a sermon." Drawing on Miroslav Volf (a theologian associated with the sociocultural and, occasionally, practice theoretical paradigms), Pleizier argues that practices are structured in relation to norms, governed by constitutive beliefs, rules of conduct, and normative convictions about what is right action. Practices are shaped by beliefs and vice versa. Since preaching is a social practice, Pleizier also prefers to talk about "homiletic interaction" rather than "preaching." The object of study is what the preacher and listener do together in interhuman communication.[32]

One of the reasons that communication theory alone is insufficient in the study of homiletic interaction, according to Pleizier, is because the idea of communication rarely is reflected upon. Pleizier draws on John Durham Peters to note that the concept of communication often is associated with an ideal of "angelic communication," in which perfect and mutual understanding is the goal, and the solution to almost any problem is better communication. However, in practice, there is a fundamental brokenness to human communication. Pleizier describes this insight into the limitations of communication as an eschatological notion. For him, therefore, it is better to study preaching as a social act because such an approach does not involve ideals.[33]

The theory that Pleizier describes, based on his interviews with listeners, outlines the practice of listening religiously as a process in three stages: opening up, dwelling in the sermon, and actualizing faith. Notably, Pleizier also uses spatial metaphors. His final chapter discusses how preaching should provide "a sacred canopy," a "home" for homeless believers in a secular world.[34]

The third conversation partner, Wilfried Engemann, was briefly introduced in Chapter 2, where I described his model of the preaching event. In his book *Homiletics: Principles and Patterns of Reasoning* (2019), which is the English translation of *Einfürhrung in die Homiletik* (2011), Engemann describes preaching as a process of comprehension and communication that is subdivided into stages of text interpretation and text production. Within these, as previously mentioned, he breaks down the preaching event further into four phases.[35]

Even if Engemann does not explicitly work with practice theory, he comes close. In his understanding of preaching as dialogue, he points out that dialogicity is created when listeners are seen as constitutive participants in the sermon, not as

---

[32] Pleizier 2010, 21–33.
[33] Pleizier 2010, 31–56.
[34] Pleizier 2010, 284–288.
[35] Engemann 2019, 1–14.

containers for the preacher's theological knowledge. Furthermore, drawing on John L. Austin, J. R. Searle, and Jürgen Habermas's speech act theories, Engemann understands preaching as not just a transfer of information but as acting and performative communication.[36]

Notably, this understanding of preaching leads Engemann into a discussion on what he calls "the virtual perspective." Drawing on the work of Ilona Nord, he refers to the sermon as the construction of a world, a virtual reality or "the world as it is *perceived or imagined, wished for or believed in.* It is a reality as a necessarily insinuated, effective field of reference of our existence." This virtual reality affects how we see and act in the "real," material, and corporeal world.[37] Engemann's brief discussion on the preaching event's virtual aspects points to potential (and exciting!) overlaps between the two scholarly conversations under consideration here. With this thesis, I hope to show more clearly how.

Engemann outlines a theology of preaching based on the relationship between communication and the following four theological aspects: Christological/pneumatological, creation-theological, eschatological, and ecclesiological.

According to Engemann, communication is personal, and people appear as themselves only in relation to other people—in other words, through communication. Theologically, this is understood as an expression of the incarnation of God in Christ. Likewise, a sermon in the Holy Spirit is "the *communication of the gospel within a qualified space of relationship and encounter between people.*"[38] Thus, as previously mentioned in Chapter 2 and in Article D, Engemann focuses primarily on relations and interactions between humans.

Communication in preaching is also "acting communication." This expression of creation theology takes the creation narrative in Genesis 1 as portraying a speech act par excellence. In the same way that God calls into existence, sermons call people into their own lives. Engemann points out that listeners often find themselves in circumstances where the future seems "closed," a "hopeless, frozen present" in which there is no space for development. In such a situation, a sermon has "anticipatory power" and can contribute to an opening up of the future. Referring to Grözinger, he underlines how a sermon can point to "God's horizon of possibility." This sense of possibility informs the idea that preaching is "committing communication." Engemann relates this to what he calls "eschatological earnestness," a reminder of the preacher's task to make listeners aware of their

---

[36] Engemann 2019, 159–188, 226–257.
[37] Engemann 2019, 205–206.
[38] Engemann 2019, 494.

responsibility toward themselves, others, and God, ultimately calling them to "a decision for or against God."[39]

Finally, preaching is "mandated communication," which relates to ecclesiology. Like the homileticians discussed in the previous chapter, Engemann considers the sermon to have a "church-shaping function [...], and through this, it has a determining influence on the nature of the church: the sermon clarifies what the church is all about and what it means to belong to her. The church becomes visible in her preaching. The sermon is a prominent expression of the essence of the church."[40]

To Engemann, this raises the question of who gets to preach. He discusses the concept of the priesthood of all believers, concluding that the point of it is not that everybody should preach but that all baptized are called to communicate the gospel in practice or "to participate willingly in a gospel-based discourse on freedom and love." The person who takes on the office of a preacher needs to have an inner and outer calling, and possess knowledge of how to deal "with the matter of the gospel in a theologically correct and homiletically skillful manner" alongside the interpretative traditions confessed by their church. Since the preacher's office is legitimated by function, these issues are "self-regulating." In his discussion, Engemann underlines the importance of preachers acting as theologians who underpin the sermon with sound theology.[41]

The fourth and final conversation partner is practical theologian Sabrina Müller, who, in her book *Lived Theology: Impulses for a Pastoral Theology of Empowerment* (2021), underlines the importance for practical theological engagement with practices, in particular in relation to the existence of digital culture and spaces. Digital media are a reminder to practical theologians that someone interested in religious practices cannot look solely at what goes on in the local congregation. Moreover, digital media have contributed to a situation in which theology is no longer constructed solely by pastors, church leaders, and theological faculties. Therefore, it is vital for practical theologians to study lived theology and describe how lived theology comes about.[42] This thesis contributes to that through its practice theoretical approach.

---

[39] Engemann 2019, 499–501.

[40] Engemann 2019. 502.

[41] Engemann 2019, 502–515. Quotation p. 515.

[42] Sabrina Müller, *Lived Theology: Impulses for a Pastoral Theology of Empowerment* (Eugene, Oregon: Cascade Books, 2021), 1–10.

Although Müller does not explicitly set out to discuss the practice of preaching, her argument is of relevance to this thesis due to her definition of "lived theology": the priesthood of all believers' opportunity to express themselves theologically. According to Müller, the priesthood of all believers must not be reduced to volunteers who only do practical and diaconal work. This would be to overlook their function as priests who are called to stand before God and express themselves theologically. Müller argues that it is crucial to acknowledge and recognize lived theology since it makes this priestly function apparent to the priesthood of all believers—and theologically empowers them to practice it. As Müller puts it: "When lived theology is perceived and taken seriously as theology, it becomes an aspect of empowerment."[43] As the priesthood of all believers grows into this calling, social media can provide a training ground where they can practice theological literacy, not least since it is a space with lower stakes than an onsite church context. Müller also calls for a pastoral theology that teaches pastors to recognize lived theology. This would enable pastors to move away from the idea of the pastor as a lonely specialist—and toward an attitude of dialogue, reciprocity, and resonance.[44]

3.2 Preaching in Digital Culture and Spaces

The first strand in Nordic homiletical research that Lorensen identifies was an empirical turn toward the interaction between listeners and preachers. The other strand was the interaction between preaching and contemporary societal events or currents—which, in the case of this thesis, means digital culture.

If "the practice of preaching" is a comparatively established and distinct discussion in the field of homiletics, "preaching in digital culture and spaces" is not—as of yet. It is clear, however, that the pandemic supercharged homiletical interest in preaching in digital culture and spaces. Judging from paper presentations on research initiatives in recent conferences in the field of homiletics, the coming years will see a surge in publications on the topic, hopefully sparking a much-needed conversation.

The fact that there is not yet an established scholarly discussion does not mean that there has not been scholarly work done. It is just that this research has been part of many different scholarly conversations and rarely brought together. In this section, I will offer an overview of the current state of scholarly discussion by mapping and categorizing various contributions. In the first section (3.2.1), I will

---

[43] Müller 2021, 64.
[44] Müller 2021, 75–84.

discuss three common ways for scholars to engage with preaching in digital culture and spaces. In the second section (3.2.2), I will identify three fields that previous research on preaching in digital culture and spaces has related to. In the last section (3.2.3) I will summarize in what ways this thesis contributes to the scholarly conversations on the practice of preaching in digital culture and spaces.

3.2.1 Common Ways to Engage with Preaching in Digital Culture and Spaces

As briefly mentioned in the introduction, one common way for homileticians to engage with preaching in digital culture and spaces has been to discuss digital media as part of the cultural context *outside* the church. In parity with, for example, secularization and pluralism, digitalization is something that preachers feel they need to respond to. Their responses and recommendations vary. Either digital culture is something that poses a threat (digitality is something that distracts from the word of God and true community), or it represents a form of communication that preachers can learn from in order to preach more effectively—or both.[45]

A prominent example is homiletician David Lose, who touches upon the subject in his *Preaching at the Crossroads,* where he discusses why the Gospel does not seem to appeal to people anymore as a meaning-making source. According to Lose, part of the problem is that digital media floods us with information and offers an uncountable number of competing narratives. The result has been shifts in worldview: from a sense of obligation to a "what's in it for me" attitude; from identity as something received to identity as something constructed; and from valuing tradition to valuing experience. However, the culture promoted by digital media does not only run unidirectionally as a challenge to preaching—it could also be an inspiration for the type of preaching Lose advocates: "participatory preaching" with "interactive sermons" that engage the listeners. However, Lose ultimately concludes that digital media only serves as a metaphor, not as something that could be a crucial part of the preaching event.[46]

Homiletical works that engage with preaching in digital culture and spaces as something *inside the* church are just as scarce. While the statement of Sunggu A.

---

[45] David J. Lose, *Preaching at the Crossroads: How the World and our Preaching is Changing* (Minneapolis: Fortress Press, 2013); *Text Messages: Preaching God's Word in a Smartphone World,* ed. John Tucker (Eugene, OR: Wipf and Stock, 2017); Wolfgang Beck, "Die Macht der Couch: Homiletische Lerneffekte entstehen an Orten moderner Medien," *Communicatio Socialis* 50:1 (2017), 113–124; *The Worlds of the Preacher: Navigating Biblical, Cultural, and Personal Contexts,* ed. Scott M. Gibson (Grand Rapids, MI: Baker Academic, 2018).

[46] Lose 2013, 86–95.

Yang that "not a single publication can be found in the market that is dedicated to online preaching"[47] is slightly exaggerated, he nevertheless has a point. Digitally-mediated preaching has been "virtually ignored"—pun, perhaps, intended.[48]

Building on the categories I present in an overview of online preaching in the forthcoming *Oxford Handbook of Digital Theology*, I have identified three common ways for scholars to engage with digitally-mediated preaching: "message-oriented," "media-oriented," and "ontology-oriented." In practice, the line between these is not clear-cut, as contributions often combine approaches from all categories. However, there is usually one category that dominates.[49]

In the "message-oriented" category of approaches, the center of attention is the message itself, and "homiletics is homiletics" no matter which media types are used. There are a few differences, possibilities, and challenges pertaining to the performance of the sermon, but all in all, digital media is merely a tool for preachers to do what they have always done.[50] Representing this view is homiletician Lisa Kraske Cressman, who states: "The reasons we preach and the components that constitute a sermon are unaffected by the medium. The word of God is transmitted just as efficaciously whether told as a story in ancient times, read silently in a Bible a hundred years ago, or listened to in a podcast today."[51]

In the "media-oriented" category of approaches, it is the media that is the main locus of interest. After all, as Marshall McLuhan famously stated, "the medium is the message."[52] An example of a commonly used family of theories deployed to this end is the "media as environment" theories.[53] Prevalent are variations on Walter Ong's theory of orality and literacy—which is quite natural since these concepts have been widely used in the field of homiletics. For example, media theories significantly impacted David Buttrick's influential oral/aural-oriented phenomenological homiletics of the 1980s.[54] Moreover, it has often been used by theologians and church historians to understand the relationship between the church and

---

[47] Yang 2021, 75.

[48] Tripp Hudgins, "Preaching Online," *Anglican Theological Review* 101:1 (2019), 79.

[49] Mannerfelt, "Online Preaching," forthcoming.

[50] Denis J. Bekkering, "From 'Televangelist' to 'Intervangelist': The Emergence of the Streaming Video Preacher," *Journal of Religion & Popular Culture* 23:2 (2011), 101–117.

[51] Kraske Cressman 2021, 46–47.

[52] Marshall McLuhan, *Understanding Media: The Extensions of Man* (Corte Madera, CA: Gingko Press, 2003).

[53] Knut Lundby and Giulia Evolvi, "Theoretical Frameworks for Approaching Religion and New Media," in *Digital Religion: Understanding Religious Practice in Digital Media*, eds. Heidi Campbell and Ruth Tsuria, 2nd ed. (London & New York: Routledge, 2022), 233–249.

[54] Lorensen 2014, 73–75. Lorensen quotes Walter Ong's *Orality and Literacy* on p. 75.

media.[55] An important topic of discussion is change: how do the affordances of digital media affect things like the sermon's form and content?[56] An example is my own case study of sermons conductd by the lead pastor of the mega-church, Hillsong Sweden. I use developments based on Ong's secondary orality theory to analyze how digital culture shapes the preaching practices of the pastor and the content of the sermon.[57]

In the "ontology-oriented" category of approaches, contributions center on the sacramentality of the word and the relationship between "real" and "virtual." The doctrine of the incarnation is commonly used to emphasize the contrast between real and virtual. An example of this approach is homiletician Luke A. Powery, who, in the book *Ways of the Word: Learning to Preach for Your Time and Place* (2016), devotes a chapter to the subject "Preaching and Technology." Powery states that there is "a historical tension" between technology and preaching, because technology shapes and controls the practice of preaching. Powery lists the losses and gains technology brings to bear on preaching. With technology, we might leverage new learning styles that can benefit preaching in the local church and wider spreading of the gospel. But concurrently, we might lose incarnational preaching, which "requires a body, as evidenced in God's sermon in Jesus Christ

---

[55] Peter Horsfield, *From Jesus to the Internet: A History of Christianity and Media* (Chichester, West Sussex: Wiley Blackwell, 2015); Dennis Ford, *A Theology for a Mediated God: How Media Shapes our Notions About Divinity* (London. Routledge, 2016).

[56] Ryan P. Burge and Miles D. Williams, "Is Social Media a Digital Pulpit? How Evangelical Leaders Use Twitter to Encourage the Faithful and Publicize Their Work," *Journal of Religion, Media & Digital Culture* 8:3 (2019), 309–339; Pauline Cheong, "Tweet the Message? Religious Authority and Social Media Innovation," *Journal of Religion, Media and Digital Culture* 3:3 (2014), 1–19; Mogomme Alpheus Masoga, "Effectiveness of WhatsApp Homiletics in the Era of COVID-19 in South Africa," *Pharos Journal of Theology* 101 (2020), 1–16; Anna-Katharina Lienau, "Kommunikation des Evangeliums in social media," *ZThK* 117 (2020), 489–522; Kerstin Menzel, "More than the Argument of Experience? Preaching with Episodes from Everyday Life on Instagram," paper at the *Societas Homiletica* conference "Preaching towards Truth," Budapest 12–18 August 2022; David Plüss "The Dialogue Form of Online Preaching. Case Studies," paper at the *Societas Homiletica* conference "Preaching towards Truth," Budapest 12–18 August 2022; Mannerfelt 2022, 6–27. Susan Codone, "Megachurch Pastor Twitter: An Analysis of Rick Warren and Andy Stanley, Two of America's Social Pastors," *Journal of Religion, Media and Digital Culture* 3:2 (2014), 1–32.

[57] Frida Mannerfelt, "Back to the Roots or Growing New Branches: Preaching, Orality and Mission in a Digital Age," in *Missio Dei in a Digital Age*, eds. Jonas Kurlberg and Peter M. Phillips (London: SCM Press, 2020), 195– 220. These features have been observed in other empirical studies of online preaching. See, for example, Clint Bryant and Mohammed Albakry, "'To be real honest, I'm just like you': analyzing the discourse of personalization in online sermons," *Text & Talk* 36:6 (2016), 683–703); Lienau 2020, 489–522.

called the incarnation. The Word event is incarnational, thus preaching is as well. [...] Real human bodies, as opposed to virtual realities and bodies, are essential for the preaching ministry."[58] Consequently, according to Powery, digitally-mediated preaching may be used as a supplement, but if it replaces onsite preaching, the core identity of preaching is lost, along with humanity, community, spiritual growth, and depth.[59]

However, a few ontology-oriented homileticians see virtuality as a continuation of the intellectual tradition that sees the real and being as mediated. Demonstrating this approach is the homiletician whom the aforementioned Engemann referred to, Ilona Nord. In her book *Realitäten des Glaubens: Zur virtuellen Dimension christlicher Religiosität* (2008), Nord outlines a practical theological approach to virtual reality as digitally-mediated communication spaces. In one of the chapters, she discusses the implications of this for homiletics. That discussion was later developed in the article "Experiment with Freedom Every Day: Regarding the Virtual Dimension of Homiletics" (2011). Nord argues that the experience of digital mediation teaches preachers and their listeners something fundamental about the preaching event: that it is about "realms of possibility." A sermon should of course always relate to the experiences of the listeners' lives, but it also needs to refer to a virtual reality, one that is connected to what we can see and touch, but which also reaches beyond that. Nord writes: "In the world of faith, it is not just that which we can actually see before us that is valid. What is often more important is something which is quite literally virtual, i.e., that which is available to us because there exists a possibility that it exists." In fact, for Nord, the experiences of digital mediation even strengthen our ability to acknowledge the possibilities of God, not least by helping listeners identify as a child of God.[60]

As Tone Stangeland Kaufman and I discuss in a forthcoming article, several of these ways of engagement with digitally-mediated preaching come with potential problems. The message-oriented approach tends to ignore the significance of media, while the media-oriented approach tends to overemphasize their significance. Meanwhile, the ontology-oriented approaches (of Powery's kind, for instance) tend to dismiss digitally-mediated preaching altogether on the basis of theological

---

[58] Luke A. Powery, "Preaching and Technology," in *Ways of the Word: Learning to Preach for Your Time and Place*, eds. Luke A. Powery and Sally A. Brown (Minneapolis: Fortress Press, 2016), 215.

[59] Powery 2016, 209–234.

[60] Ilona Nord, *Realitäten des Glaubens: Zur virtuellen Dimension christlicher Religiosität* (Berlin: De Gruyter, 2008); Ilona Nord, "Experiment with Freedom Every Day: Regarding the Virtual Dimension of Homiletics," *Homiletic* 36: 2 (2011), 31–37.

ontology. In the article we argue for socio-material approaches as a fourth option, offering Bruno Latour's Actor-Network Theory as an example of how fruitful such an approach might be. The Schatzkian practice theoretical approach of this thesis is another example embodying such an approach.[61]

3.2.2 Common Fields for Research on Preaching in Digital Culture and Spaces

Regardless of approach, scholars who have engaged with digitally-mediated preaching are mainly found in three fields: homiletics, digital religion, and digital theology. However, there are also examples from fields as diverse as language studies, religion and popular culture, studies in information seeking, and studies in World Christianity.[62]

Within the field of homiletics, there are a few larger studies of the practice of preaching in digital culture and spaces. A work already mentioned is Casey Thornburgh Sigmon's thesis Engaging the Gadfly: A Process Homilecclesiology for a Digital Age (2017). Sigmon claims that preaching has been caught in a pulpit-pew binary and that homiletics needs to let go of a number of assumptions about preaching, namely where and when preaching might occur, and by whom. Drawing on process theology, she formulates a theology of preaching and ecclesiology for a digital age—a "homilecclesiological vision."[63] Notably, Sigmon refers to Gaarden's and Lorensen's article about listeners as authors and suggests that perhaps technology could offer an opportunity for preachers and listeners to collaborate even further.[64] Sigmon writes:

> The capacity of the message to be impacted by the laity, directly, is a value in homilecclesiology. This is more than a conversational sermonic approach. This is a call to imagine the dialogue as sermon, wherein our very life of prayer, experience, and study is the sermon preparation and the insights that emerge in the dialogue are indeed lifted up as

---

[61] Frida Mannerfelt and Tone Stangeland Kaufman, "Understanding the Paradox of (Im)Perfection: A Socio–material Approach to Digitally-Mediated Preaching," (forthcoming).

[62] Bryant and Albakry 2016, 683–703); Bekkering 2011, 101–117; David H. Michaels, "Dipping Into a Shallow Pool or Beginning a Deeper Conversation: A Case Study of a Minister's Engagement with the Internet for Preaching," *Journal of Religious & Theological Information* 8:3–4 (2009), 164–178; Asamoah-Gyadu Kwabena, ""Get on the Internet!' Says the LORD': Religion, Cyberspace and Christianity in Contemporary Africa," *Studies in World Christianity* 13:3 (2012), 225–242.

[63] Sigmon 2017, 13.

[64] Sigmon 2017, 107–108, 142–143.

the aim of the sermon. The aim is discovered, mutually, rather than deduced by one and assented to the many.[65]

As shown in the quote, Sigmon's theology of preaching suggests that digital technology might enable a deeper collaboration that better achieves the dialogic ideal of mutuality. It also serves as a reminder that Sigmon's contribution—like Powery's chapter and Nord's article—is formulated from a theoretical/theological vantage point. While they give examples of how their theologies of preaching might turn out in practice, they neither conduct nor draw on empirical studies of the phenomenon they discuss.

This corresponds with Tim Hutching's broader observations about the quality of research conducted on online communities. In his contribution to the volume *What Really Matters: Scandinavian Perspectives in Ecclesiology and Ethnography* (2015), Hutchings states that theological claims are usually not anchored in empirical studies. He writes: "Christian theologians have rarely tried to use ethnography to support arguments on either side."[66] Hutchings asserts that ethnography can never replace theological reflection, but it might serve in the evaluation of theological claims. Empirical studies can shed light on a theological debate.[67]

However, there *are* a few larger empirical studies, done in the field of homiletics, to draw on. Alison Witte's case study *Preaching and Technology: A Study of Attitudes and Practices* from 2013 examines how digital technology affects preaching as a genre and as rhetorical practice. Witte found that an understanding of genre affects the adoption of digital tools. Drawing, among others, on Ong's theory of orality and literacy, Witte found that her preachers and congregants—for historical and theological reasons—thought of preaching as an oral genre, and since they wanted to preserve existing practices, beliefs, and values, they saw digital technology as peripheral and supplementary. Witte concluded that as long as preachers and congregations have these expectations, the preacher does not have the *ethos* (or authority) to speak effectively in a digital context. However, she predicted that the genre of preaching was about to be radically reshaped by new technologies, and that more studies are needed.[68]

---

[65] Sigmon 2017, 156.

[66] Tim Hutchings, "Ethnography, Representation, and Digital Media," in *What Really Matters: Scandinavian Perspectives in Ecclesiology and Ethnography*, eds. Jonas Ideström and Tone Stangeland Kaufman (Eugene, Oregon: Pickwick Publications, 2015), 227–228.

[67] Hutchings 2015, 233.

[68] Alison Witte, *Preaching and Technology: A Study of Attitudes and Practices*, Ph.D. thesis, (Bowling Green State University, 2013).

Another empirical study of the practice of preaching is presented by Ramona Hayes in her thesis *Digital and Analog Preaching in a Multi-media World* from 2018. Hayes examines the reception of different kinds of sermon styles among "analogs" (people who were formed primarily through the communication patterns of the written word) and "digitals" (people formed by digital communication patterns). Again, the orality and literacy theory of Walter Ong is at play here. Notably, the focus of Hayes's study is preaching to listeners in a local church, not in digital spaces. She states: "To be clear, I am not proposing to incorporate various forms of digital media into sermons. I am searching for non-digital ways to craft a sermon that will resonate with Digital listeners and enhance their reception and understanding of the sermon while also appealing to Analog listeners."[69]

A third example is Anna Katharina Lienau's article "Kommunikation des Evangeliums in social media" from the beginning of 2020, in which she observes and interviews eleven Instagramming pastors as they attempt to communicate the gospel through social media. Lienau found that pastors mainly use teaching and preaching to communicate the gospel. Similar to my findings in the case study of the Hillsong preacher above, she, too, found that the preaching she observed is practice-oriented, done through storytelling, focused on modeling the everyday life of a Christian, and open to dialogue with followers in the commentary field.[70]

In addition to these three larger empirical studies, there are several smaller studies, often done as part of research reports on worship during the COVID-19 pandemic.[71] However, common to most of these empirical studies is a lack of deep engagement with theological reflection.

In light of the above overview, what can we say? Scholars in the field of homiletics that have engaged in research on the practice of preaching in digital culture and spaces do so *either* from a theological point of view with little or no empirical studies *or* from an empirical point of view where theological perspectives are few or even missing. I could not agree more with the previously mentioned statement from Yang: "a concrete theology of online preaching, as well as applicable homiletical strategies, are greatly needed."[72]

---

[69] Ramona Hayes, *Digital and Analog Preaching in a Multi-media World*. D.Min. Thesis. Luther Seminary, 2018.

[70] Lienau 2020, 489–522

[71] Hudgins 2019, 79–88; *Når folkekirken skal spille efter reglerne – men uden for banen: Folkekirkens håndtering af coronaperioden i foråret 2020* (Aarhus Folkekirkens Uddannelses- og videnscenter, 2020), 167–233.

[72] Yang 2021, 75–90.

In his article "The Word Digitized," Yang offers an outline of what such an approach could look like, adopting Karl Barth's threefold definition of God's Word as a starting point. According to Barth, the Word exists and presents itself in Scripture (the written Word of God), in Christ (the revealed Word of God,) and in preaching (the proclaimed word of God). These three forms are analogous to the doctrine of the Trinity: they are separate but exist only in relation to each other. The Word of God is characterized by certain traits through its three forms: immutable, reliable, present, and transformative. Yang adds a fourth dimension: "The Word digitized," which contains all three other forms—but digitalized. However, when digitalized, the Word of God is at risk of taking on other problematic traits, and so it is essential to adapt digitally-mediated preaching to the immutability, reliability, and so on that defines its pre-digitized forms. The theology of preaching is used to analyze different preaching styles.[73] With his article, Yang provides an interesting example of how normative and formal theological voices come into conversation with the lived theology embodied in practices. This thesis aims to contribute with another example in this lineage of normative/lived theological fusion.

The second field in which scholars have engaged in the study of preaching in digital culture and spaces is digital religion. "Digital religion" is an established field for research at the intersection of religion and digital media. In the 2012 landmark volume, *Digital Religion: Understanding Religious Practice in New Media Worlds,* the editor Heidi Campbell defines digital religion as the technological and cultural space that is evoked when we talk about how online and offline religious spheres have become blended."[74] The subtitle is telling. Digital religion is highly interdisciplinary, gathering scholars from various fields with a common interest in practices and a focus on how digital technology and environments shape religious groups and cultures—and vice versa.

The second revised edition describes the development of the field over time. The key issues remain community, identity, ritual, authority, and embodiment. The development of the field is described in terms of waves, but alongside the descriptive, categorical, and theoretical waves, the editors Heidi Campbell and Ruth Tsuria identify a fourth wave: the convergent. Increasingly, digital religion scholars are turning their attention to media practices in everyday life, while maintaining their distinctive focus on identity, community, and religious authority.[75]

---

[73] Yang 2021, 75–90.
[74] Campbell 2012, xx.
[75] Campbell and Tsuria 2022, 1–22.

In the field of digital religion, relevant research has been done that informs this thesis, especially the body of work that focuses on megachurch preachers who use social media platforms like Twitter.[76]

An exemplary work is the case study conducted by media and communication scholar and professor in Engagement and Innovation, Pauline Hope Cheong, where she analyzes the Singaporean megachurch pastor Kong Hee's use of Twitter, and how the practices of his Twitter authorship point to the changing nature of sacred texts and religious authority. Cheong identifies various kinds of scripture use—to quote, extract, remix, and recontextualize—and discusses the implications for clerical authority. According to Cheong, religious authority is communicatively constructed and emergent. Through their tweets, pastors build trust by showcasing scriptural expertise and reinforcing epistemic authority. However, this social media-mediated trust also increases these pastors' dependence on their church and Twitter followers to validate their authority.[77]

In other words, digital religion is a relevant conversation partner for this thesis through its focus on practices and authority. However, as seen in the example of Cheong, the practice of preaching (or, as it is called in her article, tweeting) in digital culture and spaces is used as an opportunity to shed light on concepts relevant to the field of digital religion—like authority—but not as a contribution to discussions on the practice of preaching in a practical theological sense. In addition, digital religion explicitly delineates itself from theology. For example, in the historian of religions Gregory Price Grieves's chapter in *Digital Religion*, he stresses that digital religion is *not* theology.[78] Additionally, the journal most associated with the discourse of digital religion, *Journal of Media, Religion and Digital Culture*, emphasizes on its homepage that they decline theological contributions: "Studies of any religious tradition, medium or geographical region are welcome. [...] Theological writings will not normally be accepted for publication."[79]

The third field in which scholars engage in the particular conversations that are relevant to this thesis is digital theology. Digital theology is related to digital religion. In their description of the various waves of digital religion research, Campbell and

---

[76] See for example, Cheong 2014, 1–19; Codone 2014, 1–32; Burge and Williams 2019, 309–339; Mark Ward, "The PowerPoint and the Glory: An Ethnography of Pulpit Media and Its Organizational Impacts" *Journal of Media and Religion* 14:4 (2015), 175–195.

[77] Cheong 2014, 1–19.

[78] Gregory Price Grieves, "Religion," in *Digital Religion: Understanding Practice in Digital Media*, eds. Heidi A. Campbell and Ruth Tsuria, 2nd ed. (New York & London: Routledge 2022), 25–39.

[79] *Journal of Religion, Media and Culture*, https://brill.com [Accessed 16 January 2023].

Tsuria mention an emerging fifth wave that is even more interdisciplinary than previous ones and which focuses on finding new methods or adapting existing methods to the study of digital religion. The previously mentioned *Third Space of Digital Religion*, in my view, is exemplary of a fifth-wave approach. According to Campbell and Tsuria, a further feature of this fifth wave is an emphasis on more specialized subfields, such as digital theology.[80]

Campbell's and Tsuria's identification of this multidisciplinary fifth wave shows that the line between digital religion and theology may not be so clear-cut.[81] The authors of the 2019 article "Defining Digital Theology" are not sure there are clear boundaries here, either. The previously mentioned Phillips and Kurlberg, along with theologian Kyle Schiefelbein-Guerrero, state that digital theology relates to digital religion but argue for the uniqueness of digital theology as a space with a particular openness to theological reflection. For them, "theology is not the same as the sociology of religion or information studies, or communication studies. Theology is the critical study of the nature of God, of God's interaction with the world, or of the world's exploration of the mystery of faith."[82]

In their description of how this field has developed, Phillips, Kurlberg & Schielfelbein-Guerrero also use the concept of waves (in accordance with the digital religion discourse). However, they mention that the differences between waves are methodological and typological rather than chronological. Research has been done and is still ongoing simultaneously across all four categories. Therefore, they prefer to use the word "levels." The fours levels are DT1) the use of digital technology to teach theology; DT2) theological research enabled by digitality or digital culture; DT3) intentional, sustained, and reflexive theologically-informed engagement with digitality/digital culture; and DT4) a prophetic re-appraisal of digitality in light of theological ethics.[83]

Digital theology is thus a relevant conversation partner for this thesis, particularly in its focus on theological reflection in relation to digital culture. However, this is still a relatively new and emerging field. While scholars have contributed with theological reflections on digital culture, and these are certainly relevant to

---

[80] Campbell and Tsuria 2022, 3–21.

[81] Campbell and Tsuria 2022, 12. See also Stephen Garner, "Theology and New Media," in *Digital Religion: Understanding Religious Practice in Digital Media*, eds. Heidi Campbell and Ruth Tsuria, 2nd ed. (London & New York: Routledge), 266–281.

[82] Peter M. Phillips, Jonas Kurlberg & Kyle Schiefelbein-Guerrero, "Defining Digital Theology: Digital Humanities, Digital Religion and the Particular Work of the CODEC Research Centre and Network," *Open Theology* 5 (2019), 37.

[83] Phillips, Kurlberg and Schiefelbein-Guerrero 2019, 29–43.

this thesis, few have engaged explicitly with the practice of preaching. Among these few is the previously mentioned Ilona Nord. Still, she enters the conversation from a theoretical and theological vantage point and does not engage in empirical studies. In other words, contributions from the field of digital religion have included empirical studies of the practice of preaching in digital culture and spaces, while contributions from digital theology have mainly focused on theological reflection. Thus, the pattern found in the field of homiletics, in which the focus is on either practices or theology, resurfaces in digital religion and digital theology.

3.3 In Sum

In this chapter, I have presented the two homiletical discussions I want to contribute to: first, the ongoing and established conversation among Scandinavian homileticians on "the practice of preaching"; and second, the emerging conversation about "preaching in digital culture and spaces." While it is not yet a proper scholarly conversation where scholars directly discuss with each other within established norms, scholarly work nevertheless has been done. I have identified three common approaches (message-oriented, media-oriented, and ontology-oriented), alongside three main fields (homiletics, digital religion, and digital theology), in which research on preaching in digital culture and spaces has been conducted. I have also identified a pattern shared across each of these, in which studies of the practice of preaching in digital culture and spaces tend to focus either on practices *or* theological reflection, but rarely both together.

I stated that this thesis wants to contribute with the following: 1) a discussion on how to research preaching, both in its local and digitally-mediated forms; 2) an empirical and theological study of the practice of preaching that is up-to-date, and looks into digitally-mediated preaching in mainline Protestant denominations (but not the evangelical mega-church context) with a special focus on digitally-mediated preaching that is part of the Sunday Service (i.e., not just a general category inclusive of all preaching on Twitter or other social platforms); and 3) a discussion on co-authorship and deep relationality. Within this strand of homiletics, there is a presumption that materiality matters. I want to provide insight into *how* it matters and what the consequences might be through the example of digital technology.

4. On Methodology and Methods

This chapter focuses on methodology and method. As sociologist Patricia Leavy points out in her book on research design, these are not the same thing. Methodology is a plan for how research should proceed, given certain ontological and epistemological considerations. In essence, methodology is when the researcher matches method to theory. A method is a tool for data collection, and the use of that tool (for example, the proceedings of an interview) will differ depending on the methodology.[1]

This thesis is situated in a practice theoretical paradigm. In the following, I will elaborate on practice theory in practical theology—and the epistemological implications of the methodology and research design this implies. This resulting thesis, therefore, takes shape as a multicase study consisting of several case studies, each centered on a particular issue. Finally, I will describe the methods used to generate and analyze the source material—in short, why I chose to do what I did and how I did it.

4.1 Considering Methodology

Methodology rests on epistemology. Since epistemology itself has been a matter of fierce debate in the field of practical theology for the last decades, it is necessary to start this section by accounting for the epistemological groundwork of research design considered as such (4.1.1). Next, I will account for my methodological considerations and presuppositions in research design (4.1.2), research questions (4.1.3), and the kinds of conclusions I am able to make (4.1.4).

---

[1] Patricia Leavy, *Research Design: Quantitative, Qualitative, Mixed Methods, Arts-based, and Community-based Participatory Research Approaches* (New York/London: The Guilford Press, 2017), 10–17.

4.1.1 Epistemological Groundings

As mentioned in Chapter 2, there has been a turn to practice in practical theology.[2] As a result, the number of practical theologians who work with qualitative methods has increased.[3] This raises a question that practical theologians have struggled with for at least two decades: how to account for the relationship between practice and theology?

In his overview of this discussion, practical theologian Pete Ward points out that this relationship is often uneasy, since both qualitative methods and theology carry epistemological force shaped by disciplinary norms and conventions. Qualitative methods rely on observation and empirical evidence, which do not always sit well with theology's emphasis on revelation and rationality. According to Ward, this awkward relationship has often been solved through correlation, in which qualitative research and theology are separated and engaged with in different steps of the research process—as seen, for example, in models like *the pastoral cycle*. The general idea is to generate empirical knowledge first, *then* engage with theological reflection.

However, according to Ward, theologians who engage with qualitative research soon discover that it is an excellent tool for exploring an often overlooked theology, namely a theology situated in social and cultural locations, performed by individuals and communities. This realization actualizes questions about theology—particularly whether it is possible to learn anything about God using qualitative methods. Based on Trinitarian and Christological thought, some theologians claim that it indeed is possible. They argue that the divine is present and active in the depths of human experience and practices. In other words, they aim to collapse the binary positions generated by the correlation described above.[4]

I argue that aiming for collapsed correlation in studies of digitally-mediated practices is essential. In a discussion on normativity and the question of precedence, the previously mentioned Stangeland Kaufman shows that correlation

---

[2] Bobrowicz and Mannerfelt 2021, 47–68; Stangeland Kaufman and Danbolt 2020, 6–18.

[3] Pete Ward and Knut Tveitereid, "Introduction," in *The Wiley Blackwell Companion to Theology and Qualitative Research*, eds. Pete Ward and Knut Tveitereid (Oxford: Wiley Blackwell, 2022), 1–4.

[4] Pete Ward, "Theology and Qualitative Research: An Uneasy Relationship," in *The Wiley Blackwell Companion to Theology and Qualitative Research*, eds. Pete Ward and Knut Tveitereid (Oxford: Wiley Blackwell, 2022), 7–15.

models tend to give precedence to theology over practices.[5] As discussed in Chapter 2, digitally-mediated practices are often assessed from a normative and formal theological point of view with little or no regard for lived theology as it is practiced on the ground, often resulting in the dismissal of digitally-mediated practices altogether. Working with a correlation model would thus put me in an untenable position where I run the risk of designing a research project with only one outcome. But how to conceptualize a collapsed correlation?

In the last decade, practice theory has surfaced as a fruitful collapsed correlation approach. In the volume *Practice, Practice Theory and Theology: Scandinavian and German Perspectives,* mentioned in Chapter 2, Ulla Schmidt argues for the benefits of practice theory.[6] Schmidt points out that practical theologians that have turned to practice generally claim that knowledge comes from doing. Knowing something is knowing how to relate to, use, or act with something. They challenge the modern, enlightenment understanding of knowledge as an internal representation of outer reality and something you can have independent of context. However, they are not particularly explicit about the precise nature of practical knowledge. How are knowledge and practice integrated? According to Schmidt, practice theory can, in fact, provide an explanation. She refers to Reckwitz's account of three different kinds of knowledge in relation to practices (interpretive, methodical, motivational-emotional) as an example.[7]

An alternative practice-theoretical account would be Schatzki's concept of "practical intelligibility." According to Schatzki, practical intelligibility—why it makes sense to perform an action— depends on particular, contextual states of affairs and ways of being. "State of affairs" are shaped and formed by previous practices and consist of things like prior experiences and preconceptions about how the world works. "Ways of being" are desires and beliefs one expects to achieve through practices. Such desires are also created through and sustained by practices—for example, participating in religious rituals.[8]

Furthermore, according to Schmidt, practice theories not only provide an account of the relationship between knowledge and practice but also shed light on the relationship between practice and *theological* knowledge. From a practice

[5] Tone Stangeland Kaufman, "From the Outside, Within, or in Between? Normativity at Work in Empirical Practical Theological Research," in *Conundrums in Practical Theology (Theology in Practice)*, eds. Joyce Ann Mercer and Bonnie Miller McLemore (Boston: Brill, 2017), 134–162.

[6] Schmidt 2022, 41–45.

[7] Schmidt 2022, 46–50.

[8] Schatzki 2010, 111–127.

theoretical perspective, practices involve theological knowledge enacted through constellations of materiality, embodiment, sociality, and knowledge. However, practice theory also serves as a reminder of something Schmidt claims practical theologians tend to overlook: that all practices cannot immediately be considered *theological* knowledge. While practices certainly generate and shape theology, there is no guarantee that they will—or that the lived theology they embody is not manipulative and unjust. Discernment, therefore, is pivotal.

In the correlation model, normative theology (doctrine, for instance) would serve as a corrective. Still, from a practice theoretical perspective, there are no sources of theological knowledge that are pure and untouched by practices, which can then serve as a neutral point of departure from which to evaluate the lived theology at issue. Doctrines and other normative theological sources are also shaped by practices situated in time and space and, therefore, may also be fraught. Drawing on practical theologian Elain Graham, Schmidt finds a solution to this apparent lack of evaluative standing in the constant process of change that is the inherent nature of practices. Since theological knowledge is a practice that is contextual, provisional, reflexive, and engaging in alterity, there is a constant negotiation between different sources of theological knowledge. And these correct each other.[9] This thesis adheres to this epistemology and understanding of theological knowledge—and grounds its methodology in it.

4.1.2 Designing a Multicase Study

If we start with the idea of practices as a source of (theological) knowledge entangled and situated in context, then case studies are an excellent methodological choice for investigations and analysis. Education scholar Helen Simons defines a case study as "an in-depth exploration from multiple perspectives of the complexity and uniqueness of a particular project, policy, institution or system in a 'real-life' context. It is research-based, inclusive of different methods, and is evidence-led."[10] Case studies' focus on "complexity and uniqueness" points to their usefulness in a project that wishes to attend to multiplicity. Moreover, its attention to "real-life context" sits well with the epistemological starting point of this thesis—that knowledge is intrinsically situated and entangled in materiality.

---

[9] Schmidt 2022, 46–50.

[10] Helen Simons, "Case Study Research: In-depth Understanding in Context," in *The Oxford Handbook of Qualitative Research*, ed. Patricia Leavy, 2nd ed., (New York: Oxford University Press, 2020), 681.

Another expert in case study research, education scholar Robert E. Stake, further underlines epistemological reasons for doing case studies. He writes: "Qualitative understanding of cases requires experiencing the activity of the case as it occurs in its contexts and particular situation. The situation is expected to shape the activity, as well as the experiencing and the interpretation of the activity."[11] In addition, according to Stake, case studies emphasize the sequentiality of happenings in context.[12] This makes case studies suitable for a research project interested in the interpretative and communicative process of "the preaching event."

Furthermore, case studies have a dynamic interplay between case and theory. According to Stake, case studies can both generate theory *and* question theory. While case studies cannot produce generalizable knowledge, it is possible sometimes to see recurring patterns (the same thing happens over and over in one case, or the same thing happens in several different cases) that might result in, for example, the outlines of a theory. Case studies may also be used to modify or even question theories.[13] According to historian Michael M. Widdersheim, the dynamics between theory and case are especially beneficial in historical case studies, where the general overview of the history and the particular complexity of the cases come into fruitful conversation.[14]

For all these reasons, I designed this thesis as a case study. However, due to unique and unforeseen circumstances, it was re-designed into what Stake calls "a multicase study." A multicase study research design consists of several cases that share a common characteristic or condition and serve as examples of a "quintain," a phenomenon or issue.[15] The circumstances that caused the change were the COVID-19 pandemic.

Early on, I decided to write an article-based thesis. This was due to the object of study. Technological development happens so fast that it can be difficult for a scholar to keep up. New technology creates new questions, and the results of a study are soon outdated by the next technological advancement.[16]

In other words, I did not want to end up in a situation where the questions and results of a monograph might be more or less obsolete before they were even

---

[11] Robert E. Stake, *Multiple Case Study Analysis* (New York, London: The Guilford Press, 2006), 2–3.

[12] Robert E. Stake, *The Art of Case Study Research* (Thousand Oaks: Sage 1995), xi–xii.

[13] Stake 1995, 7.

[14] Michael M. Widdersheim, "Historical Case Study: A Research Strategy for Diachronic Analysis," *Library and Information Science Research* 40:2 (2018), 144–152.

[15] Stake 2006, 5–6.

[16] Stirling 2016, 62.

published. In light of this, it seemed better to write an article-based thesis that would enable me to adjust to changes and be part of an ongoing discussion throughout the whole Ph.D. process. As it turned out, the changes were more disruptive than anyone could have imagined.

On March 11th, 2020, the World Health Organization declared a global pandemic. Governments around the globe imposed severe societal restrictions—even lockdowns. This prompted churches to transition to digital platforms in many countries, including Sweden. For me, one result of this shift was that mid-way through my Ph.D., the practice of preaching I had set out to research underwent a radical transformation. This had devastating effects on my research project. The carefully crafted case study research design, tailored to pre-pandemic practices, became outdated when these practices radically changed. In addition, the transformation raised a series of new questions. And when half of the participants dropped out because they did not have the time and energy to participate in a research project while dealing with a societal crisis, I realized I had to start over.

The pandemic closed doors, but it also opened new doors. The fact that suddenly almost *all* preaching became digitally-mediated generated an enormous amount of new practices to study. Furthermore, the pandemic sparked scholarly interest in the effects of the digital transition churches were embarking on en masse and created a need for persons with a special interest in digitally-mediated practices and digital theology. Soon I became involved in three research initiatives, where I was allowed to include perspectives and questions related to my research interests and use the source material for my thesis. In short, it meant that I was able to conduct not just a case study but a multicase study.

In his description of multicase studies, Stake identifies triangulation as an advantage. Triangulation is the process of using multiple perspectives to clarify meaning and verify the repeatability of an observation or interpretation. While each case is valuable on its own, a cross-case analysis in which several cases are analyzed in relation to each other adds an extra dimension. Having more than one case study of the same quintain enhances the researchers' ability to confirm, assure, or add nuance to findings—or even question them.[17] In addition, I gained another advantage: the ability to adjust and develop my thoughts over time. When Stake conceptualizes multicase studies, he imagines a research project involving several researchers who simultaneously make their case studies.[18] However, a single person cannot conduct several case studies at once. They must be done one after another.

---

[17] Stake 2006, 33–35.
[18] Stake 2006, 17–22.

As a result, in my case, the cross-case analysis also became diachronic and allowed for a discussion on changes over time.

This multicase study consists of different kinds of case studies of the practice of preaching in digital culture and spaces. Handbooks on case studies usually distinguish between instrumental and intrinsic case studies. *Intrinsic* case studies are only interested in describing the particular case itself, while *instrumental* case studies use the case as an

instrument to accomplish something else. There are also collective case studies in which there is coordination between individual cases. [19]

The cases involved in this thesis are, as is often the case with the digital, in-between. Every case is unique since the site of the social always is particular and unique. These case studies of digital spaces are, in that sense, intrinsic. However, due to the commonality of the digital media arrangements involved, the cases inevitably become instrumental case studies of digital culture.

One of the case studies is also historical. A historical case study is a study that considers cases from the distant past to the present. It is suitable for addressing questions related to change, continuity, development, and evolution. According to Widdersheim, historical case studies combine the best of two worlds. They study both the past and the present, use both existing data sources and create new ones, and construct specific and general knowledge types.[20]

The four kinds of case studies that are included in the multicase study of this thesis are:

Article A – a historical case study of four female preacher's practices of preaching. Here, cases and theory inform each other. This article describes changes over time—for example, how authority is practiced and construed.

Article B – a contemporary collective case study of the practice of preaching with a focus on the preparation phase in the digitally-mediated preaching event.

Article C – a contemporary collective case study of the practice of preaching with a focus on the verbalization phase in the digitally-mediated preaching event. Among other things, it pays attention to how authority is practiced and construed.

Article D – a contemporary collective case study of the practice of preaching with a focus on the realization phase in the digitally-mediated preaching event.

---

[19] Stake 1995, 3–4.
[20] Widdersheim 2018, 144–152.

4.1.3 What Kind of Questions? On Research Questions

A central part of any research design is the research questions. In case studies, especially multicase studies, they are pivotal. Case studies often generate enormous amounts of data, and the research questions enable the researcher to prioritize relevant data. In multicase studies, they also serve to hold all the cases together. Since case studies focus on complexity, several sub-questions—focused on relevant issues in the quintain—typically contribute to answering an overarching question.[21] This is also the strategy of this thesis. There is one overarching research question and three sub-questions whose content was chosen in relation to the theoretical paradigm (practice theory) and issues currently discussed in the field.

The research questions are also designed in light of the scarcity of prior research. In her handbook on research design, Patricia Leavy stresses that in cases where there is little prior work to draw on, it is common to design research projects with the purpose of exploring, describing, and/or understanding, and to conduct qualitative research that takes particular interest in thick descriptions of phenomena and the task of unpacking meaning (like case studies) with research questions that start with "how" and "what."[22]

Consequently, the overarching research question in this thesis is: *What characterizes the practice of preaching in digital culture and spaces?* The sub-questions that focus on relevant issues in relation to the quintain are:

a) *What characterizes the practices in the digitally-mediated preaching event?*

b) *What kinds of authority are practiced by preachers in digital culture and spaces?*

c) *Which theological features are salient in the practice of preaching in digital culture and spaces?*

Here, one might object and ask if these kinds of questions are not too banal and descriptive for a thesis. However, as Schatzki points out, the line between "how?" and "what?" questions as only generating descriptions, while "why?" questions generate "meatier" accounts of causation, is not as clear-cut as it is sometimes made out to be. Some "how?" questions provide explanations. Or, as Schatzki puts it:

---

[21] Stake 2006, 4.

[22] Leavy 2017, 3–5, 72.

> If casual explanations mention that which is responsible for things, that on which they depend, then answers, not just to why-questions (and not all why-questions at that), but also to how-questions qualify.[23]

In other words, *what* and *how* questions ask about steps in the process—and *why* questions do not always do that. Instead, *why* questions tend to ask for things like chief factors or factors responsible, and since the theoretical answers provided tend to depend heavily on the disciplinary home of the researcher, they can inadvertently reduce the range of possible answers.[24]

4.1.4 What Kind of Conclusions? On Generalization

Research questions are not the only important consideration for methodology and research design. It is just as important to be clear on what kind of answers—what kind of knowledge—the inquiry will generate. What kind of conclusions may be drawn?

Answers are often discussed in terms of generalization. Simons above offers an overview of different ways to argue for generalizability in case studies. One strategy is to design a collective case study, in which the researcher can show that "this happens in more than one case." Other strategies are to argue for: *naturalistic generalization* (if the description is detailed enough, then others in similar situations can recognize similarities and differences), *situated generalization* (the practitioners in the field trust the researcher who generated the results), or *concept- and process generalization* (that even if the case itself is not generalizable, the concepts and processes that emerge from the study will be).[25]

However, Simons points out that it is also possible to question why case studies (and qualitative research in general) should discuss generalizability at all. If a case study is about the particular, would it not be better to aim for the best particularity possible instead? She writes:

> If we are able to capture and report the uniqueness, the essence of the case, in all its particularity and present it in a way we all can recognize, we will discover something of universal significance. This is something of a paradox. The more you learn in depth about the particularity of one person, situation or context, the more likely you are to discover something universal.[26]

---

[23] Schatzki 2019, 119.
[24] Schatzki 2019, 119–120.
[25] Simons 2020, 676–703.
[26] Simons 2020, 696.

In the particular, something universal resides, and there is no need to argue for generalizability. The universal is an emergent property of the particular. Putting aside this possible foundation, however, other options appear for a case study researcher who doubts the need for generalizability in qualitative studies. For example, education scholars Yvonna Lincoln and Egon Guba argue for another criterion to evaluate qualitative research: trustworthiness, achieved through credibility, dependability, confirmability, and transferability.[27] Trustworthiness is connected to the way the case study was conducted. Uwe Flick, professor of qualitative research in social science and education, argues that the relevant question is not whether or not the conclusions of the case study are generalizable—it is the quality of the study itself. Which cases, what were they selected for, and how do they relate to theory?[28]

From the perspective of the practice theoretical epistemological starting point of this thesis, the case studies all aim for "best particularity." In particularity, there are nevertheless universal traits. The nature of the phenomenon under investigation serves to underscore this point. As argued earlier, there is a commonality to digitally-mediated practices because they involve a materiality that is the same across contexts and which is embedded in how the technology functions: it spreads the same content across many contexts and thus contributes to common cultural reference points.

However, trustworthiness is needed to achieve this best (possible) particularity. Sociologist David Silverman lists criteria for designing trustworthy and credible qualitative research. Silverman suggests building upon existing knowledge, articulating the connections between theory and data, being transparent in research design, material, and analysis, accounting for alternative explanations and negative cases, including concrete observations and quotes instead of the researcher's descriptions, describing expected findings, and specifying limitations of research as things that all contribute to validity and reliability.[29] The following section is intended to do just that.

4.2 Considering Methods

In this section, I will account for sampling and methods involved in generating and analyzing the source material. While these procedures are also described in

---

[27] Yvonna Lincoln and Egon Guba, *Naturalistic Inquiry* (Beverly Hills, CA: Sage, 1985).

[28] Uwe Flick, *An Introduction to Qualitative Research*, 4th ed. (London: Sage, 2009), 30–31.

[29] David Silverman, *Interpreting Qualitative Data*, 5th ed. (London: Sage, 2014), 75–85.

each article, the descriptions found there are generally short due to the length restrictions of the article genre. In what follows, I will give a more thorough account
of these procedures. In particular, I would like to elaborate on the ethical deliberations involved in these case studies.

Therefore, this section begins by describing issues pertinent to ethical considerations (4.2.1). Next, I discuss sampling (4.2.2). The choice of Swedish Protestant
churches is motivated and discussed, and the sampling procedures in each article
are accounted for more thoroughly than a journal article allows. Lastly, I account
for the procedures for generating and analyzing the source material (4.2.3).

4.2.1 Ethical Considerations

When considering research design, the researcher makes choices that shape the research process. Therefore, Stangeland Kaufman and Ideström liken the researcher
to the Gamemaker in Hunger Games.[30] Although I prefer to use the less violent
analogy of a computer game developer, I still find it a helpful way to speak of what
is at stake. Design choices made by the game developer set the parameters for how
participants can interact, respond, move, and behave. In particular, they decide
whose voices are to be heard and in what manner. It is a tremendous responsibility,
both in gaming and in research design, not least because in the latter, these choices
affect not just the outcome of the research project but also the participants.

Ideström and Stangeland Kaufman identify four normative dimensions in
qualitative theological research projects that often come into play and which the
researcher must pay attention to. Firstly, *evaluative normativity*, as in using academic and ecclesial authorities as the normative standard. Secondly, *prescriptive
normativity*, as in the researcher giving concrete suggestions on how something
ought to be done or understood. Thirdly, *rescriptive normativity*. The researcher
must be aware that when you describe the field, you also contribute to shaping or
re-shaping the norms of the field. Fourthly, *emergent normativity* is the normativity that emerges as the researcher gives priority to different voices. Ideström and
Stangeland Kaufman underscore that the researcher cannot step out of the role of
Gamemaker. Because of that, the researcher needs to engage in reflexivity.[31]

---

[30] Jonas Ideström and Tone Stangeland Kaufman, "The Researcher as a Gamemaker – Response," in *What Really Matters: Scandinavian Perspectives on Ecclesiology and Ethnography*,
eds. Jonas Ideström and Tone Stangeland Kaufman (Eugene, Oregon: Pickwick Publications,
2018), 173.

[31] Ideström and Stangeland Kaufman 2018, 173–180.

In her contribution to the previously mentioned *Wiley Blackwell Companion to Theology and Qualitative Research* (2022), Stangeland Kaufman lists five aspects of reflexivity that researchers need to take into consideration when designing and engaging in qualitative research: *personal reflexivity* (the social location of the researcher), *ecclesial reflexivity* (how the researcher is shaped by her own church tradition), *relational reflexivity* (the researchers' relation to the participants in the research project), *epistemological reflexivity* (what kind of knowledge is created through the choice of research design and methodology—in particular, whose voices are included), and *sociological epistemology* (the researchers' position and affiliations in the academic field). According to Kaufman, three things are pivotal in reflexivity: making the implicit explicit, empathic curiosity, and collaboration and collegial communities.[32]

In practice, these ethical considerations usually concern four themes: informed consent, invasion of privacy, harmfulness, and deception. However, as literature on methods in qualitative research on digital media phenomena often points out, the media and the medium complicate matters.

The goal of informed consent is to ensure that participants fully understand what they are participating in, the extension and consequences of their participation, their right to withdraw, and how to withdraw their consent. In relation to digital settings, this can get complicated. For example, how do you gain informed consent when you might not know the participant's identity (because they may be using aliases or avatars)? How do you know they are eligible, old enough, or even able to consent? In addition, ensuring, verifying, and documenting that participants have read and understood consent information is more complicated in digital ecosystems. The same issues arise with withdrawal and debriefing. Have they understood how to withdraw? How can the researcher know if someone is withdrawing because they experienced harm in any way?[33]

Complications might also occur in relation to the second theme: invasion of privacy or confidentiality. To get informed consent, you need to uncover a person's identity, and in the process, you jeopardize the very confidentiality you wish to protect.[34]

---

[32] Stangeland Kaufman 2022, 111–120.

[33] Claire Hewson, "Ethics Issues in Digital Methods Research," in *Digital Methods for Social Science: An Interdisciplinary Guide to Research Innovation,* eds. Helene Snee et al. (London: Palgrave Macmillan 2016), 206–213.

[34] Mark D. Jones, "Ethical Issues in the Study of Religion and New Media," in *Digital Religion: Understanding Religious Practice in Digital Media,* eds. Heidi Campbell and Ruth Tsuria, 2nd ed. (New York: Routledge 2022), 259.

Ensuring confidentiality is, on the whole, more complicated in digital environments. Potential hackers, transmission errors, or third-party control (server hosts) all underscore the responsibility of the researcher to take extra care to pseudonymize data in case it leaks. Digital technology also makes data traceable and searchable, which means that the researcher must be careful in the dissemination phase of research. For example, a quotation that appears online is easy to Google. Even if the ideal for ensuring validity is "show, don't tell," the researcher may have to retreat to summarizing content to ensure confidentiality, given the unique challenges presented by digital content.[35]

Confidentiality is linked to the third theme, harmfulness. Although participants in digital ethnography may not risk physical harm, the nature of digital media makes it easier for people to come across the published results, easier to find out who said or did something that might be considered controversial or stupid, and easier to ruin someone's reputation through revealing who said and did what. Serious harm may come to people if confidentiality is not protected.[36]

Deception, the fourth theme, also poses new challenges. Digital technologies encourage research with so-called non-obtrusive methods, where data is created or even "harvested" at a distance without the participants knowing their data is so easily accessible. However, it is not always easy to discern if, for example, a Facebook post is a document or the thought and actions of an individual, or if the digital platform is to be considered a public space or sacred ground. Accordingly, there is a risk that participants may feel deceived by a researcher.[37] In a recent Swedish example, a researcher was able to collect and analyze Facebook profile pictures without the participants' knowledge or consent. While it might be formally legal to do so since information on a Facebook page is technically considered public in Sweden, the participants might (as in this case) feel it is discomforting, unethical, and strange.[38]

The previously mentioned Hutchings discusses how these challenges could come into play in relation to research on religion, using examples from his research on online communities to highlight the issues involved. In his discussion on "Ethnography, Representation, and Digital Media," Hutchings considers three kinds of representation. Firstly, the *representation of the researcher to the field site.*

---

[35] Hewson 2016, 206–213.

[36] Jones 2022, 257–258.

[37] Hewson 2016, 206–213.

[38] Johanna Holstein, "'Snygghetsstudien' i Lund utreds – bilder användes utan vetskap," *SVT Nyheter*, 4 November 2022, *https://www.svt.se/nyheter* [Accessed 19 March 2023].

Hutchings points out that while it is possible to "lurk" or use a different identity in many digital spaces, participating as a stranger in a Christian community for any extended period is often difficult. Sooner or later, you are forced to engage in conversation and account for who you are and why you are there. Hutchings points out that being an insider does not necessarily have to be a disadvantage from a research perspective. An outsider who does not share core beliefs might be treated with suspicion or exposed to conversion attempts. In addition, while an insider might have to sacrifice distance, she may, on the other hand, find herself in a unique position to gain insights and opportunities for participation.

Secondly, *the researcher's representation in and for the field site*. Participants in a study might see the researcher as part of their group and expect the researcher to represent them. Hutchings found this particularly common in his research on online churches. He was approached by people who had suffered and been marginalized in onsite churches, and who wanted him to tell their stories. They expected that he should function as an advocate, attract publicity, and demonstrate credibility for online churches—serving as a kind of public relations arm for their particular point of view.

Thirdly, *representation of the field site to others*. As in all ethnography, the researcher sometimes shares preliminary representations with research participants and asks for their thoughts and comments. Hutchings suggests that digital ethnography offers new ways to enable even more direct forms of representation. The researcher could include the participants' own representations (for example, videos or narratives) without being filtered through the researcher. Researchers could also have a research blog to discuss preliminary results and representation with other academics and interested people.[39]

In my own studies of digitally-mediated preaching practices, I encountered similar challenges as Hutchings. In the following, I will give an account of these and other challenges in the different case studies, and articulate how they affected the research design, methods, and outcomes of the projects.

4.2.2 Sampling

As mentioned in the first section of this chapter, a crucial question in every case study is "Which case?" When it comes to sampling, handbooks usually give the same advice as Stake: because case studies take an interest in the complex, unique, and particular, it is no use trying to choose "typical" cases that aim to be

---

[39] Hutchings 2018, 227–246.

generalizable. While case studies may be useful in formulating a theory, the researcher still cannot lay claim to generalization. If you aim for that, case studies are unsuitable research designs. Instead, according to Stake, sampling should be made to maximize what might be learned.[40]

Silverman mentions three kinds of sampling. Firstly, *random sampling*, which is possible only in some cases—for example, if you have done a survey with quantitative methods and randomly pick a few participants for in-depth interviews. Secondly, *purposive sampling*, which is a careful selection in relation to the purpose of the study. Thirdly, *theoretical sampling* in relation to a specific theory.[41]

The four case studies in this thesis use different types of samplings. However, they all have one thing in common: they all study Swedish Protestant churches from across five different denominations. In this section, I will elaborate on the motivation for this sampling and provide more information on the specific contexts—or the organizational structures—that the denominations and congregations in question operate within. Finally, I will elaborate on the sampling in each article.

Swedish Protestant Churches

The choice of Sweden is due not just to the fact that the author of this thesis is Swedish but also because the use of digital technologies is highly dependent on the national context.[42] Geography, economy, and politics affect how people use digital technology. For instance, digitally-mediated preaching during the pandemic was practiced very differently in Swedish congregations (situated as they are in a rich country that has spent years, and billions of krona, in securing high-speed internet and relatively stable access to energy, with public Wi-fi accessible almost anywhere and a population who can generally afford iPads and computers)—especially when compared to a congregation in, say, a favela in Brazil (where most of the members may be poor and depend on smartphones for internet access, and whose electricity and Wi-Fi are lacking). In the first case, a twenty-minute live-streamed sermon might seem like a great idea; in the second case, it may be impossible.[43]

---

[40] Stake 1995, 4.

[41] Silverman 2014, 56–69.

[42] Hine 2015, 7–8; Pink et al. 2016, 8–9.

[43] The example is based on Luiz Coelho's presentation in the "International Panel: 4 Regional Reports: Preaching & Worship in Times of the Corona Crisis" during the *Societas Homiletica* 2020 online conference "Words in Times of Crises" 10–12 August 2020.

Sweden is one of the most digitalized countries in the world.[44] Professor in technology history, Nina Wormbs, argues that official discourse in Sweden is characterized by an ideology of advancement, where new technology is assumed to be clean, effective, and correct.[45] This is mirrored by the digitalization strategy of the Swedish government. The statement that until the 2022 election was found on a Swedish government portal is telling:

> The vision is a sustainably digitalized Sweden. The overarching goal is that Sweden will be the best in the world to use digitalization's possibilities. Digitally competent and confident people can push for innovation, where purposeful leadership and infrastructure are essential conditions.[46]

In other words, given the high degree of digital penetration, the Swedish context is inherently interesting to explore for someone (like myself) interested in digital cultures and spaces.

However, as the previously mentioned Jonas Kurlberg, and World Christianity scholar Alexander Chow, found in their comparative study of churches' transition to digital platforms in Britain, Sweden, Singapore, and Hong Kong during the first months of the COVID-19 pandemic, Sweden's prominence in digitalization does not necessarily mean that the Protestant churches' use of digital media was cutting edge. Perhaps surprisingly, they found that Protestant churches in Sweden were the *least* innovative in their digital transition strategies. The authors argue that this was partly due to the nature of the restrictions in Sweden during the early stages of the pandemic. Since most churches could gather up to fifty people in person, many churches opted for the "mobile phone camera in the corner" option for those unable to attend physically, recording or live-streaming the full local service. But Kurlberg and Chow also point out that there appeared to be a theologically motivated reluctance towards digital technology in Sweden, including a pastoral concern for digital outsiders (i.e., for those who lack access and/or the skill to use digital technology). In light of this, I found the Swedish context even more intriguing.

---

[44] European Commission, *Digital Economy and Society Index (DESI) 2022, https://desi-sweden* [Accessed 8 December 2022].

[45] Wormbs 2022, 11.

[46] Regeringskansliet, *För ett hållbart digitaliserat Sverige – en digitaliseringsstrategi,* https://digitaliseringsradet.se/media/1191/digitaliseringsstrategin_slutlig_170518–2.pdf [Accessed 22 April 2023]. My translation. "Visionen är ett hållbart digitaliserat Sverige. Det övergripande målet är att Sverige ska vara bäst i världen på att använda digitaliseringens möjligheter. Digitalt kompetenta och trygga människor har möjlighet att driva innovation där målmedveten ledning och infrastruktur är viktiga förutsättningar."

My choice to focus on Protestant churches was purposeful in several other aspects: the conditions of the researcher (I am an ordained pastor in CoS and have knowledge of and access to the field); the conditions of the context (Sweden is a predominantly Protestant country); the conditions of the research school I was part of (it was created to conduct research on Free churches—in particular, the Uniting Church in Sweden); and the conditions set by the more extensive research projects within which the various source materials were created (all three were financed by and focused on Protestant churches).

To be clear: in relation to Swedish Protestant churches, I am an insider. Arguably, I am an insider when it comes to digital media and technology, too. While I am too old to be a digital native, I am a gamer and relatively knowledgeable about digital technology. As Hutchings mentioned, this is not necessarily a disadvantage since being an insider can facilitate access to other kinds of source material unavailable to outsiders. In her work on "ethnographic theology," practical theologian Natalie Wigg-Stevenson has argued that practical theologians can make methodological use of their insider knowledge through their embodied habitus.[47] Being an insider is not only helpful in the process of generating source material, according to Wigg-Stevenson, but it could also be an advantage in the process of analysis itself. As Stangeland Kaufman and I discuss elsewhere, in cases like these, theories such as Actor-Network theory—or, perhaps more to the point of this thesis, Schatzki's version of practice theory—become even more critical since they aid the researcher in discovering aspects of the familiar that they otherwise would be blind to.[48] I argue that choosing a theoretical paradigm that stresses the situated, relationally-produced qualities of knowledge further encourages what Wigg-Stevenson calls an "epistemological humility."[49]

The four case studies each engage with the following Swedish Protestant churches. In Article B, the Church of Sweden[50] (CoS) and Uniting Church in Sweden[51] (UC, a merger of the Swedish Mission Covenant Church, Methodist Church in Sweden, and Baptist Union of Sweden). In article C, CoS, UC, The

---

[47] Natalie Wigg-Stevenson, *Ethnographic Theology: An Inquiry into the Production of Theological Knowledge* (New York: Palgrave Macmillan, 2014), 45–62.

[48] Mannerfelt and Stangeland Kaufman (forthcoming).

[49] Wigg-Stevenson 2014, 170.

[50] Svenska kyrkan.

[51] Equmeniakyrkan.

Swedish Pentecostal Movement[52] (PM), Interact[53], and Swedish Mission Alliance[54] (SMA). Article D compares two congregations in CoS. Article A, with its historical and diachronic approach, uses a variety of cases from Sweden. Among them are a case from CoS and one from the Swedish Holiness Union that later became part of SMA.

Choosing Protestant churches in Sweden was purposeful, and the choice itself relates to the practice theory paradigm that is foundational to this thesis. As mentioned in Chapter 2, practices are organized, and in the practice of preaching, theology—in particular, ecclesiology –is arguably a crucial aspect of that organization. The state of affairs and ways of being that surround and interpenetrate the practice of preaching affect how it is carried out. This is implied and briefly discussed throughout the articles, but just as with various other tangential (to this thesis) ethical considerations, the analysis in the articles is not particularly thorough. Therefore, I would like to give an overview of the main characteristics of the five denominations represented in the case studies. I have chosen to structure this account into two sections. First, I will sketch the main characteristics of CoS, followed by the main features of the four other denominations, which all belong to the family tree of Free Church denominations. While there are differences between and within these denominations, I will argue that they share several traits that motivate grouping them together.

Church of Sweden

The Church of Sweden (CoS) is one of the largest Lutheran churches in the world. Statistically speaking, the majority of the 10,4 million population (5,6 million) belong to the former state church.[55] In 2019 (before the pandemic), 40% of all children born in Sweden were baptized in CoS, and 35% took part in confirmation.[56] Since 2000 CoS is not formally a state church, but unlike any other denomination

---

[52] Pingströrelsen.
[53] Evangeliska Frikyrkan.
[54] Svenska Alliansmissionen.
[55] Svenska kyrkan, *Statistik*, *https://www.svenskakyrkan.se/statistik* [Accessed 2 January 2023]; Statistiska Centralbyrån, *https://www.scb.se* [Accessed 2 January 2023].
[56] Svenska kyrkan, *Döpta, konfirmerade, vigda och begravda enligt Svenska kyrkans ordning år 1970–2020, https://www.svenskakyrkan.se/filer/1374643* [Accessed 23 February 2023].

in the country, it is regulated by constitutional law, and the head of state (Sweden is a monarchy) is obliged to be a member.[57]

The "Church of Sweden Law" states that the church is "Lutheran" and "evangelical," but also "nationwide," meaning that parishes are understood in terms of geographical territory.[58] Every square inch of the country is divided into parishes, and CoS is responsible for the country's graveyards and funeral services. Due to the fact that several surveys show that a low percentage of CoS members believe in key historic tenants of Christianity, or even a general belief in God or the divine, the church is often characterized by "belonging without believing."[59]

According to the ecclesiastical order of CoS, the parish is the primary unit of church organization. Parishes are further organized into 13 dioceses, each under the supervision and leadership of a bishop. CoS also has an Archbishop (whose digitally-mediated preaching practices are under consideration in Article A).[60] However, these parish units vary widely in size from a couple of hundred villagers, a handful of employees, and one church building (as is the case in some of the parishes in the region of Småland that are part of the case in Article C), to parishes with thirty thousand members, sixty employees and five church buildings (like the parishes in Stockholm that are part of the cases studied article B and D). In addition to multiple church buildings, parishes often also manage parish homes and/or vicarages. Regarding resources, CoS is relatively wealthy and can afford many employees (as seen in Article D)—at least the larger parishes.

The Church of Sweden Law also states that CoS is a "folk church." This concept has influenced the ecclesiology of the CoS since the beginning of the 20th century.[61] For some, the folk church is seen as a middle ground in-between other traditions and spiritualities, which are sometimes expressed in terms of "high church" (emphasizing sacraments, ordination, and the common—"catholic"—tradition) and "low church" (inspired by pietist and revivalist movements). However, there

---

[57] For an overview of the Swedish and Scandinavian historical and contemporary ecclesial context, see Kirsten Donskov Felter, Ninna Edgardh and Troen Fagermoen, "The Scandinavian Ecclesial Context," in *What Really Matters: Scandinavian Perspectives in Ecclesiology and Ethnography*, eds. Jonas Ideström and Tone Stangeland Kaufman, (Eugene, Oregon: Pickwick Publications, 2018), 5–14.

[58] *Lagen om Svenska kyrkan* (1998:1591).

[59] For an overview of relevant research, see Isabella Kasselstrand, "Nonbelievers in the Church: A Study of Cultural Religion in Sweden," *Sociology of Religion* 76:3 (2015), 275–294.

[60] *Kyrkoordning för Svenska kyrkan* (Verbum: Stockholm, 2023), 7.

[61] Jonas Ideström, *Folkkyrkotanken – innehåll och utmaningar: En översikt av studier under 2000-talet* (Uppsala: Svenska kyrkan, 2012), 5.

are countless other traditions within CoS congregations in Sweden. For example, the diocese of Växjö, in which the source material used in Article C was generated, is usually described as consisting of three areas with different spiritualities: one where high church spirituality dominates; one where a spirituality that resembles the Free-churches dominates; and one where the spirituality of an older Lutheran pietist revival movement, centered on the Lutheran confessional writings, dominates.[62]

However, in practice, these ecclesiological categories are blurred and blended. For example, in the research project, *Church in Digital Space* (where the source material for Article D was generated), three different conceptions of folk church emerged as operant in the digitally-mediated practices of seven Stockholm congregations.[63]

Nevertheless, the three folk church models observed in these seven congregations shared some basic assumptions. Firstly, 'folk' were understood as individuals and groups in the context where the church acts, not in an essentialist way as "the people of Sweden."[64] Secondly, the church exists to give the gospel in its many forms to 'folk'—that is, everyday people. Thirdly, the church's mission is to contribute to expanding the kingdom of God. However, these congregations differed in their opinion on *how* this is done and *what* and *who* constitutes the church—in other words, in what forms the gospel may be transmitted, and what role the visible church (as in the community gathered for worship) plays in this transmission.

The first operant model observed is the "folk church as an address in everyday life." It builds on the folk church theology of Einar Billing and Gustaf Wingren. In this model, the church's identity is grounded in its mission to reach out with the gospel. *How* this is enacted is not important so long as the gospel is heard by 'folk.' Addressing 'folk' with the gospel in their everyday life is a goal in itself, and

---

[62] Carl Henrik Martling, *Fädernas kyrka och folkets: svenska kyrkan i kyrkovetenskapligt perspektiv* (Stockholm: Verbum, 1992), 158–160.

[63] Jonas Ideström and Tone Stangeland Kaufman, "Hur framträder kyrkan i de digitala rummen? – kommunikation, teologi och folkkyrkotankar," in *Kyrka i digitala rum: Ett aktionsforskningsprojekt om församlingsliv online*, eds. Sara Garpe and Jonas Ideström (Uppsala: enheten för forskning och analys, 2022), 31–43. See also Frida Mannerfelt, "Between Ritual and 'Advertisement': Theological Negotiation in the Development of Digitally Mediated Worship Services at the End of the COVID-19 Pandemic," paper presented at the *Global Network of Digital Theology* online conference "How Theology and Faith Practices shape Digital Culture," 7–9 July 2022, *https://gonedigital*

[64] Decidedly not akin to the "blood and soil" conceptions of the Nazi volk, to be clear.

the results do not have to be measured or defined. It is primarily in this mediation of the gospel that the church becomes the church.

The second model is the "folk church as sacramental enactment." It resembles the first model in the sense that the mediation of the gospel is a goal in itself, and its effectiveness does not have to be measured. In other words: the church's primary task is to ensure the gospel is proclaimed and enacted. The difference lies in *how* it is done. Here, the folk church model depends on ideas from the ecumenical and liturgical movements. Since "the medium is the message," you cannot extract the message from the traditional practices of the church and simply allow it to take new shapes and forms. The liturgy of the worship service, rather, is a necessary part of the mediation of the gospel. However, this model of the folk church does not, unlike the third model that follows, emphasize the visible community.

The third model is the "folk church as a visible community." This model emphasizes the relationships and community through which the gospel is understood to take form and be administrated. Often the gathered and visible worshipping community takes precedence as the place where the church becomes the church. A subsequent emphasis on liturgy—the visible community "doing church together"—resembles the second model. But it also resembles the first model by allowing for a plethora of ways to enact the gospel's message. It is the underlying purpose beneath this that is distinctive to the third model: for 'folk' to become, explicitly and recognizably, part of the visible community.[65]

Regarding liturgy, the CoS church ordinals state that the worship service—primarily the Sunday service—is the center of the church's life. There is a liturgical handbook that pastors are obliged to follow, albeit with some allowable variation. In examining the worship service in CoS 1968-2008, the practical theologian Ninna Edgardh lists several features that characterize the worship service in CoS congregations. Over four decades, there has been a shift from uniformity to greater variation, from solely verbal communication to communication through things like music, symbol, movement, and silence. In addition, there has been a conscious effort to incorporate inclusive language alongside intense development and revisions of liturgical handbooks to emphasize the worship services as anchored in the local community. During this forty-year period, there has also been increased participation in the Eucharist, as well as the active participation of laypeople and a greater, more active involvement of women.[66]

---

[65] Ideström and Stangeland Kaufman 2022, 33–34.

[66] Ninna Edgardh, *Gudstjänst i tiden: Gudstjänstliv i Svenska kyrkan 1968–2008* (Lund: Arcus förlag, 2010), 197–198.

In her studies of participation in CoS, religious education scholar Caroline Gustavsson Klintborg points out that active participation is often understood as normatively good, particularly when parishes envision what development might look like for worship services. However, according to Klintborg, it is often quite unclear what, exactly, participation means. In church documents and theological literature, it is often associated with building relationships within the congregation and contrasted with "watching."[67]

In his description of the CoS worship service, practical theologian Mikael Löwegren highlights the inspiration from the liturgical and ecumenical movements for liturgical reform and Eucharistic revival in CoS during the 20th century. The high church movement emphasized ecumenical orientation toward the Church of England. Archbishops such as Nathan Söderblom (1866–1931) envisioned CoS as a church uniquely called to act as a middle way between the catholic and evangelical.[68] That CoS has a legacy of ecumenicism is evident, not least in the fact that CoS was chosen to host the 2017 Lutheran and Catholic joint commemoration of the Reformation.

When it comes to the characteristics of preaching in CoS, my analysis of homiletical literature used in the education of CoS pastors from 1903-2013 points to a shift from message-oriented preaching to relation-oriented (or media-oriented) preaching, starting in the 1970s. From being heavily influenced by German homiletics in which the ideal was a deductive, theocentric, and message-oriented sermon, CoS homiletics became heavily influenced by the *New Homiletic* movement of the 1970s, with its focus on the relationship between the preacher and listeners, and where the ideal sermon was understood as a mutual dialogue.[69]

The homiletical literature, in particular, older books from the first part of the 20th century, is critical of the style of preaching in pietist and revival movements— or "preaching outside of the Church," as Fredrik Sjöberg would have it in his 1923 book—as it is emotional, intimate, free form, biblicist and "far from Luther."[70]

Finally, the origin of the name "Church of Sweden" is telling. For a long time, it was just "the Church (in Sweden)." The Christianization of the region started in the 9th century, and after the reformation in the 16th century, a state church was

---

[67] Caroline Gustavsson, *Delaktighetens kris: Gudstjänstens pedagogiska utmaning* (Skellefteå: Artos, 2016), 29–42.

[68] Mikael Löwegren, "Gudstjänst i Svenska kyrkan," in *Kristen Gudstjänst - en introduktion*, ed. Stina Fallberg Sundmark (Skellefteå: Artos, 2018), 103–130.

[69] Mannerfelt 2018, 123–158.

[70] Mannerfelt 2018, 123–158; Fahlgren 2006a, 57–58.

formally consolidated, led by the king. The need to define itself from other churches emerged in relation to pietist and revivalist movements.[71] The name "Church of Sweden" first appeared in a legal text in 1860 (in the first Dissenter Acts).

Free Churches

The four other churches under consideration in this thesis—UC, PM, Interact, and SMA—have their roots in pietist and revivalist movements which arose in the 18th and 19th Centuries. The Swedish Mission Covenant grew out of revival movements within the CoS, while the Methodist and Baptist churches were the result of missions from abroad—typically from Germany, as well as England and the United States.[72] In Sweden, these Protestant churches are often referred to—and self-identify as—"Free churches," where "free" signals an emphasis on freedom in structure, leadership, and liturgical forms, as opposed to the structures in churches like CoS.[73] Of course, "free" also indicates free of ties to the state.[74]

The concept of "Free churches" has been questioned for good reasons. It is unfair to define denominations in relation to a majority church instead of on their own merits. Additionally, the concept tends to hide the diversity that exists in these denominations, despite the catch-all umbrella term of "Free churches." Church historian Joel Halldorf and theologian Fredrik Wenell discuss alternative concepts to better describe these kinds of churches in Sweden, including "Believer's church" (based on the understanding of the church as a community in which all members profess a personal faith in Christ), non-creedal (since several of these churches reject official documents such as creeds or liturgical handbooks), or "evangelical." Halldorf and Wenell still opt for Free churches for historical reasons and since evangelical implies a broader circle of churches.[75] Elsewhere, Halldorf

---

[71] Donskov Felter, Edgardh and Fagermoen 2018, 5–14.

[72] Joel Halldorf and Fredrik Wenell, "Introduction," in *Between the State and the Eucharist: Free Church Theology in Conversation with William T. Cavanaugh*, eds. Joel Halldorf and Fredrik Wenell (Eugene, Oregon: Pickwick Publications 2014), 6.

[73] Christopher J. Ellis, *Gathering. A Theology and Spirituality of Worship in Free Church Tradition* (London: SCM Press 2004), 25–27.

[74] *Vägmärken för baptister: Tro frihet gemenskap: Svenska baptistsamfundet 1848–2012* (Karlstad: Votum Media, 2016).

[75] Halldorf and Wenell 2014, 6–8.

suggests that using the concept "Free Churches" in plural could serve as a reminder to both authors and readers of the plurality represented by this appellation.[76]

While there is a great deal of diversity among the Free church denominations, there is also good reason to group them together under a common concept. As I have discussed elsewhere, these churches share many ecclesiological, liturgical, and ethical convictions, and there is a well-documented interplay of overlapping ideas, practices, and members between these denominations.[77]

According to the Swedish Christian Council, the Swedish Free churches have around 235.000 members across different denominations.[78] They are often members of a joint association of some form. The Free churches in the case studies in this thesis are all organized as associations with a board.[79] The congregations vary in size, from just a handful of persons to around five thousand. However, as the categories of "size" in the survey *Free Churches in Times of Corona* indicate, large congregations are not very common. There were four categories in the survey, with the category of the largest number, "more than 300 members," only indicated by a few Free church congregations. Most of these congregations manage only one building that contains both the church's primary space for worship, as well as other spaces for gathering. Compared to CoS, there are few employees, and congregation members do most of the necessary work together with a pastor.

In the survey mentioned above, practical theologian Ulrik Josefsson identified five themes that characterize Free churches' ecclesiology. It is simultaneously "personal" and "communal." Personal faith is pivotal, but this faith is enacted both through personal and collective experience. Personal relationships and community thus shape personal faith. In other words, the personal is dependent on the community, and the community is dependent on the personal. According to Josefsson, Free churches' ecclesiology is, to a high degree, a *communio* ecclesiology. Furthermore, Free churches' ecclesiology is characterized as "active." There are

---

[76] Joel Halldorf, "Mötet i frikyrklighet och väckelse," in *Kristen Gudstjänst – en introduktion*, ed. Stina Fallberg Sundmark (Skellefteå: Artos, 2018), 140.

[77] Mannerfelt 2022, 93.

[78] *Sveriges Kristna råd*, Frikyrkor, *https://www.skr.org* [Accessed 13 March 2023]. However, as ØivindTholvesen states in his report on the development in the Free Churches during 2000-2020, there are other ways to define "Free Churches." Apart from Free Churches that are members of SCC, there are Free Churches within the Lutheran family of denominations and Free Churches that are not connected to denominations (and thus not counted). In addition, there are many who take part in the congregational life of the Free Churches without being full members, such as children and youth. Öivind Tholvesen, *Frikyrkoundersökningen: En rapport on frikyrkornas utveckling i Sverige 2000–2020* (Örebro: Frikyrkosamrådets styrelse, 2021), 8–11.

[79] Fahlgren 2006a, 65.

strong expectations that personal faith should lead to active involvement. This is connected to the fourth feature of Free churches' ecclesiology identified by Josefsson: "mission." Free churches emphasize working for revival in a society where people are Christians in name only. Finally, this ecclesiology is "entrepreneurial," oriented toward action.[80] Notably, the emphasis on mission has generally led to a fuller embrace of media and innovation in Free churches. They have traditionally been quick in appropriating media in service of the gospel—and doing so quite skillfully.[81]

In my own contribution to the report, "Old and New Habits: The Transition to Digitally-Mediated Worship in Four Swedish Free Church Denominations during COVID-19," I identified additional core components of Swedish Free Churches' spirituality. Drawing on practical theologian Ulla Bardh, I argue that the community—in particular, the community gathered for worship—functions like a sacrament: a sign and a tool for Christ's presence in the world. Secondly, church growth is sometimes associated with a powerful ideal of participation and engagement. Thirdly, spirituality is expressed and shaped by the liturgy employed and practiced in local congregations. Drawing on Halldorf and Fahlgren, I point to three strands in Free church liturgy: one that practices "classic" Free church liturgy with a special focus on preaching; one ecumenically-inclined strand that emphasizes Eucharist and liturgy; and one inspired by neo-Pentecostal worship that emphasizes charismatic practices and contemporary worship music. A final core component of Free Churches' spirituality is an emphasis on responding to the sermon.[82]

Characteristic of preaching in the Free Churches context is, according to Fahlgren, its close connection to the context in which it is performed. In his

---

[80] Ulrik Josefsson, "Bilder av församlingen: Frikyrklig ecklesiologi under och genom pandemin," in *Svensk frikyrklighet i pandemin: En studie av församlingen i corona och corona i församlingen*, eds. Ulrik Josefsson and Magnus Wahlström (Forskningsrapporter från Institutet för Pentekostala Studier, No 9, 2021), 60–89.

[81] Fredrik Stiernstedt, "Free Churches of the Air: the History of Community Radio in Sweden," *Historical Journal of Film, Radio and Television* 41:2 (2021), 317–337; Gunnar Hallingberg, *Läsarna: 1800-talets folkväckelse och det moderna genombrottet* (Stockholm: Atlantis bokförlag, 2011); Gunnar Hallingberg, *Moderna läsare : 1900-talets frikyrklighet som kulturbygge* (Stockholm: Atlantis bokförlag, 2016); Harry Lenhammar, "Tryckpressarna i kyrkans och väckelsens tjänst," in *Sveriges Kyrkohistoria: Folkväckelsens och kyrkoförnyelsens tid*, ed. Oloph Bexell (Stockholm: Verbum, 2003), 306–315; Joel Halldorf *Biskop Lewi Pethrus: Biografi över ett ledarskap. Religion och mångfald i det svenska folkhemmet* (Skellefteå: Artos, 2017), 110–111, 134–135, 137; Fahlgren 2006a, 74–80.

[82] Mannerfelt 2022, 107–114.

historical case studies from the 1850s to 1960s, he identifies several types of preaching, but each share a common denominator: they occur in a "meeting" or "gathering." The gathering can take place at a home, mission house, chapel, tent, or barn, but no matter where it happens, people are gathered to be presented with a message. It is an address to the individual centered on their meeting with God and God's meeting with them. The ideal of "free" is also reflected in the sermon, where the preacher is often appreciated for using a casual, conversational style. Music is sometimes used to create an atmosphere intended to enhance the sermon's message, and attract listeners.[83]

In his case study of the preacher Frank Mangs (1897-1994), Runar Eldebo describes the background preaching context of this Free Church preacher along similar lines. Mangs migrated between churches—he was a member of CoS, Swedish Mission Covenant Church, and Swedish Mission Alliance, and preached in other Protestant church contexts as well—and was influenced by preaching in pietist and revival movements. Preaching in the pietist movements focused on *ordo salutis*. The purpose of preaching was not distributing grace, as in CoS, but the transformation of the human will. The sermons took as their starting point the fallen human situation, which required a calling forth into conversion and renewal. Preaching in the revival movements aimed to persuade and convince, often through intense emotion. The sermons were structured to create a need in the listener, eventually leading to an invitation to faith and conversion. Eldebo characterizes them as anthropocentric and listener-oriented in the sense that the preachers take a special interest in *how* the sermon reaches the listener—in order to bring about the salvation of the individual.[84]

According to social work scholar Charlotta Carlström, the Free Churches have another common denominator in their normative views of heterosexuality and marriage. Drawing on Andersson, Roland Spjuth, and Fredrik Wenell, she points to how conservative interpretations of the Bible and theological doctrines, as well as an emphasis on personal experience, have sustained these norms around

---

[83] Fahlgren 2006a, 58–64.

[84] Runar Eldebo, *Den ensamma tron: En studie i Frank Mangs predikan* (Örebro: Libris, 1997), 113–130.

sexuality.[85] However, according to theologian Anders Gerdmar, there is also a strong movement within the Free Churches to question these traditional views.[86]

As this brief overview of the Swedish Protestant churches found in the case studies of this thesis demonstrates, there are several differences between CoS and the four Free churches under consideration here. However, while CoS and these Free Churches historically (and sometimes contemporaneously) define themselves in opposition towards each other, these Protestant churches have, in practice, often been intertwined, with overlapping memberships or members switching between them.[87] For this reason, their inclusion in this thesis is not an accident. The relationship between these Swedish Protestant churches is a purposeful part of my work and also, if I may, fascinating in its own right.

There is yet one more motivation for my intentional inclusion of Cos and Free church congregations in my sampling: the need for more research on Free churches. CoS is comparatively very well-researched. As the former state church, now a majority church, it has often been prioritized in academic research. The church itself also prioritizes research and has the resources to do so. It runs its own research unit and offers different kinds of research scholarships, and CoS pastors are eligible to apply for Ph. Ds as a matter of course, given the educational requirements of ordination in the church. On the other hand, the Free churches have historically been much more skeptical of the academy, particularly in the Pentecostal branches. Lack of economic resources and other particular circumstances, such as the fact that academic education and research have generally prioritized CoS Lutheran theology and ignored Free churches, along with the fact that you do not need an academic degree to become a pastor in these churches, has resulted in a situation in which Free churches are much less likely to be meaningfully included in research.

Fahlgren identifies another contributing reason for this research exclusion. According to him, Free churches often lack the kind of source material that practical

---

[85] Charlotta Carlström, "Queer desires and emotional regimes in Swedish Free-Church contexts," *Theology & Sexuality* 27:2–3 (2021), 188–203. See also Charlotta Carlström, *En villkorad gemenskap: Hbtq, sexualitet och kristen frikyrklighet* (Stockholm & Göteborg: Makadam förlag, 2023).

[86] Anders Gerdmar, *HBTQ och Bibeln: Svärdet genom svensk kristenhet* (Uppsala: STH Academic, 2023).

[87] Ulla Bardh, *Församlingen som sakrament: Tro dop, medlemskap och ekumenik bland frikyrkokristna vid 1900-talets slut* (Uppsala: Uppsala universitet, 2008), 4–18, 81–82. Jessica Moberg, *Piety, Intimacy and Mobility: A Case Study of Charismatic Christianity in Present-day Stockholm*, Ph.D. thesis (Södertörn: Södertörn College 2013), 191–192.

theologians traditionally have focused on. As Fahlgren has pointed out, Free churches are "non-creedal churches." A symbol of freedom is not having creeds, liturgical handbooks, or other binding documents, which are the traditional "stuff" of much theological academic analysis. However, the turn to practices in recent practical theological circles now releases better methodological resources to research Free churches.[88] Through their sampling, Articles A, B, and C contribute to the much-needed practical theological engagement with Swedish Free churches.

Sampling in the Four Case Studies

While all four articles engage with the practice of preaching in digital culture and spaces in Swedish Protestant churches, each case has its own distinctive structure. In this section, I will succinctly describe the reasoning behind the sampling in each case study, focusing on the ethical considerations in each case.

For Article A, I used a *theoretical* sampling that used secondary orality theories as an organizing principle. As stated in the article, I chose cases of the practice of preaching by preachers before, during, and after the so-called "Gutenberg parenthesis." Since the first purpose of the article was to modify—cultivate—a theory, I chose so-called "deviant" cases with which to test the theory. In the case of the theory at issue, which appears to presuppose a Western, white, male, educated subject, there were several options for what "deviant" could mean. I opted for "female" since gender is a critical issue in the context of Swedish Protestant churches—and because, as the previously mentioned Lövheim has pointed out, gender is still often overlooked in studies of religion, media, and culture.[89]

In relation to the second purpose of the article approach, which was to test the modified theory by applying it to the case of a female preacher in digital culture, the sampling was *purposeful*. In the Swedish context, it was highly topical since the preacher in question—the Archbishop of CoS—had drawn much attention in the media because of her choice to quit Twitter due to the massive amount of online hatred directed at her.

For Article B, I used *purposeful* sampling. Since the aim of the article was to discuss the theology that had been done and what kind of theology that *could* be done, in relation to the COVID-19 pandemic and digital spaces, I chose to focus on congregations in areas hardest hit by the pandemic, and among congregations

---

[88] Fahlgren 2006a, 21–22.

[89] Mia Lövheim, "Introduction: Gender – a Blind Spot in Media, Religion and Culture?," in *Media, Gender and Religion: Key Issues and New Challenges*, ed. Mia Lövheim (London & New York: Routledge, 2013), 1–14.

that were generally so large they found it necessary to go digital (and had the resources to do so). These were found in the three largest cities in Sweden.

In the flood of blog posts and other texts from digital theologians during the first weeks of the pandemic, the Ascension of Christ was often mentioned in passing as a viable source for theological reasoning. When I mentioned this in my lectures and musings on digitally-mediated church and worship in my Swedish context at the time, it propelled interesting discussions with listeners and readers. Consequently, I decided this project would consider sermons from the Feast of Ascension. To restrict the number of Bible texts involved in the theologizing process, I chose to compare CoS and UC, who use the same lectionary. While UC preachers are not obliged to use the lectionary, they often do. The article shows that only a few UC preachers chose to preach on other Bible passages during this feast day.

However, Ascension is not just any day in Protestant churches in Sweden. In CoS, it is quite common to have the worship service outside—for example, in a garden. Since it was challenging to broadcast or livestream outside, and the government proscriptions at the time allowed people to gather outside without numerical restriction, some CoS congregations cancelled digitally-mediated services and only held onsite services on this day. In UC, the usual preacher is usually away at the yearly church joint conference on Ascension Day. As a result, it is quite common to invite guest preachers—but since the pandemic made it difficult for guest preachers to travel, some Ascension services were canceled altogether. As a result of these challenges, and to get enough material, I also decided to include sermons from the Sunday before Pentecost into this project. The Bible texts and themes are closely associated, and some of the UC preachers who had not been able to speak about the Ascension on Ascension Day chose to do so on the following Sunday instead.

The sampling involved much reflection on normativity. First, there were questions of normativity within UC itself. While the church is a merger of three denominations (Swedish Mission Covenant Church, the Baptist Union in Sweden, and the Methodist church in Sweden), there are still differences between specific congregations and preachers due to the differing traditions in the founder churches. To complicate things further, one of the founder churches brought significantly more congregations to the merger. A case study of UC could thus have easily ended up looking into only one of the "streams" that form the tripartite tradition of UC. However, by choosing samples from the three largest cities in Sweden, where all three founder churches are represented, I was able to avoid this problem.

Second, as mentioned in the previous section, CoS is a much bigger church than UC, and if I were to include *all* the CoS sermons preached in these areas in the given time frame, CoS preachers would have drowned UC preachers out. Therefore, I opted to let the number of available UC sermons decide the number of CoS sermons, resulting in digitally-mediated sermons from 12 UC and 14 CoS preachers. In addition, I asked six CoS preachers who were preaching onsite, and whose sermons would not be recorded, for their sermon manuscripts. The idea was to be able to compare onsite with online sermons. However, in the analysis of the sermons, it turned out that there were few differences, neither between onsite/online nor between CoS/UC. Therefore, I decided to include them all in my analysis.

The sampling in Article C was also *purposeful*, primarily in relation to the research project *Congregational Change in Times of Crisis*. The project was initiated by the CoS bishop in the diocese of Växjö, Fredrik Modéus, and the diocese lecturer and professor in church history in Lund, Erik Sidenvall, shortly after the WHO declaration of COVID-19 as a pandemic. The purpose of the project was to examine how congregations act in times of societal crisis. Sidenvall quickly gathered a group of researchers (Ulrik Josefsson, Jonas Ideström, and me), and due to the competencies and the research interests of the group, the project developed into a comparative study of 24 congregations from 5 Protestant denominations in the region of Småland: CoS, UC, PM, Interact and SAM. In other words, the sampling was made within the overarching research project's framework to compare CoS and the Free churches. The researchers chose the congregations in consultation with each denomination's leadership to ensure variety in size and spirituality. Just as with the sampling of Article B, we ensured that all three founder church traditions in UC were represented. Likewise, the diocese of Växjö took care to include congregations from all three traditions of CoS spirituality previously mentioned. This was done not for the study to be generalizable but to maximize what might be learned—in the interest of complexity and particularity, which are the watchwords of all case studies.

This consultation with church leadership proved very fruitful. They had valuable knowledge of the unique situations represented by each congregation and were able to direct us to meaningful cases—not just congregations that had done well but congregations that struggled with problems and conflicts. The consultation was also helpful in a situation where the sampling needed to be as fast as it was accurate—because, at that point, we assumed the pandemic would be over soon.

In other words, the sampling was not done directly in relation to the purposes of the article or the thesis. However, it serendipitously served the purposes of this thesis, too, since one of the significant congregational changes in this crisis was the transition to digital spaces.

Article D, finally, also used *purposeful* sampling in relation to the purposes of a larger research project. The *Church in digital space* project was initiated by the CoS bishop of the Stockholm diocese, Andreas Holmberg, and led by his theological advisor, Sara Garpe, and the previously mentioned Ideström. The purpose of the project was to find ways for CoS to use learnings from the digital transition prompted by the pandemic to find sustainable and theologically-informed ways to keep the digital church doors open in the future.

The sampling was made in relation to the research design of the project as an "action research" project. Action research starts from the assumption that research can contribute to solving real-world problems and developing practical knowledge and skills—and includes the further conviction that participants themselves possess knowledge that could contribute significantly to the research process and its actionable aims. Because of these foundational convictions, research in this paradigm is a highly collaborative process of interpretation and reflection in which the practitioners contribute with their experience and knowledge alongside researchers who draw on their own resources, like methods, theories, and research from other contexts.[90] This dynamic was also reflected in the sampling procedure.

The project and its purposes were presented to all vicars in the diocese, together with an invitation to apply for participation. From among the unusually large number of applications, eight congregations were selected. In addition, five researchers were engaged (Ideström, the previously mentioned Stangeland Kaufman, Bible scholar Rikard Roitto, Ph.D. student Simon Hallonsten, and me) along with employees of the diocese, and the CoS research unit—in all around 70 people. The project was divided into phases, where phase 2 consisted of smaller,

[90] Sara Garpe, Jonas Ideström and Frida Mannerfelt, "Att vara kyrka i digitala rum," in *Kyrka i digitala rum: Ett aktionsforskningsprojekt om församlingsliv online*, eds. Sara Garpe and Jonas Ideström (Uppsala: Svenska kyrkan, 2022), 6–18. As stated in the introduction, the research project was inspired by Theological action research (TAR), as well as methods and concepts developed by Jonas Ideström and bishop Andreas Holmberg; Watkins 2020; Jonas Ideström, "Implicit Ecclesiology and Local Church Identity. Dealing With Dilemmas of Empirical Ecclesiology," in *Ecclesiology in the Trenches: Theory and Method under Construction*, eds. Sune Fahlgren and Jonas Ideström (Eugene OR: Pickwick Publications, 2015), 121–138; Andreas Holmberg, *Kyrka i nytt landskap: En studie av levd ecklesiologi i Svenska kyrkan* (Skellefteå: Artos Academic, 2019).

directed case studies. By this point, one congregation had already decided to leave the project.

Before the start of phase 2, the researchers presented areas of interest to the remaining seven congregations. The project leaders then listened to the congregations to hear what they were interested in and matched researchers and congregations based on both responses. Roitto and I ended up collaborating with the congregations in Täby and Järfälla in a project on interaction, synchronicity, and integrity in pre-recorded, digitally-mediated worship services.[91]

Just as with Article C, the sampling was not done directly in relation to the purposes of my thesis. And yet, because I had stated in my presentation to the congregations that my main interest was the practice of preaching in digital culture and spaces, and the participating practitioners shared this interest, the sampling ended up serving the purposes of the thesis as well.

4.2.3 Generating and Analyzing Material in an Ethical Way

In case studies, you generally use multiple kinds of materials and methods in order to triangulate results and analysis. Standard methods are observations, interviews, and the analysis of documents. You commonly analyze the source material (or data) in steps: first via initial sense-making, then through an identification of themes in which the material is broken down into segments (coded or categorized), and finally with an examination of patterns and relationships between the segments.[92] This thesis is no exception to the rule.

In this section, I will describe the procedures employed for generating and analyzing source material, with a special focus on the ethical dimensions involved in the process. And where I deem that the articles may be a bit frugal with information, I will also provide additional information.

For the historical case study in Article A, whose purpose was to adapt a theory of orality and literacy, I chose to rely on the existing work of other scholars, who specialized in studying the preacher in question, to describe the cases. In my analysis, I also applied a variety of theoretical lenses to conceptualize the case findings. Of particular relevance to the purposes of this thesis are Pamela E. Klassen and Karen Lofton's discussion of authority as derived from both the body and

---

[91] Mannerfelt and Roitto 2022a, 47–60; Mannerfelt and Roitto 2022b, 61–79.
[92] Simons 2020, 681 (676–703).

practices, as detailed in their chapter "Material Witnesses: Women and the Mediation of History."[93]

To analyze the contemporary case of a female preacher enmeshed in digital culture, I used newspaper articles by and about her in combination with observation of her social media accounts on Twitter and Instagram. However, this raised ethical concerns about consent and deception. As mentioned earlier, digital platforms allow researchers to "lurk"—observing conversations and social practices without the participants' knowledge. In this case, I deemed that the social media accounts under observation were clearly at the more "public" end of the privacy scale because the names on the accounts contained "bishop" and "archbishop," indicating that the posts and the profile were created in the official capacity of her office as a church leader. As shown in the article, this case was analyzed using a theory developed out of orality and literacy.

Article B posed a similar problem. Did the sermons count as "public enough," or did I have to contact the preachers to ask for consent? I opted for the former for two reasons. Sermons are generally considered public speech, and most of these sermons were published on the congregations' official websites and social media accounts. In addition, my analysis did not concern anything other than the preacher's words, re-presented in print for the purposes of my analysis, which would make it very hard for a reader of my work to identify or recognize the preacher in question. It would also be nearly impossible to trace quotations back to their original sources, even with the aid of search engines, because the quoted material relies on transcriptions of orally-delivered speech.

However, there were a few situations where I did ask some preachers for consent. In a few of these cases, the congregations did not publish sermons publicly. They only live-streamed their services to people in their local congregation, and you had to have a particular link to get access. In these cases, I wrote to the preacher and asked if I could attend and record the audio of the sermon. In other cases, I had to ask onsite-only preachers for their sermon manuscripts.

Because the source material was gathered this way, I faced a classic problem for homileticians when it came time for analysis. Is it possible to compare the product of the preparation phase (the manuscript) with the product of the verbalization phase (the spoken word of the delivered sermon)? Given that the purpose of my analysis here was to examine the theologizing that occurred in the sermons, thus

---

[93] Pamela E. Klassen and Karen Lofton, "Material Witnesses: Women and the Mediation of Christianity," in *Media, Religion and Gender: Key Issues and New Challenges*, ed. Mia Lövheim (New York: Routledge, 2013), 53–63.

putting theological content at the center of my analysis, I deemed that any differences between prepared notes and delivered speech would not pose any significant problems. However, in light of my later findings in Article D, I would now think twice about replicating this approach since the co-preaching feature in the verbalization phase in a digitally-mediated sermon tends to amplify the differences between the manuscript and delivery.

The sermons were analyzed through the conceptual lens of "theologizing" as a way to scrutinize the interpretation process in the preparation phase of the sermon. I drew on Jonas Ideström's description of the practice of theologizing in my work here, but, since the word limits on Article B were quite severe, I would like to elaborate at more length on the concept.

Ideström draws on Bruno Latour—as already mentioned, a theorist often associated with practice theory –to show how theology is "done." It is a continuous meaning-making process that emerges in social practices in which the bodily and the material are actors too.[94] Ideström also draws on the hermeneutics of Gordon Lathrop's liturgical theology and his concept of "juxtaposition." Bible texts are juxtaposed against human lives and experiences, and in the interaction between text, symbols, objects, and humans, "a dialogue of holy things" occurs. To Ideström, this is not just a process that takes place in the framework of the liturgy. It is a hermeneutical process that also occurs daily concerning everyday activities and objects. The process does not happen automatically, however. It takes a conscious effort.[95]

Notably, according to Ideström, the process of theologizing is capable of opening up a "room of possibilities" ("möjlighetsrum").[96] In other words, his conception of theologizing bears resemblances to the thinking of homileticians like the earlier mentioned Gaarden and Pleizier, who described the interaction between the preacher and listeners in the realization phase.

The results of my analysis were discussed in light of Ascension theology. Here, I wanted to bring the lived theology expressed in the sermons into conversation with normative theology. As stated in Chapter 2, discussing how lived theology sits within wider theological conversations is crucial. Ethical questions arose, however. Was I using normative theology to evaluate the homiletical theology of the preachers, and if so, was that not unfair? The second research question in the

---

[94] Jonas Ideström, *Ikoniska kartor: Att göra teologi I kyrkans vardag* (Stockholm: Verbum, 2021), 28–38, 51.

[95] Ideström 2021, 81–91.

[96] Ideström 2021, 41–47, 176.

article was formulated especially with this concern in mind—*How could theology continue to be done in a digital culture?*—striving for a constructive approach that took into consideration the fact that any discussions I undertook would be a continuation of certain theological interpretative practices that are now flourishing, and not an attempt to use normative theology as a cudgel or contrast, to which inferior interpretations were measured.

Another ethical question was if I could provide a fair analysis of the UC preachers. From a broad perspective, I am an insider in Protestant churches. However, from a narrower point of view, I am, in actuality, an insider in only one of the churches, CoS. To those in the UC, I could be considered, justifiably, an outsider. But when I found very few differences between the preachers in the two churches, I became worried that I had overlooked something and that my outsider status might be obscuring something from me in regard to UC preachers and sermons. In this case, the collegial community of the research school (where there were several UC insiders who aided me) was crucial to ensuring that I did not misinterpret the UC preachers.

The source material in Article C consists of interviews. Homiletical studies of sermon reception and listening practice are traditionally interview studies, and the *Congregational Change* project offered an opportunity to do just that. As the pandemic continued, so did the study, and the research group decided to expand its scope to include interviews with employees and active members of the congregations. The interviews were conducted a year into the pandemic, during the spring of 2021. With the permission of the senior researchers on the project, I included a few questions about sermon reception in these interviews. In all, I conducted 40 interviews with 64 people. The employees were interviewed individually, and the active members were interviewed in groups of 2–3 persons. These 14 group interviews with 29 members (listeners) provided the source material for the article.

The process of generating the source material was approved by the Swedish Ethical Review Authority (SERA).[97] The employees served as gatekeepers to the listeners, akin to how church leadership originally provided suggestions for which congregations to focus our study on. While there was a risk that the employees would provide us with participants that would not air critique, we realized that other methods of approaching informants would likely not secure a broader range of opinions. In addition, the employees could be assumed to practice pastoral care for their members, which would lower the possibility of including informants who

---

[97] Dnr 2020-06823. Approval date 16 February 2021.

were vulnerable or otherwise not suitable for the study. This was, after all, happening amid a pandemic that had robbed people of social life. An open invitation to an interview study could potentially attract vulnerable persons searching for company.

After their own interviews, the employees were asked to suggest 3–5 active members of their congregation who they thought would make suitable interview subjects. About half of them provided such suggestions. The suggested members were contacted individually via e-mail with information about the research projects. (The employees knew who would potentially be invited to participate but not who accepted the invitation.) If the suggested members showed interest, they received a phone call in which I gave the same information about the research project that appeared in the e-mail and ensured that they knew what the project was about, how their personal information was being handled, and how to withdraw consent. The phone calls also allowed potential participants to get answers to any questions they had.

Once I knew who among the suggested persons wanted to participate (and had excluded persons I deemed not eligible for the study), the groups of 2–3 interviewees then decided on a time and place for the interview. The interviews were semi-structured and lasted no more than 90 minutes, even if I did not get to ask all the questions in the questionnaire.

In an interview, the interviewer and the interviewees create knowledge together—and this epistemological dimension is crucial to my own understanding of what took place between us during these interviews. The knowledge created as a result is, as Steinar Kvale and Svend Brinkman state, "created, relational, conversational, contextual, linguistic, narrative and pragmatic."[98] Or, to speak in a more Schatzkian mode, knowledge is created in the practice of systematic and purposeful inquiry and conversation. Since I view knowledge as co-constructed, I wanted to ensure that the participants were allowed to linger on topics that were important to them and not force or rush the conversation just to be able to tick all the boxes in the questionnaire. I also always included a final question in which I asked if there was anything they thought was missing from the questionnaire that would be essential to include in the interview to understand what it was like to "do church" in their context during this particular time.

Allowing the participants space to make their own contribution was also important because I once again was caught in a situation where I was an insider to

---

[98] Steinar Kvale and Svend Brinkman, *Den kvalitativa forskningsintervjun* (Lund: Studentlitteratur, 2014), 69–80.

the CoS interviewees and an outsider to the Free church interviewees. In some interviews, I had to ensure I was "intentionally naïve" and not take things for granted.[99] In some interviews, I had to be careful not to let my CoS habitus cloud my interpretations of the Free church interviewees' statements. In addition, there was also a power dynamic to consider. To the CoS participants, I could potentially be seen as a representative of church leadership. To the Free church participants, I could potentially be seen as a representative of the formerly oppressive state church. Before and during the interviews, I took great care to introduce myself as a researcher, clarify my role and task, and act in such a manner that the interviewees felt that they were talking to a researcher, not a representative of CoS leadership.

In addition, two other ethical dilemmas arose during the interviews. One resembled the situation Hutchings described. The interviewees desired someone who could speak for them—in particular, the participating employees who were tired and frustrated. It was common for them to cry during the interviews, especially when I asked them what the pandemic was doing to them as pastors, deacons, and teachers. During the fall of 2021, when the interviews were conducted, and as a result of what I'd discovered, I decided to write a debate article on exhaustion among employees and volunteers.[100]

The other dilemma was that I had started impacting the research field. The many lectures I had given during the year, the interviews in church-oriented newspapers, and my teaching in the summer course *Church and Theology in Times of Pandemic* with hundreds of students had begun to give me—as practical theologian Ninna Edgardh named it in a review of the anthology *Corona och kyrkorna* (Churches and Corona)—a reputation for being "something of an expert on church and digitalization."[101] This affected some of the interviews, in which interview subjects referred to my analyses ("It was like you described it"), used the concepts I had taught them, and so on. In this case, I sought advice from the senior researchers in the research group, who advised me to address the issue when it arose in the interviews and formulate follow-up questions to better uncover the interviewees' own words and experiences as a check to ensure they were not merely parroting my own ideas back to me.

The interviews were transcribed, and the transcribed texts were the object of analysis. To ensure the confidentiality of the participants, they are referred to as a

---

[99] Stangeland Kaufman 2022, 113.

[100] Frida Mannerfelt, "Kan vi tala om trötthetsskulden," *Dagen* 13 August 2021.

[101] Ninna Edgardh, "Ett snabbt sammanställt men viktigt tidsdokument," *Svensk kyrkotidning* 117:10 (2021), 319.

group. As seen in article C, I based the analytical questions on Schatzki's practice theory and discussed the findings in light of recent homiletical research on listening practices. As previously mentioned, in analyzing case studies conducted in a field familiar to the researcher, theories aid in rendering the familiar "unfamiliar." Here, practice theory created a much-needed distance, not least to the CoS portion of the material.

As stated in the article, the source material for Article D was created between August 2021 and February 2022. The SERA also approved this procedure.[102] During that period, researchers and practitioners met once a month. At the first meeting, the researchers observed the practitioners' online and onsite practices and conducted semi-structured individual interviews. We gathered statistics, edited recordings of the worship services, and took screenshots of their publications on social media. At the second meeting, the researchers presented a preliminary analysis of what they had seen and heard and offered theories for the practitioners to respond to and reflect on. A month later, the researchers returned for another round of individual interviews, observations, etc. The source material thus consists of a variety of materials, transcriptions of individual and group interviews, protocols of observations onsite and online, and recordings of worship services.

Since this study concerned only CoS, I did not have to negotiate the insider/outsider dynamic. However, I did have to manage the problem of being in a context where I might be blind to certain aspects because they were too familiar to me. Throughout this process, my co-researcher, Rikard Roitto, proved to be a valuable ally in generating source material. As an outsider, he was able to make observations and ask questions that I had not considered.

While the *Church in digital space* project was designed as an action research project, the research design of article D was that of a case study. Consequently, the material was analyzed using Heidi Campbell's work on authority and Religious Digital Creatives (RDCs), as well as Engemann's conceptualizing of the preaching event, and further developed in light of a Scandinavian homiletical strand I labeled "polyphonic preaching." Again, these theories served to estrange me from the familiar in the analysis process—a necessary stance for a researcher, even a sympathetic one, to take at times.

The action research design also actualized ethical dilemmas. In an action research project, you research *with* the practitioners. Since they are co-researchers, pseudonymizing them would be against the core principles of action research. On

---

[102] Dnr: 2021-03608. Approval date: 9 August 2021.

the other hand, we were keen to include interviews with worship service participants—which, according to the law, require confidentiality. To ensure listeners' confidentiality and give as much credit to our co-researchers as possible, we decided to refer to practitioners using work titles and the names of their respective congregations, for example, "pastor in Täby." The same principles are used in the article.

4.3 In Sum

In this chapter, I have accounted for methodological considerations and why I find practice theory to be a fruitful way to account for the relationship between practice and theology—namely, that it collapses correlation through conceiving of *all* knowledge, be it the 'normative' theology in doctrines or the lived theology in practices, as something that arises through practice.

Furthermore, I have described the research design as a multicase study on the quintain of the practice of preaching in digital culture and spaces. As such, it consists of several case studies that examine various important aspects of the quintain. I have accounted for the sampling choice of Swedish Protestant churches and given an overview of the historical, sociological, and theological characteristics of the five denominations involved.

Finally, I have given a supplementary account of the procedures used to generate and analyze the source material in each article, with particular attention to the ethical considerations that the restricted length of the articles did not always allow for.

Now we turn to the cross-case analysis of this multicase study and the conclusions of the thesis.

5. On Conclusions

In this chapter, I will summarize what I perceive to be my main contributions to the scholarly conversations outlined in chapter 3. The chapter is divided into three sections. In the first section (5.1), I will present the results of this multicase study of the practice of preaching in digital culture and spaces. Through a cross-case analysis of the findings in the four case studies of the articles, I will answer the three sub-questions that, in turn, enable me to answer the overarching research question about what characterizes the practice of preaching in digital culture and spaces. I will argue that the practice of preaching in digital culture and spaces is characterized by "co-preaching."

In the second section (5.2), I will delve deeper into the overarching research question and discuss the implications of co-preaching in relation to the findings in the articles. As mentioned in Chapter 3, homileticians have begun to pay more attention to the deep relationality of the practice of preaching and point to the fact that materiality matters. I will contribute to the conversation by discussing the consequences of that interdependence, using digital media material arrangements as an example. In the third and final section (5.3), I will contribute to the conversation on how to research the practice of preaching, in both its local and digitally-mediated variations. Throughout, I will suggest areas for further research.

5.1 Co-preaching: The Results of a Multicase Study

In this section, I will present the results of a cross-case analysis of the cases described in the four articles and argue that the practice of preaching is characterized by co-preaching. As discussed in Chapter 4, these results are not generalizable in the sense that they apply to all cases of preaching in digital culture and spaces. Since all practices are situated and indissolubly entangled in their context, the results are particular to that context too. However, as previously noted, the particular holds something universal. Especially in the case of digital media that possess common and global features due to the fact that their material arrangements are the same across the globe.

The analysis is done in awareness of the potential challenges of cross-analysis. The aforementioned Stake cautions against a tendency to focus only on what is common and not what is unique to each case. Researchers must remember that some of the important findings will be context-bound and perhaps only appear in one of the cases. Therefore, to catch a fuller understanding of the quintain, they need to make a careful review of the details in the analysis and not let go of the site-specific experiences.[1]

As mentioned in Chapter 4, there is also a diachronic dimension to this cross-case analysis. This means that I will not just point out similarities and differences, but I will also occasionally point out shifts and developments over time—not least developments in my own line of thinking.

The section is structured in relation to Schatzki's practice theory, where the three components of a practice—materiality, human agency, and organization—will be discussed in turn. As mentioned in Article C, such a division of indissolubly entangled components will always be somewhat forced, but may be done for analytical clarity.

5.1.1 Materiality

This section will focus on the first sub-question—What characterizes the practices in the digitally-mediated preaching event?—and examine material arrangements in the three phases of the preaching event, *the preparation phase, the verbalization phase*, and *the realization phase*.

In Chapter 3, I referred to discussions on materiality in the practice of preaching and showed that homileticians interested in practices have increasingly begun to explore the material arrangements that might play a part in the preaching event. Pleizier, who emphasizes the "homiletical interaction" between preacher and listener, also points to the importance of the community in which both are situated.[2] Engemann, whose main actors in the preaching event are the preacher, the listener, and various texts (written and spoken), mentions the role of "the situation" in the process.[3] Lorensen, who speaks of an interaction between the preacher, listener, text, and God, discusses the importance of bodies and mentions that other material arrangements might play a part in the meaning-making process.[4] Gaarden, finally, describes the reciprocal interaction between the listener and the preacher

---

[1] Stake 2006, 39–77.
[2] Pleizier 2010, 21–33.
[3] Engemann 2019, xix–xx.
[4] Lorensen 2014, 21–41.

and sees the preacher as "a tool" in the meaning-making process. She also mentions in passing that the space of the local church also plays a part in the construction of meaning.[5]

Moreover, homileticians like Stangeland Kaufman, Mosdøl, and Rystad have used practice theory (and "socio-material sensibilities") to show that material arrangements *do* play an important part in the practice of preaching.[6] Rystad concludes: "Preaching happens in relation to listeners and the church room, and the preacher always preaches with mediational means, including language."[7] To this conversation, this thesis brings a clearer understanding of the ways in which materiality actually interacts with the preaching event, as well as a discussion of what the consequences might be for the practice of preaching taken as a whole.

Turning an eye to the materiality of the preaching events examined in these cases discloses the significance of all kinds of material arrangements in the complex interpretation and communication process of the preaching event as such. In other words, as I have demonstrated, digital media reveals the importance of materiality in the practice of preaching generally, no matter where it is situated.

Moreover, in several of these cases, the involvement of the material arrangements of digital media increases the interaction and interdependency with materiality in the practice of preaching. Notably, the particular materiality of digital media impacts the outcome of the preaching event in different ways, depending on which kind of material arrangements are involved. In other words, there is a variety of possible consequences and involvements, depending on the type, form, or functionality of the digital media used by listeners and churches in the case studies.

In *the preparation phase*, the results of Article B suggest that the process of interpreting the Bible texts and tradition is impacted by the new material arrangements incorporated into this phase because of the pandemic. In *the verbalization phase*, materiality also plays a significant role in the cases under consideration in this thesis. This is particularly evident in the case discussed in Article D, in which attentiveness to the material arrangements of digital media highlights how the verbalization phase seemingly is a verbalization *and visualization* phase in all preaching, no matter where it is situated.

As discussed in Articles C and A, there is a multiplicity in digital media arrangements—and different kinds of setups tend to lead to different outcomes in

---

[5] Gaarden 2021, 69–73.

[6] Rystad 2020, 1–12, Stangeland Kaufman 2021, 7–18; Stangeland Kaufman and Mosdøl 2021, 91–112.

[7] Rystad 2020, 122.

the delivery of a sermon. Article C addresses this multiplicity in the verbalization phase by referring to various categories of online preaching. The results of the analysis of the theory of secondary orality in Article A point to the importance of paying attention to multiplicity when considering space, body, and genre of communication. The preacher in the contemporary case receives online hate when she preaches through public statements about faith on Twitter but is welcomed and encouraged to preach through narratives with the authority from her body and practices on Instagram. In the case of Article D's study of pre-recorded worship services, the particular properties of the digital media material arrangements involved launch a second verbalization and visualization phase during the editing process.

However, despite the variation that results from different material arrangements, several of the cases have one thing in common: the inclusion of other (new) material arrangements in the verbalization phase. Examples include artwork in the churches or artifacts like a tiny toy car that the listeners normally would not see during the sermon. The preachers tend to use these kinds of material arrangements as visual aids to accompany their words, and the co-preachers strive to enhance and enrich the preacher's words in the editing process through a visual representation of these material arrangements.

In Article D, I discuss how this might delimit the verbalization phase. I refer to Johannes Stückelberger's observation that in a digitally-mediated sermon, the gaze (and thus the interpretation process) of the listener is controlled by the camera person and the editor—the listener is not able to let her gaze wander around the church building like she might have been accustomed to doing, after all.[8] However, the findings in Article C question this conclusion. Stückelberger—and I—overlooked the fact that the realization phase is characterized by multiplicity. The idea that the gaze of the listener is controlled presupposes that the listener only looks at and interacts with the screen in front of them—whereas the listeners in article C testified to how plenty of other material arrangements interacted with the sermon, in particular everyday arrangements. In digitally-mediated sermons, the listener does not necessarily have *fewer* material arrangements to interact with—often, they have *more*.

Moreover, being able to direct the gaze of the listener to certain material arrangements and exclude others might not be a disadvantage in some cases. For instance, artwork in church buildings may sometimes contradict the preacher's

---

[8] Johannes Stückelberger, *Liturgie in virtuellen Räumen: Der Raum in Online-Gottesdiensten https://www.liturgik.unibe.ch* [Accessed 26 August 2022].

words. An example I have discussed elsewhere is the altarpiece of the Holy Trinity church in Malmö, Sweden. Its large altarpiece from the 1930s depicts a blond Jesus welcoming children into the light while turning away from stereotypically depicted Jews, who are standing in the shadows pointing angrily at Jesus. Thus, the preacher's efforts to verbalize the gospel in a way that welcomes the other and with respect for Christian roots in Jewish faith and Scriptures, often clashes with the altarpiece's visualization of a replacement theology that demonizes the other.[9] In this case, a digitally-mediated preaching event could better facilitate interactions between the words of the sermon and more suitable material arrangements other than the altarpiece.

In *the realization phase,* the material arrangements of digital media fuel the listeners' insight into the impact of material arrangements on their listening practices in general, but also on their interpretation and meaning-making process. The digital mediation of the preaching event makes them realize how important the church building and the material arrangements inside it are—including the bodies of the community and the preacher.

The digital mediation of the preaching event also leads to the inclusion of other material arrangements. Some, like hymnbooks, Bibles, candles, or designated spaces for prayer and worship, are included in order to reproduce the practices of the local church. But there are several examples of the inclusion of new material arrangements, often belonging to the category of the everyday, such as the couch or kitchen table. These everyday material arrangements can distract, obstruct, or aid in reaching the desired end of the practice of listening to a sermon, depending on how the listeners engage with them.

Just as in the other phases, there is a multiplicity that characterizes how various digital media setups lead to different outcomes for listening practices. For example, material arrangements that increase a sense of community (like gathering the family or using digital platforms that allow for interactions like comments, chat functionality, etc.) also boost the chances that digitally-mediated preaching is perceived as "working."

---

[9] I used the example of his painting in the seminar "Att tala väl om den Andre – judisk-kristen dialog utmanar kristna förkunnare" ("to speak well of the other – Jewish-Christian dialogue challenges Christian preachers") (29 March 2022) where I was invited to give a response to the recently released commentary on Bible texts in the lectionary of CoS and UC. The commentary gathers texts from a blog, aimed to give examples of how to "speak well" of Jews and Judaism when preaching on Bible passages that traditionally have been used to speak pejoratively or even antisemitic about Judaism. *Tala väl: Predikokommentarer i Krister Stendahls anda*, ed. Helene Egnell (Uppsala: Bibelsällskapets förlag, 2021).

In sum, the digitally-mediated preaching event is characterized by interaction and interdependence with material arrangements—consequently drawing attention to how all preaching events, no matter where they are situated, are indissolubly entangled with material arrangements and thus impacted by them. Throughout the articles, I have shown some of the ways in which material arrangements matter. Buildings, individual and collective bodies, art, objects, artifacts, and technology all play a role in how practices are carried out and in the outcome of the interpretation and communication processes of the preaching event. As the practice theory approach of the thesis discloses: material arrangements are entangled and embedded into all practices, including the practice of preaching. They always have been, and they always will be.

The particular arrangements of digital media appear to increase the interaction and interdependence with materiality in the preaching event. This occurs because the digital mediation itself is so clearly, well, mediated by materiality, but also because digital mediation makes it possible to introduce other new material arrangements into listening practices that were not previously possible in the local church context, for instance. The interdependence between humans and material arrangements in the practice of preaching is thus amplified.

5.1.2 Human Agency and Interaction

In this section, I will discuss human agency in relation to the first and second subquestions. First, I will examine human agency in the three phases of the preaching event. Second, I will examine what kinds of authority are practiced by preachers in digital culture and spaces.

Human Agency in the digitally-mediated preaching event. As mentioned in the section above, many of the homileticians involved in the "preaching as a practice" conversation have shown that there is an intense interaction and interdependency between preachers and listeners. The results of my cross-case analysis support their arguments. As I have shown in Article C, the listeners engage in chains of actions with others and material arrangements in various ways to uphold the proper ends of the listening practices. Listeners collaborate with the preacher in order to make the sermon "work."

Furthermore, the cases under consideration in this thesis show that human actors adapt and adjust their interhuman actions in relation to digital media material arrangements. Digital mediation of the preaching event does not only affect human agency in relation to materiality; it also affects how humans interact with other humans. Notably, interaction and interdependency could both increase *and* decrease. Just as with materiality, the digitally-mediated preaching event could be said to amplify the interactive and interdependent features of the sermon, drawing more human actors into the practice of preaching. However, depending on the characteristics of the digital media arrangements and the way humans interact with them, these interactive features could also be diminished and decreased.

In the description of *the verbalization phase* in Article D, this dynamic is particularly evident. Take the digital media arrangements of pre-recorded worship services. Here, the digitally-mediated preaching event is characterized by collaboration and negotiation between various kinds of digital strategists (pastors, musicians, religious educators) and digital spokespersons (technicians and communications directors). The article also suggests other ways for more people to be actively involved in the verbalization and visualization process, for example, through comments on social media.

As the description of *the realization phase* in Article C shows, the preaching event is indeed about interaction and collaboration. In order for the sermon to "work" and the third room of preaching to open up, listeners need to engage and interact in certain ways with the words and visuals. This supports the claim of Lorensen and Gaarden that the listeners are indeed authors of the sermon.[10]

However, the multiplicity of digital media arrangements corresponds to a multiplicity of ways in which humans choose to act. Interaction and interdependency were not always increased. The findings in Article C show that in some cases, digital mediation could lead to increased individualization, especially in cases where listeners were alone and/or the sermon was mediated as a one-way or pre-recorded broadcast. For instance, listeners could lapse into the disengaged passivity of "merely watching a screen," or struggling to navigate what to them are confusing interfaces. Notably, listeners in these cases sometimes adapted and adjusted their actions in relation to the (new) material arrangements in order to be better able to interact with the preachers' words and reach the desired ends of their listening practice.

None of the articles in the thesis examine the actions of preachers in *the preparation phase*. Other studies, such as Lienau's study of how pastors communicate the gospel on Instagram (see section 3.1), show that digital mediation can enable and encourage the inclusion of others—and thus increase interaction and interdependence—in this phase as well.[11] Sigmon (see section 3.2) argues similarly, giving

---

[10] Gaarden and Lorensen 2013, 29–41.
[11] Lienau 2020, 489–522.

examples of how she herself and others has been using social media to involve others in the preparation phase.[12] However, in one of the rare case studies of preachers' use of digital media in this phase, David H. Michaels finds that ministers typically use the internet for information-seeking rather than conversation.[13] This indicates that digital mediation in the preparation phase might not necessarily lead to increased interaction and collaboration with other humans. Rather, it could merely recapitulate the same kind of lonely interaction with (the material arrangements of) textual sources that are often common in (non-digitally-mediated) sermon preparation. Notably, Michaels' study was published in 2009, when digital media arrangements were significantly different compared to Sigmon's study, from 2017 and Lienau's, from 2020. This is clearly an issue that warrants further research. In anticipation of that, my instinct is to argue that human agency in the preparation phase seems to be characterized by the same features as those previously noted in the realization phase—i.e., that any increase or a decrease in interaction and interdependence is dependent on which digital media are involved and how humans choose to interact with them. However, when addressing answers to the second sub-question of this thesis—what kinds of authority are practiced by preachers in digital culture and spaces—I argue that when it comes to the practices of preaching under consideration in this thesis, an increase is more common.

The preacher's authority in digital culture and spaces. As indicated in Chapters 2 and 3, the preacher's authority is a key question when it comes to the practice of preaching in digital culture and spaces. Witte found in her study from 2013 that preachers of digitally-mediated sermons did not enjoy the same authority they typically received in non-digitally-mediated spaces due to historical and theological expectations of the sermon as a genre. She predicted this "authority deficit" would change over time as digital media reshaped these expectations.[14] Based on the findings in my cross-case analysis, they now have.

The authority of the preacher is discussed in Articles A and D. Both articles come to the same conclusion: in digital culture and spaces, the practice of preaching is characterized by relationality and negotiation. In other words, they support the findings of, for example, Cheong, who found that the Tweets of the megapastor under consideration in hers work contributed to negotiating and validating

---

[12] Sigmon 2017, 201–215.
[13] Michaels 2009, 164–178.
[14] Witte 2013.

the pastor's authority—effectively making his authority more dependent on the validation of his followers.[15]

Yet these two case studies are the first (Article A) and last (Article D) I conducted—and so helpfully illustrate both the development of how religious authority is conceptualized in the field of digital religion as well as the refinement of my own line of thought regarding the issue of authority in digitally-mediated preaching.

In Article A, I draw on the work of the previously mentioned Klassen and Lofton to cultivate an approach rooted in the theory of secondary orality. The historical case studies of female preachers indicate the need to attend to the ways authority is being construed, and as I wrote up the main part of this analysis in early 2019, Klassen's and Lofton's chapter in the 2016 anthology *Gender, Media and Religion* "Material Witnesses: Women and the Mediation of History," provided the best tool I could find for adopting an analytical framework.

The key aspect of Klassen's and Lofton's argument that I picked up was, in short, the idea that throughout the history of Christianity, women have relied on the material witness of their bodies to construe authority. Two other common ways of exhibiting authority—authority from (theological) education and ecclesial authority (for example, being ordained)—have often excluded women. Hence, women draw on "the matter of their lives," their bodies and practices, as a foundation for their testimonies of the Christian faith.[16] The two authors claim that the Christian doctrine of the incarnation gives special weight to material witness. However, there is also a paradox here. The same body that potentially gives women authority is, at the same time, the very reason women do not get authority in the first place. Furthermore, such body-oriented authority is fragile. There is a fine line between using your body and life as grounds for faithful witness, and instead becoming a "commodity," a brand, open to the charge of self-promotion. If witness is deemed as self-promotion, authority is lost.

Klassen and Lofton argue that, from the 20th century onward, the material witness of women has evolved from being a critical component of their religious practice to being the *only* expectation for their Christian identity. In addition, the same unstable paradox remains. as prevailing cultural winds continue to force women to walk the line between "reverent witness and shameless self-promoter." At the end of the chapter, Klassen and Lofton discuss how critical comments on social

---

[15] Cheong 2014, 1–19.

[16] Throughout their chapter, Klassen and Lofton use the words "testimony" and "witness," but on one occasion, they talk about "preaching women."

media testify to "the fragile authority of a woman intent on melding motherhood, sensuality and piety in a material, yet virtual Christian witness." Referring to the work of Mia Lövheim on female bloggers, they argue that the "ethical space" that women create in digital spaces through narratives of personal experience, inviting their audience to share personal confessions and make strong declarations of one's views, is especially unstable since all materiality, bodies included, are questioned in digital space.[17]

Klassen's and Lofton's focus on gender, the authority of bodies as mediated through material witness, and a thoroughly historical perspective all contributed to the development of my own interpretation of secondary orality theory in Article A.

But two things bothered me. Firstly, there seemed to be a missing component in their construal of authority, one that neither educational, ecclesial, nor embodied authority could account for. In the case of the 19th-century evangelist Nelly Hall's practice of preaching, it was not just body and practices that were important in the construal of authority. It was also numbers. Her authority as a preacher was also based on metrics: how many people would come and listen to the sermon and surrender their lives to Christ? Klassen and Lofton hint at this feature in their analysis of Mary Lena Street Lewis Tate (1871-1930), a preacher living at approximately the same time as Nelly Hall. According to the authors, Tate's and other women's success lay in their ability to self-mediate in the process of spreading the gospel. However, they do not discuss the metric aspect of authority.

Secondly, the case study of Antje Jackelén, a preacher in the secondary orality of digital culture, points to another missing component in Klassen's and Lofton's account. In earlier work, I drew on the analysis described in Jackson W. Carroll's *As One with Authority* to discuss how the preacher's authority is practiced.[18] Carroll distinguishes between "official" and "personal" authority, authority based on representing the sacred, and authority based on expertise. Official authority comes from meeting the training requirements of a given denomination or ecclesiastical body and being officially appointed—for example, through ordination. Personal authority is based on a pastor's personal qualities, whereby they gain trust and establish authority through thoroughly relational means. Carroll claims that all Christian denominations give increasingly more weight to personal authority,

---

[17] Klassen and Lofton 2013, 53–63.

[18] Frida Mannerfelt, "Hör ni som har öron: En studie av samtalets funktion för nutida predikan," Master thesis (Lund: Lunds universitet, 2017); Frida Mannerfelt, "Hör ni som har öron!," *Svensk kyrkotidning* 114:11 (2018), 324–327.

forcing pastors to "earn the respect and trust of their parishioners by their personal attributes regardless of the standing that their office may give them."[19] This notion of earned authority resembles Klassen's and Lofton's description of authority as based in practices and the material witness of the body.

Like Klassen and Lofton, Carroll discusses the instability and potential downsides of this kind of authority. Since personal authority is upheld through trust, pastors need to continually garner it. They could thus be tempted to shy away from doing and saying things that might jeopardize that trust—like making tough but necessary decisions that parishioners might not like, or preaching uncomfortable truths they might not want to hear. In other words: *vox pulpiti* is at risk of becoming *vox populi*. This resembles Klassen's and Lofton's observation that authority from a material witness is reliant on the validation of others.

However, Carroll points to another problem with personal authority: it not only makes the preacher vulnerable, it also puts the preacher in a position of power that they may be tempted to think they have earned—and, therefore, may be tempted to take advantage of. The risk is enhanced by the fact that an important component of the pastor's authority is their vocation as a representation of the sacred. This can create a depth of trust that leaves others highly vulnerable to exploitation.

In other words: while Klassen's and Lofton's account in many ways resembles Carroll's, I found that it puts too much emphasis on how the person wielding authority can find that authority made vulnerable—and neglects how a personal, negotiated authority also could potentially put a person in a position of power such that their followers and others around them are, too, made more vulnerable to abuse.

Heidi Campbell's 2021 book, *Digital Creatives and the Rethinking of Religious Authority,* offered a theoretical framework for conceptualizing the metric and relational aspects of authority that I observed. As discussed in Article D, Campbell describes different kinds of authority that emerge through the practices of religious digital creatives. She identifies authority as role-based (akin to Weber's account of authority) and as a power struggle (corresponding to Foucault's account of authority). But she also finds two other kinds of authority that address the missing aspects in Klassen's and Lofton's account: *algorithmic authority* and *relational authority.*

---

[19] Jackson W. Carroll, *As One with Authority: Reflective Leadership in Ministry*, 2nd ed. (Eugene, Oregon: Cascade, 2011), 36–51.

According to Campbell, algorithmic authority extracts and determines value by nonhuman, computer-driven entities such as search engines. What is considered authoritative is based on programmatic ranking and reputation systems found online—as determined by, for example, the number of followers and "likes." Algorithmic authority is often measured by one's visibility online and the search engine or Google-ranking prominence of the content produced. This authority is confirmed in numerical terms by an "unbiased" computer ranking, or the number of links or endorsements received from others online.[20]

The authority Campbell discusses here is described as a new way of structuring authority, as opposed to the "traditional" forms of authority as role-based, rooted in power, or relational. However, the rationality behind this "new" kind of authority –visibility and numbers—bear a resemblance to the kind of metric authority that Nelly Hall wielded in her day. This would suggest that algorithmic authority might not be such a new phenomenon after all.

Here one might object that this overstates the case. In digital culture's version of metric authority, the argument might go, authority is understood as confirmed by computers and not by other humans. Judging from the results of the research project *Church in digital space*, one thing does not exclude the other. The fact that a given digitally-mediated sermon attracts a large number of listeners may both be attributed to algorithms *and* to the fact that other humans consider the preacher's words powerfully inspired by God. Nonetheless, the concept of algorithmic authority brings into the spotlight another kind of authority at play that seldom is recognized, neither in the fields of digital religion nor homiletics.

The fourth type of authority is, according to Campbell, identified by digital religion scholars in their studies of digital religious practices. This is a negotiated authority arising from the interaction between a speaker/author and their audience. She labels it relational authority. In her description, Campbell refers to a paper presented at a conference in 2019, where Mia Lövheim describes authority as relational, established through a person's ability to express authenticity and exhibit certain values in communicative relationships.[21] This notion of authority contains the mutual, reciprocal features I noted in the case study of Article A.

Lövheim's conference presentation is not available as text, but she develops similar thoughts in a later article. In this article, Lövheim and her co-author, sociologist of religion Evelina Lundmark, discuss a certain type of authority that

---

[20] Heidi Campbell, *Digital Creatives and the Rethinking of Religious Authority* (London & New York: Routledge, 2021), 9.

[21] Campbell 2021, 26–28.

emerges in digital media: a relational, co-affected authority forged via constant connectivity with the audience. Drawing on their research of female bloggers and vloggers, Lövheim and Lundmark claim that a certain kind of religious authority emerges from these digitally-mediated interactions. This authority is not dependent on formal training or positions sanctioned by religious institutions (in other words, the educational and ecclesial authority Klassen and Lofton speak about) but on dynamic interaction that requires trust, respect, and confidence from the audience. A crucial component of this authority is thus the performance of certain values that generate trust, respect, and confidence. One way this was done was through the sharing of personal everyday experiences, which established dialogue and intimacy with their audiences. The women became authorities as they enacted certain shared values, namely authenticity and vulnerability, in a particular social setting. In other words, the vulnerability they were exposed to in digital spaces was not simply a potential problem along the lines discussed above—it was, in fact, the very means by which the authenticity that forged their authority was demonstrated. Lövheim and Lundmark devote a section of their work to "tracing relational authority through history." In this section, they draw on Klassen and Lofton, connecting Klassen's and Lofton's observation that women's authority often comes from their bodies, experiences, and practices to their own concept of relational authority.[22]

The two case studies in Articles A and D show that the authority practiced by preachers in digital culture and spaces was characterized by relationality, orientation toward practice, negotiation, and collaboration. As mentioned in both articles, there were other kinds of authority simultaneously at play. The preacher in Article A drew on educational and ecclesial authority, and the religious digital creatives in Nacka and Järfälla describe role-based and algorithmic authority. However, in these case studies, the most apparent kind of authority was relational and practice-oriented.

Finally, both articles highlight the fact that the negotiations taking place in the creation and re-creation of authority do not necessarily involve equals. There are likely asymmetries in the power relations between the people involved. In the case of Article A, the body of the preacher creates a power asymmetry that affects how authority is distributed and practiced. Arguably, there are similar power asymmetries at play in the negotiation of authority in Article D, not least because the digital strategists (in particular, the pastors) could be said to wield ecclesial and

---

[22] Mia Lövheim and Evelina Lundmark, "Gender, Religion and Authority in Digital Media," *ESSACHESS, Journal for Communication Studies* 12:2 (2019), 24–31.

educational authority, while the digital spokespersons (technicians and communications directors) primarily have to rely on practice-oriented authority. In the negotiations that characterize the practice of preaching in the digitally-mediated worship services described in Article D, these power dynamics reasonably affect the outcome of those same negotiations.

In sum, the cross-case analysis of human agency in the different phases of the digitally-mediated preaching event supports the claim that the practice of preaching is characterized by interaction and interdependence between preachers and listeners, no matter where it is situated. Furthermore, the analysis suggests that digital mediation could increase these features, not least because it tends to involve more persons in the interpretative and communicative processes (and not just in terms of vaster potential audiences, either, but also in the mediation of technicians, camera operators, digital strategists, etc.). Notably, there were also instances where interaction and interdependence *decreased* due to digital media material arrangements and/or human agency. However, in relation to the preacher's practice of authority— a central aspect of the constellation of practices labeled "the practice of preaching"—interaction and interdependence surface as defining features in the case studies considered in this thesis.

5.1.3 Organization

As mentioned in Chapter 2, practices are organized. The intimate entanglement of the components of a bundle of practices means that if material arrangements and/or chains of actions change, the overall organization of these things is likely to change, too. Central to the ways of being and state of affairs that organize the practice of preaching is theology. This section answers the third research question by focusing on salient theological features in the practice of preaching in digital culture and spaces—in particular, the theology *shaped by* the materiality and agency involved in these practices. In Articles B and C, that shaping process is described as a sort of pedagogy of the virtual and/or the situation that impacts theological interpretation. I will also put "lived theology" in conversation with "formal" and "normative voices of theology."

However, before I get to that, it is important to point out that theology, of course, also *shapes* the interaction with digital media arrangements and, thus, the practices of preaching. As shown by Heidi Campbell, religious communities perform a "religious social shaping of technology" (RSST) in which the historical and cultural contexts of a religious community and its values impact how they negotiate the use of new media.[23] Additionally, there is—as always— multiplicity at work here, too. Since this shaping is only mentioned but not discussed in any depth in the articles, I would like to give a few examples of how that multiplicity comes into play through a short discussion on how differences in theology and ecclesiology contribute to the differences in practices noted in Article C.

Theology as shaping practices. As I show in Article C, there are some differences in practices that are arguably caused, at least in part, by the theological and ecclesiological organization (or RSST) of CoS and the Free churches.

One important difference is the digital media material arrangements of the particular listeners represented in the study. Free church listeners commonly participated from the couch with their families while the CoS listeners were usually alone. This distinction reflects the ecclesiology and organization of the churches and their congregations. As mentioned in chapter 4 in the section on sampling, the core features of Free church ecclesiology and spirituality are engagement and participation, and the gathering of the community functions as a sacrament in which personal faith and community mutually shape each other. Typically, the Free church interviewees would be part of the lay leadership and be heavily involved in the congregation. In addition, there is a strong emphasis on marriage and family in this tradition, whereby the family is itself considered a crucial community where personal faith is shaped. Consequently, the most common way for Free Church members to interact with digital media arrangements was to set them up in a way that allows the family to gather around them.

In CoS, a church with more resources and personnel and consequently less dependent on laypeople, the interviewees would typically be engaged in one or even a few church activities—but not with the same intensity as their Free church counterparts. Often, they were also either significantly younger or older than those in the Free church. Several of the older listeners were widowed. The younger CoS members were often involved in their church communities only after confirmation. Since most of the members in CoS are in the category of "belonging without believing," the CoS interviewees were more likely to be the only ones in their family who "belonged and believed." Therefore, they were also more likely to be worshipping alone.

These theological and ecclesiological differences could also be said to have impacted what listeners thought was missing from the overall church experience

---

[23] Heidi Campbell, *When Religion Meets New Media* (London & New York: Routledge, 2010). The religious social shaping of technology (RSST) was observed also in the *Church in Digital Space* project. Mannerfelt & Roitto 2022b, 60–67.

when the sermon was digitally-mediated. As I have demonstrated in Article C, the Free churches interviewees, with their emphasis on personal faith and their traditional understanding of the practice of preaching, were more likely to mention their personal response to the sermon. In the former state church of CoS, such expressions of personal faith are not as emphasized or expected. Due to the typical CoS understanding of the practice of preaching as allowing the Word of God to do its work, especially in combination with the "folk church as an address in everyday life" and "folk church as sacramentally enacted" ecclesiologies, there was no need for such responses. However, in a context where many members are more likely to live alone or be the sole Christian in their family, it nevertheless was important to be seen and to be able to see others as part of a community.

A third difference mentioned in Article C was the fact that CoS interviewees were more prone to complaints about bad technology. Since CoS has significantly more resources than many Free churches, a fair expectation might be that these congregations would be better equipped. However, as mentioned in Chapter 4, there are significant differences in size between CoS parishes, which meant that some of the CoS parishes that took part in the research project were small, rural parishes with few employees or other resources. In contrast, the Free churches' history of appropriating new technology in the service of the gospel and mission seems to have helped pave the way for a smoother transition to digitally-mediated culture and spaces. Free churches were also more likely to have digital media of some sort in place prior to the outbreak of the pandemic. In addition, the CoS interviewees were typically older and, therefore, more likely to struggle with new technology and new interfaces.

The differences between these two church communities could also extend to other resources, such as church buildings. A CoS congregation would typically have several old (sometimes even medieval) church buildings spread over a large area, while Free churches typically would have one building from the 20ᵗʰ century. Since CoS congregations have an ecclesiological ideal of covering a territory, they tended to move equipment around to a different church (or even several churches) every Sunday—churches that sometimes did not even have Wi-fi—they were less likely to have advanced equipment and achieve good quality.

These are a few examples of how theology and ecclesiology, including the historical and cultural contexts of the churches listeners hailed from, could influence the organization of the practices of preaching in digital culture and spaces. As previously mentioned in Chapter 4, ecclesiological and theological multiplicity naturally occurs on a denominational, congregational, and individual level. With that said, I now turn to discuss which theological themes and features become most salient when the practice of preaching is situated in digital culture and spaces.

Theology as shaped by practices. A cross-case analysis of the four cases described in the articles suggests development in two directions. On the one hand, a practice- and individual-oriented theology; on the other, something I call *Third space theology*.

Beginning with the practice- and individual-oriented theology, the findings in Article B point to how theologizing on the experiences of the pandemic and digital spaces seemed to nudge listeners toward an interpretation of God's presence as a quiet whisper in the everyday life of the individual. Furthermore, the Holy Spirit was proclaimed as a promotor of personal, not communal, growth. Preachers tended to encourage the individual practice of participating joyfully in the sacrament of salvation history (through immersive imagination) while the practice of serviceability—care for others—slipped into the background.

This same theological interpretation appeared at play in the case of Article D. For example, one digitally-mediated sermon about the woman at Sychar's well in the Gospel of John was interpreted and "translated" by a digital spokesperson to fit the format of social media. In my analysis, I demonstrated how the "translation" of the content of the sermon into a shorter message that could attract potential listeners turned the sermon's "the woman *and Jesus*" into "the woman," and put the focus on the part of the sermon that centered on being freed from one's shame while omitting the other preacher's main point about spreading the message of Christ's love.

Notably, the same pattern appeared in other sermons specially tailored for social media. In my analysis of five sermons by the Swedish lead pastor in Hillsong church, an evangelical mega-church that has grown up hand-in-glove with digitalization and which has incorporated digital media as an integral part of its ministry, I observed a similar dynamic. In one of the sermons, the same Bible passage from John 4 was used by the preacher to explicate the thesis of the sermon: that it is important to speak well about each other. In the preacher's narrative, Jesus is described as focusing on what is right and positive in the woman's life, which transforms her life and leads her to run off into town to tell everyone that she has met someone who can tell her who she really is. As I pointed out in the chapter, "the biblical perspectives of forgiveness of sins (what is *not* right in humans) and the revelation of Jesus as God's Messiah (who *Christ* is) are lost in the narrative."[24]

---

[24] Mannerfelt 2020, 211–212.

In both cases, the digital media material arrangements arguably shaped the theologization process by nudging it toward an individual and practice-oriented interpretation of the Bible texts. As I point out in article D and especially in the chapter with the Hillsong sermon analysis, the affordances of digital media are far from the only cause of this phenomenon, but it certainly contributes. In Article B, these findings were briefly discussed in relation to the aforementioned Phillips research on the usage of Bible texts in digital culture and social media. Phillips found a significant shift over time to engagement with Bible verses that display practice-oriented, individualized, and anthropocentric content. This is partly achieved through decontextualization and fragmentarization, where the Bible verses are presented in such a way that their content applies to situations in general. While Phillips is careful not to blame digital culture and the affordances of social media for these features, he nevertheless argues that they are being "enhanced or magnified by contemporary media ecology."[25]

The idea that digital media is not the cause of the practice- and individual-oriented content is supported by recent Scandinavian homiletical research on the content of sermons. For example, in a study of CoS sermons during the fall of 2016, homiletician Clara Nystrand found that the sermons was highly anthropocentric.[26] Furthermore, in a comparison of sermons during the COVID-19 pandemic and the Spanish flu in 1918, Nystrand found that contemporary preaching was characterized by the notion that God is (passively) present by our side, rather than God who (actively)holds everything in God's hands, and a focus on life here-and-now, rather than eternal life.[27] Likewise, in his study of implicit ecclesiology in Annunciation sermons in Church of Norway, theologian Marius Timman Mjaaland found that in congregations that strived for church growth, the content of the sermons was characterized by short and simplified statements like "God is love." On the other hand, the sermon in only congregation that did not aim explicitly for church growth, the sermon was characterized by "a broken gospel" that provided a space for human brokenness and vulnerability, as well as community in faith,

---

[25] Peter M. Phillips, *The Bible, Social Media and Digital Culture* (London & New York: Routledge 2019), 91–92. Quotation p. 92.

[26] Clara Nystrand, "Nöd och nåd i aktuell svensk predikan," in *Årsbok för svenskt gudstjänstliv* 93, ed. Stephan Borgehammar (Skellefteå: Artos, 2018), 163–185.

[27] Clara Nystrand, "Predikans ärende i tider av pandemi: Lidande, hopp och evighetens horisont under corona och spanska sjukan," in *Corona och kyrkorna: Lärdomar, digitala möten och beredskap för nästa kris*, eds. Sune Fahlgren, Elin Lockneus and Daniel Strömner (Stockholm: Libris, 2021), 235–256.

hope and trust in God's promises.[28]In other words, the tendencies toward a prac-tice- and individual-oriented theology is already present in the practice of preach-ing.

The second salient theological feature identified in the cross-case analysis is "Third space theology." The concept is inspired by Echchaibi and Hoover's *Third space of Digital Religion*. As described in Chapter 2, they use the "third space of digital religion" to designate a space that is co-generative, interactive, negotiated, and characterized by an "in-between-ness" that reflects the experience of being in the borderlands. Furthermore, the "located logic" of the third space of digital reli-gion is described by the authors as something that enables reflectivity and an open-ing up to imagining possibilities.[29]

Echchaibi and Hoover's notion of the third space of digital religion bears a re-semblance to Nord's argument that I refer to in Chapter 3 and Article C. Nord argues that the experience of virtual spaces might teach listeners and preachers to see the sermon as a creative space in which they are able to "imagine mankind into God's horizon of possibilities."

As seen in Article B, the located logic of the third space of digital religion could be said to promote theological thinking about in-betweens, limits, and thresholds. It draws attention to presence and absence and points to absence in presence; it brings out eschatological interpretations of the Eucharist and inspires theologizing on *Kairos* as an upheaval of time; it accentuates the universal aspect of the church; it draws attention to what the theologian Vitor Westhelle calls "tangential space"—that is, the limits of the spatial *eschaton* where the marginalized other is.[30]

In Article B, this "third space theology" (lived theology) is put in conversation with Ascension theology (formal and normative theology). As seen in Chapter 3, Creation theology and Process theology are more common formal and normative theological sources in the scholarly conversations about the practice of preaching and preaching in digital culture and spaces. Engemann draws on Creation theol-ogy to conceptualize the "acting communication" that takes place in the preaching event, and Gaarden finds Scandinavian Creation Theology (SCT) a potentially vi-able source to draw on as well. Gaarden also mentions Process theology, which is the theology out of which Sigmon builds her "homilecclesiology."

---

[28] Marius Timman Mjaaland, "Prekenen som hendelse: Analyse av fire prekener på Maria-budskapsdag," *Teologisk tidsskrift*, 9:2 (2020), 22–37.

[29] Echchaibi and Hoover 2023, 1–8.

[30] Vitor Westhelle, *Eschatology and Space: The Lost Dimension in Theology Past and Present* (London: Palgrave MacMillan, 2012), 73–83.

I would argue that Ascension theology offers something unique as a for-mal/normative voice in the conversation that is worth exploring further, not least in relation to materiality.

When it comes to Creation theology, both versions come with potential issues, albeit in different ways. In Engemann's account, Creation theology is primarily about the performative function of words.[31] As discussed earlier, materiality tends to be a mere backdrop.

Gaarden, on the other hand, refers to Creation theology as understood in a Scandinavian theological tradition that truly emphasizes materiality and creation. It underlines the presence of God in all creation and emphasizes creation as the starting point for all theological reflection.[32] As the theologians Niels Henrik Gregersen, Bengt Kristensson Uggla, and Tryggve Wyller state in the introduction to the Scandinavian Creation Theology (SCT) landmark volume *Reformation Theology for a Post-Secular Age: Löstrup, Prenter, Wingren, and the Future of Scandinavian Creation Theology*, "creation constitutes the universal horizon for any Christian theologizing regarding Christ and church, baptism and salvation." Here, the spiritual and temporal are indissolubly entangled, and neither can be reduced to the other.[33] In this capacity, it is—as I have discussed elsewhere—a promising theological conversation partner for the practice of preaching in digital culture and spaces.[34]

However, as Phillips points out in a discussion on Gregersen's work on "deep incarnation" (God being incarnated in all of Creation), the *Logos* mentioned in the first chapter of the Gospel of John does more than infuse creation with God's pres-ence. It is also incarnated in the *sarx* of Jesus. According to Phillips, sometimes a deeply incarnational theology (such as SCT) diminishes the *particular* incarnation of Jesus Christ by translating *sarx* as "materiality" instead of "flesh" to underscore God's presence in *all* existence. Instead, Phillips calls for theological reflection that

---

[31] Engemann 2019, 499–501.

[32] Gaarden 2021, 128.

[33] Niels Henrik Gregersen, Bengt Kristensson Uggla, and Tryggve Wyller, "Reconfiguring Reformation Theology: The Program of Scandinavian Creation Theology," in *Reformation Theology for a Post-Secular Age: Lögstrup, Prenter, Wingren, and the Future of Scandinavian Creation Theology*, eds. Niels Henrik Gregersen, Bengt Kristensson Uggla, and Tryggve Wyller (Göttingen: Vandenhoeck & Ruprecht, 2017), 11–34. Quotation p. 21.

[34] Frida Mannerfelt, "Människa och kristen 3.0: teologisk ontologi för en digital kultur och det digitala rummet," in *Människa och kristen idag: Skapelseteologiska perspektiv på samtiden*, eds. Johanna Gustafsson Lundberg and Frida Mannerfelt (Stockholm: Verbum, 2021), 207–234.

emphasizes the continuity between Jesus and the cosmic Christ of the *Logos*.[35] In other words, SCT takes materiality very seriously, but the emphasis on the interdependence between God, humans, and materiality could possibly overshadow the particularity of the incarnation in Jesus Christ.

Process theology, "where everything is dynamically interconnected with God, who is the most relational reality of all," in the words of Gaarden, could also be said to have the same tendency. This dynamic becomes clear in Sigmon's account of Process theology. Drawing on mathematician Alfred North Whitehead, she defines its core as "becoming, not being." Everything comes into being in interaction with others in a "turbulent flow of an endless becoming." All things and persons flow and change—including God. God is not *before* all creation but *with* all creation in constant re-creation. "God is not an unmoved mover exercising dominion over the world," Sigmon writes. "God is caught up in the world's becoming, and the world is caught up in God's adaptive and creative engagement with the world in its becoming." In the becoming of the world, God exercises relational power, "the power to both influence and be influenced by others."[36] In other words, just as with SCT, Process theology emphasizes God's presence in all creation—with the potential result that any *particular* instantiation of that presence is devalued or diminished in importance.

Notably, in Sigmon's account of Process theology, Jesus is seen as a living word that grows in size and stature. Jesus grew, gained insight, and changed, and after his resurrection and Ascension, his body just keeps growing and changing. She writes: "His return to God only opened the path to greater works to be done in his name through his earthly body." To her, the body of Christ is no longer an individual body but a collective body that grows and changes. Furthermore, the collective body takes on different features depending on the particularities of the situation at hand: "What we describe as Christ or Logos, the embodiment of God's creative transformation in Jesus of Nazareth, takes on different nuances in different cultural settings, and may be understood in a variety of ways depending on culture and context."[37] In other words, while Sigmon takes great care to describe the body of Christ, her main interest is Christ as incarnated in the church, and the particular body of the person Jesus Christ tends once again to slip into the background.

---

[35] Peter M. Phillips, "Digital Theology and a Potential Theological Approach to a Metaphysics of Information," *Zygon, Journal of Religion & Science* 59:2 (2023), 1–19.

[36] Sigmon 2017, 56.

[37] Sigmon 2017, 68–69.

I believe these potential problems and tendencies inherent to SCT and Process theology can be overcome. However, since one of the fiercest theological critiques of digitally-mediated preaching is launched from the vantage point of the doctrine of Incarnation (as seen in Chapters 2 and 3), I wanted to supplement these other approaches with a formal and normative theological voice that takes a sturdy Christological point of departure: ascension theology. In this way, the conversation is anchored in a formal and normative theology that centers just as much on the body of Christ-the-person as the doctrine of Incarnation. In a sense, that is what Yang is doing when he draws on Barth's threefold understanding of the Word. However, Ascension theology is a broader concept and is applicable also in church traditions where Barthian theology does not hold a prominent position.

Article B outlines a few characteristics of Ascension theology. It offers an account for absence in presence, arguing that it is crucial for a proper understanding of Christ and Christ's presence. As mentioned in Chapter 2, according to Katherine G. Schmidt, the experience of the absence in presence of digital spaces is a powerful reminder of the conditions of presence, namely that it is always mediated. A correct understanding of Christ and Christ's presence is, in turn, essential for a proper understanding of the church. Unless the tension between absence and presence is upheld, there is a risk that the presence of Christ collapses into the church[38]—as Sigmon's account comes quite close to doing. According to several of the theologians mentioned in the article (Schmidt, Bible scholar Peter C. Orr, and theologian Douglas Farrow), this tendency can lead to an idealization or even idolatry of the local congregation, the sacraments, and/or the people administering them.[39]

Furthermore, the notion of absence in presence brings the universal character of the church to the fore, a feature of the church that, due to theological and ecclesiological emphasis on the local congregation during the 20th century, has been eclipsed. Notably, based on the results from Fahlgren's study described in Chapter 3, this resurgent universality seems to be a feature of other kinds of media as well. Fahlgren found that preachership in "cassette church" (preaching mediated through radio), by its very nature and form, draws attention to *ecclesia universalis*.

Moreover, a correct understanding of Christ and Christ's body is essential not only for a proper understanding of church but also for a proper understanding of

---

[38] Schmidt 2020, 134–148.

[39] Schmidt 2020, 91–104, 128–135; Peter C. Orr, *Exalted Above the Heavens: The Risen and Ascended Christ* (Downers Grove: InterVaristy Press, 2018); 37–75, 115–131, Douglas Farrow, *Ascension Theology* (London: T&T Clark International, 2011), 2–47, 65–69.

human bodies. Farrow underscores the importance of understanding the Ascension of Christ as a "transformative relocation," where Christ's physical body is located in a particular place—the right hand of God—and not just something that has vanished into space to give way for Christ's ubiquitous presence. If the Ascension is understood as a transformative relocation, it becomes clear that the Eucharist is not just about Christ coming down to the altar here and now; the Eucharist also proclaims the eschatological promise of what one day will happen to human bodies by the grace of God. According to Farrow, this affects how we perceive our own bodies and the bodies of others.[40]

Bible scholar Matthew Sleeman argues that this extends also to the "other" of creation. To him, the Ascension of Christ breaches and reforms previous demarcations of spaces, and challenges dichotomies such as "heaven and earth." Drawing on Edward Soja's concept of "third space," he calls the Ascension a theological "thirding" of the earth, which challenges the view of what is possible for earthly bodies and spaces and thus encourages care for others, including creation as a whole.[41] As I argued in Article B, the third space of digital religion might do that too. Through Ascension theology, the individual- and practice-oriented theology and third space theology— salient theological features of preaching in digital culture and spaces—gain a helpful conversation partner—one that I believe would be very fruitful to explore in further discussion.

In sum, the cross-case analysis shows how theological organization is both shaped by and contributes to shaping the practice of preaching in digital culture and spaces. In the case studies under consideration in this thesis, the practices nudge theological organization in two directions: either toward a practice- and individual-oriented theology, or toward a third-space theology characterized by in-between-ness.

Having answered the three sub-questions, I am now ready to answer the overarching research question: what characterizes the practice of preaching in digital culture and spaces? If I were to give a short, one-word answer, it would be *co-preaching*. As the cross-case analysis has shown, digital media material arrangements serve to disclose that preaching is a deeply relational and collaborative practice characterized by interaction and interdependence.

---

[40] Farrow 2011, 70–74.

[41] Matthew Sleeman, "The Ascension and Spatial Theory," in *Ascent into Heaven in Luke-Acts: New Explorations of Luke's Narrative Hinge*, eds. David K. Bryan and David W. Pao (Minneapolis: Fortress Press, 2016), 162–164, 171–172.

While certain digital media material arrangements and chains of actions could be said to promote a decrease in interaction and interdependence, the digital mediation of the practice of preaching in these four case studies, taken overall, was more likely to increase the interactive and interdependent character of the preaching event, not least by introducing even more co-preachers into it. The co-preaching character of all preaching is thus amplified and distilled in the digitally-mediated event.

5.2 Co-preaching: Implications for the Practice of Preaching

In this section, I will pursue the question of "what characterizes the practice of preaching in digital culture and spaces" and move on to a further discussion of the implications of co-preaching. What do deep relationality, interdependence, interaction, entanglement, negotiation, and collaboration mean for the practice of preaching? In the following, I will argue that it provides a space for dialogue and imagination (section 5.2.1), contributes to two kinds of ecclesiology (5.2.2), and increases the vulnerability that is a necessary condition of interdependence (5.2.3).

5.2.1 Opening a Space for Dialogue and Imagination

As outlined in Article D, one of the consequences of co-preaching is that it enables the polyphony necessary for dialogue. Here (as well as in Chapter 3), Lorensen and Rystad draw on Bakhtin to argue that genuine dialogue is dependent on polyphony. In her work, Lorensen argues that dialogue allows the other to be other and allows interaction between distinct voices without harmonizing them. However, Rystad's case study also shows that the preachers involved tended toward an imposed harmonization. Although the sermons in her study started out as polyphonic—not least through the involvement of material arrangements—the preachers concluded by speaking authoritative words ("This is the message of the sermon") that conflated what was initially many voices into one. My case study in Article D shows that this does not happen as easily in digitally-mediated preaching events. In fact, digital mediation seems to enable and encourage polyphony. More voices contribute, both humans and material arrangements of various kinds, and they do not fall into the pattern of "one singular harmonized voice," as the preachers in Rystads case study.[42]

---

[42] Rystad 2020, 45.

In addition, as shown in Article B's account of third-space theology, digital mediation also seems to encourage another feature of polyphonic preaching: carnivalization. As stated in Chapter 3, Lorensen gives the Bakthinian concept of "carnivalesque" two meanings. It can be used both to designate the situatedness of the word *and* the overturning of everyday life. Preaching is a carnivalesque genre, and "crucial elements in the carnivalized genres are threshold places, pregnant bodies, role changes, and dreams." Furthermore, the carnival carries the greatest potential for creating transformative new meaning. A carnival genre starts in the present and shapes reality based on ancient truths; it draws on experience, and it is multi-style and hetero-voiced (polyphonic).[43] Similarly, Rystad describes dialogical preaching as something that happens in between and at thresholds, particularly in settings where the preacher allows themselves to be decentered.[44] Arguably, preaching in the third space of digital religion potentially facilitates carnivalesque preaching. As argued in Article B, it puts the preacher in an in-between, a threshold, that decenters the preacher whether they want to be or not.

The "in-between-ness" of digitally-mediated preaching is also discussed in Article C, where I draw on Nord to suggest that the phenomenology, the lived experience, of virtual spaces further facilitate a crucial task of the sermon: to imagine God's possibilities for this world—or, as Lorensen puts it—to start in the present and shape reality based on ancient truths. Digital media are characterized by multiplicity and possibility; digital media arrangements could thus be argued to enable and encourage features of genuine dialogue: polyphony and carnivalization.

Here, one might object. Can there really be genuine dialogue in a mediated situation? Lorensen provides a very interesting discussion on whether or not the letters of Paul could be considered an embodied dialogue. According to her, they are. Through the letters, Paul and his readers develop a dialogue between the already said and the not yet said in the anticipated congregational response. Drawing on Lars Kjaer Bruun, Lorensen conceives of the letters as a "mixed medium reality" capable of transcending time and space. "The literacy of the letter," she writes, "opens up a temporary and alternative space in which the dialogue partners can communicate and be present to one another." To Lorensen, this might even be said to encourage dialogue: "The fact that Paul is at a distance from the congregation enables him to cultivate and deepen the 'outside' position in relation to his

---

[43] Lorensen 2014, 98–103.
[44] Rystad 2020, 122.

addressees. The outside position is essential to creative understanding."[45] In other words, the media arrangements of the letters of Paul could be said to function in the same way as the digital media arrangements in my case studies: both encourage genuine dialogue.

5.2.2 Shaping Church Community

A second implication of co-preaching is how it contributes to the shaping of church community. As discussed in Chapter 2, the practice of preaching—or, to use Fahlgren's concept, a certain preachership—always shapes a certain understanding of the church.

As with the theology discussed in section 5.1.2, the ecclesiology that is shaped by preaching in digital culture and spaces could also be said to develop in two directions. The first is toward a "weak ecclesiality" of the kind identified by Yang in his discussion. It develops in parallel with a practice- and individual-oriented theology in which community is not emphasized as a crucial component.

The second ecclesiology is shaped as third-space theology, that is, in relation to the in-between-ness nature of digital spaces. As mentioned earlier, this entails a greater attentiveness to and emphasis on the universal church. However, I argue that digital culture and spaces function in identical ways to Fahlgren's "cassette church." In Fahlgren's example, the preacher simultaneously spoke to church as *familia* and church as *universalis*.[46] Thus, the digitally-mediated preaching in the cases considered here is *not* a matter of shifting from a unilateral focus on the local church to a unilateral focus on the universal church that is not situated in the materiality of a context. Rather, it is a matter of simultaneously experiencing both expressions of church.

Another characteristic of ecclesiology shaped by co-preaching is collaboration. In the Protestant context, of which the churches in this multicase study take part, such collaboration could be understood theologically as the priesthood of all believers enacting their calling to preach the Gospel. As mentioned in Chapter 3, the role of the priesthood of all believers is emphasized by both Sigmon and Müller. Both scholars point to how digital media enables and empowers the participation of the entire church community in the practice of preaching. As seen in the same chapter, Engemann has a slightly different view. To him, the significance of the priesthood of all believers is not for *everyone* to preach. It simply means that the

---

[45] Lorensen 2014, 97–98.
[46] Fahlgren 201–246.

whole congregation is called to communicate the Gospel in the practices of their everyday lives.[47]

However, I would argue alongside Müller that digital media is now an intrinsic part of the practices of everyday life. As a consequence, theologizing is not confined only to preachers and other theologians anymore. Since this is an irrevocable change, the only option now before the church is to make the priesthood of all believers aware of their calling to theological maturity, responsibility, and productivity, and then equip them with theological literacy.[48] In Article D, I draw the same conclusions based on Sigmon's argument. A conscious, theologically-informed use of digital media can shape preaching that, in turn, shapes a church to take the idea of the priesthood of all believers seriously. Theologically educated preachers still have the crucial duty of educating laypeople for the task of interpreting and communicating God's word. Preachers should model a sound interpretation of sacred texts and dogmas as they cultivate the laypeople's capacity to do the same.[49] Notably, this negotiated and relational authority is reminiscent of the kind of authority that Rystad claims her preachers probably strive for in the space of the local church: a discourse with authority, based on trust and respect.[50]

5.2.3 Vulnerability

Sigmon's and Müller's insistence on the need to equip the priesthood of all believers to make theologically sound interpretations points to the third and final consequence of co-preaching: vulnerability. Vulnerability is a necessary condition of interdependence and interaction but is not often discussed by the scholars who engage in the conversations that this thesis wishes to contribute to. (Pleizier is an exception, given his acknowledgment of the fundamental brokenness of all communication.[51]) Based on my findings in the cross-case analysis, vulnerability is a defining characteristic of preaching in digital culture and spaces, and it pertains to both the theological content at play in digital mediation, as well as the humans involved and entangled in digitally-mediated preaching practices.

Concerning content, I have shown in Articles B and D how the gospel becomes more prone to interpretations that fit the affordances of social media. Others—involving human participants as well as the material arrangements at work—

---

[47] Engemann 2019, 502–515.
[48] Müller 2021, 44–84.
[49] Sigmon 2017, 169–187.
[50] Rystad 2020, 121.
[51] Pleizier 2010, 31–56.

have an impact on the communicative and interpretative processes of the preaching event and could obstruct the "theologically correct and skillful" handling of the gospel that, for example, Engemann advocates.[52]

But it's not just the gospel message. The preacher, too, becomes more vulnerable. This vulnerability occurs in relation to other humans but arguably also in relation to digital material arrangements. As mentioned in Chapter 1, a digitally-mediated preaching event is dependent on the media involved, media that often are invisible to its users and consumers—up until the moment they stop working, that is, or work in unexpected or unforeseen ways. As most of the preachers and human co-preachers interviewed in the case studies were unhappily aware of, digital media unfortunately often resist perfect functionality. The skip, the stutter, the buffering, the perpetually loading, the disconnect—these, too, are frequent features of a digitally-mediated experience.

The preachers were also more vulnerable in relation to other humans. As I show in Article A, a dark underbelly exists, where the unstable and negotiated authority characteristic of digital culture and spaces leads to hate and threats. The significance of this for the practice of preaching is evident in the quote from the preacher studied in the article, Archbishop Antje Jackelén:

> For a pastor, who is supposed to be open, understanding, and attentive, it clashes with your pastoral identity. To survive, you need to steel yourself and develop a thick skin. At the same time, your pastoral duty is to constantly practice attentiveness and empathy.[53]

This vulnerability experienced by the preacher could affect their empathy and willingness to listen. Furthermore, as previously mentioned, a preacher dependent on negotiated authority might be tempted to shun prophetic preaching or challenging topics, because preaching uncomfortable truths could negatively impact her relationships, especially with followers or fans online—and, thus, also impact her authority. In the interviews with preachers in the larger source material from the research project *Congregational Change in Times of Crisis* we found extreme examples of this, where a few preachers mentioned that they chose not to preach at all due to the risk of online hatred. In other words, the vulnerability associated with co-preaching could, in the worst-case scenarios, lead to silence.

Furthermore, the addition of more human co-preachers could also potentially increase the vulnerability of each of the co-preachers. As mentioned in section 5.2,

---

[52] Engemann 2019, 515.

[53] Antje Jackelén, "Ärkebiskopen: Twitter domstol och avrättningsplats," *Svenska Dagbladet* (SvD) 4 September 2016, *https://www.svd.se* [Accessed 12 December 2019].

there are rarely symmetrical power relations between the co-preachers involved in the negotiations that surround the sermon. The deliberations do not take place among equals, and the negotiations between, for example, pastors and technicians, might not be as respectful and empathetic as the ones I observed in Article D.

Moreover, listeners to digitally-mediated sermons are more vulnerable too. The listeners' vulnerability, caused in relation to digital media arrangements, are discussed in Article C. Older people with less knowledge of digital media were particularly vulnerable. This increased vulnerability unsurprisingly also pertains to people who cannot afford the expensive technology involved. In this sense, the already vulnerable become more vulnerable. As with preachers, so also listeners become more vulnerable in relation to other humans in the digitally-mediated preaching event—not least because a preacher might start considering their authority as something they have earned, looking pridefully at their follows and likes, and start abusing their authority as a result.

In sum, co-preaching could be said to open up a space for dialogue and imagination. It shapes church community in two ways: toward a weak individual-oriented ecclesiality, or toward a third-space-oriented ecclesiology that balances the local and universal properties of the church, with the result being that the priesthood of all believers are enabled and equipped for preaching the gospel. Finally, the interdependency of co-preaching causes the gospel, the preacher, and the listeners to become more vulnerable, each in their own ways.

5.3 Co-preaching: Implications for Research on the Practice of Preaching

In this third and final section, I would like to suggest some implications of co-preaching for future research on the practice of preaching.

First, co-preaching affirms the recent attention paid to materiality in recent homiletical research. The four case studies of the practice of preaching in digital culture and spaces are a testimony to how much materiality matters in the preaching event and in what ways. In future research, there is a need to further develop theoretical approaches that allow for such socio-material sensibilities. As indicated in Articles C and D, a particularly pressing question in relation to digitally-mediated preaching is to examine the impact of algorithms.

Second, this thesis has argued for the importance of not losing sight of the theology that contributes to organizing the bundle of practices in preaching. Since co-preaching introduces more human and non-human actors into the practice of

preaching, thus submitting the practice of preaching to a higher degree of negotiation and vulnerability, it is crucial for homileticians to not overlook theology—
neither the lived theology attested to in practices nor its conversation partners of
formal and normative theology.

Third, co-preaching implies the need for the study of preaching in digital culture and spaces to take into account the entanglement of human agency and material arrangements. As I mentioned in Chapter 3, practice theory offers an approach that neither ignores media (as a message-oriented approach tends to do)
nor pays too much attention to it (as media-oriented approaches often do). As
such, it offers the balanced view called for by several of the homileticians mentioned in Chapter 3. Pleizier, Lorensen and Gaarden all underscore the importance
of an orientation toward practices as a complement to communication theory.[54]
Fahlgren advocates communication theory (or theology) as a complement to practice-oriented research.[55] Furthermore, practice theory's understanding of being as
mediated helps to avoid the futile position of some (often traditional) approaches,
where real is understood in contrast to virtual.

Finally, co-preaching points to the importance for homileticians, and indeed
practical theologians, to push beyond the established categories of Scandinavian
practical theology where, for example, homiletics and liturgy sit in different boxes.
By paying attention to the concepts of practice, lived religion, and lived theology,
a fruitful conversation with other relevant academic, theological, and sociological
fields is enabled. In the case of this study, a conversation with the fields of digital
religion and digital theology was most at issue. However, as the listeners in Article
C point out, these somewhat exclusionary categories are not entirely uncalled for.
Based on that case study, the practice of preaching could be said to have a unique
character that distinguishes it from other liturgical practices. Unlike all the other
elements of the worship service, digitally-mediated preaching still "worked"!

5.4 In Sum

Based on the four case studies in this thesis and the findings of the cross-case analysis, I have suggested an answer to the overarching research question: the practice
of preaching in digital culture and spaces is characterized by "co-preaching." While
the analysis shows that interdependency and interaction with material

---

[54] Lorensen 2014, 21–41; Gaarden 2015, 47–48; Pleizier 2010, 31–56.
[55] Fahlgren 2015, 102–105.

arrangements and other humans characterize *all* preaching, these features are often amplified in digital culture and spaces.

Because of the digital media arrangements inherent to digital culture and spaces, more material arrangements and more human actors tend to be included in the various phases of the digitally-mediated preaching event. In part because of this, the authority practiced by the preacher appears more clearly as a relational, negotiated authority in digital culture and spaces. Taken together, this all tends to increase the co-preaching features of the digitally-mediated preaching event. That being said, there were also a number of instances when interaction and interdependence decreased due to digital media material arrangements and/or human agency. However, in the case studies considered in this thesis, increased and amplified interaction and interdependence were more common.

This bidirectional movement was mirrored in the cross-case analysis of salient theological features in the practice of preaching. The theological organization of the practices moved either toward a practice- and individual-oriented theology or toward a third-space theology characterized by an experience of in-between-ness and thresholds.

Moreover, when delving into the characteristics of co-preaching, a similar duality was seen in relation to church community and attitudes toward it. Notions of church trended in one of two directions, too: toward a weak individual-oriented ecclesiality or toward an absence-in-presence ecclesiology that balanced the local and universal properties of the church, in which the priesthood of all believers was enabled and equipped for preaching the gospel.

Co-preaching could also be said to encourage dialogue and imagination, because it seemingly carries the potential to prompt the polyphony and carnivalization necessary for genuine dialogue. However, I argue that increased interaction and interdependency also lead to increased vulnerability. In digitally-mediated culture and spaces, the interpretation of the gospel, and the preachers and the listeners involved, all become increasingly vulnerable to each other in various ways.

Bibliography

Ash, James, "Flat Ontology and Geography." *Dialogues in Human Geography* 10:3 (2020), 345–361.

Bardh, Ulla, *Församlingen som sakrament: Tro dop, medlemskap och ekumenik bland frikyrkokristna vid 1900-talets slut* (Uppsala: Uppsala universitet, 2008).

Beck, Wolfgang, "Die Macht der Couch: Homiletische Lerneffekte entstehen an Orten moderner Medien." *Communicatio Socialis* 50:1 (2017), 113–124.

Bekkering, Denis J., "From 'Televangelist' to 'Intervangelist': The Emergence of the Streaming Video Preacher." *Journal of Religion & Popular Culture* 23:2 (2011), 101–117.

Berger, Teresa, *@Worship: Liturgical Practices in Digital* Worlds (London/New York: Routledge, 2018).

Bobrowicz, Ryszard and Mannerfelt, Frida, "Between *Kuriaké* and *Ekklesía*: Tracing a Shift in Scandinavian Practical Theology Based on Handbooks." *Svensk teologisk kvartalskrift* 97:1 (2021), 47–68.

Boellstorff, Tom, "For Whom the Ontology Turns: Theorizing the Digital Real" *Current Anthropology* 57:4 (2016), 387–407.

Bollmer, Grant D., *Theorizing Digital Cultures* (London: Sage, 2018).

Bryant, Clint and Albakry, Mohammed, "'To be Real Honest, I'm Just Like You': Analyzing the Discourse of Personalization in Online Sermons." *Text & Talk* 36:6 (2016), 683–703.

Bucher, Taina and Helmond, Anne, "The Affordances of Social Media Platforms." In in *The SAGE Handbook of Social Media,* eds. Jean Burgess, Alice Marwick and Thomas Poell (Thousand Oaks: Sage Publications, 2017), 233–253.

Bueger, Christian and Gadinger, Frank, *International Practice Theory. New Perspectives* (Basingstoke: Palgrave Pivot, 2014).

Burge, Ryan P. and Williams, Miles D., "Is Social Media a Digital Pulpit? How Evangelical Leaders Use Twitter to Encourage the Faithful and Publicize Their Work." *Journal of Religion, Media & Digital Culture* 8:3 (2019), 309–339.

Caliandro, Alessandro, "Digital Methods for Ethnography: Analytical Concepts for Ethnographers Exploring Social Media Environments." *Journal of Contemporary Ethnography* 47:5 (2018), 551–578.

Cameron, Helen, et al., *Talking About God in Practice: Theological Actions Research and Practical Theology* (London: SCM Press, 2010).

Campbell, Heidi, *When Religion Meets New Media* (London & New York: Routledge, 2010).

— "How Religious Communities Negotiate New Media Religiously." In *Digital Religion, Social Media and Culture: Perspectives, Practices and Futures*, eds. Pauline Hope Cheong et al (New York: Peter Lang, 2012), 81–96.

— *Digital Religion: Understanding Religious Practice in Digital Worlds* (London & New York: Routledge, 2012).

— *Digital Creatives and the Rethinking of Religious Authority* (London & New York: Routledge, 2021).

Campbell, Heidi and Tsuria, Ruth, "Introduction to the Study of Digital Religion." In *Digital Religion: Understanding Religious Practice in Digital Media*, eds. Heidi Campbell and Ruth Tsuria, 2nd ed. (London & New York: Routledge, 2022), 1–15.

Carlström, Charlotta, "Queer Desires and Emotional Regimes in Swedish Free-Church Contexts." *Theology & Sexuality* 27:2–3 (2021), 188–203.

— *En villkorad gemenskap: Hbtq, sexualitet och kristen frikyrklighet* (Stockholm & Göteborg: Makadam förlag, 2023).

Carroll, Jackson W., *As One with Authority: Reflective Leadership in Ministry*, 2nd ed. (Eugene, Oregon: Cascade, 2011).

Cartwright, Nancy, "Middle-Range Theory: Without It What Could Anyone Do?" *Theoria: Revista de Teoria, Historia y Fundamentos de le Ciencia* 35:3 (2021), 269–323.

Cheong, Pauline, "Tweet the Message? Religious Authority and Social Media Innovation." *Journal of Religion, Media and Digital Culture* 3:3 (2014), 1–19.

Codone, Susan, "Megachurch Pastor Twitter: An Analysis of Rick Warren and Andy Stanley, Two of America's Social Pastors." *Journal of Religion, Media and Digital Culture* 3:2 (2014), 1–32.

Coelho, Luiz, "International Panel: 4 Regional Reports: Preaching & Worship in Times of the Corona Crisis." Presentation during the *Societas Homiletica* 2020 online conference "Words in Times of Crises," 10–12 August 2020.

Couldry, Nicholas, *Listening Beyond the Echoes: Media Ethics, and Agency in an Uncertain World* (London: Paradigm, 2006).

Couldry, Nicholas and Hepp, Andreas, *The Mediated Construction of Reality* (Cambridge: Polity Press, 2017).

European Commission, *Digital Economy and Society Index (DESI) 2022*, https://digital-strategy.ec.europa.eu/en/policies/desi-sweden [Accessed 8 December 2022].

Donskov Felter, Kirsten, Edgardh, Ninna, and Fagermoen, Troen, "The Scandinavian Ecclesial Context." In *What Really Matters: Scandinavian Perspectives in Ecclesiology and Etnography*, eds. Jonas Ideström and Tone Stangeland Kaufman, (Eugene, Oregon: Pickwick Publications, 2018), 5–14.

Svenska kyrkan, *Döpta, konfirmerade, vigda och begravda enligt Svenska kyrkans ordning år 1970–2020, https://www.svenskakyrkan.se/filer/1374643* [Accessed 23 February 2023].

Edgardh, Ninna, *Gudstjänst i tiden: Gudstjänstliv i Svenska kyrkan 1968–2008* (Lund: Arcus förlag, 2010).

— "Ett snabbt sammanställt men viktigt tidsdokument." *Svensk kyrkotidning* 117:10 (2021), 319.

Tala väl: Predikokommentarer i Krister Stendahls anda, ed. Helene Egnell (Uppsala: Bibelsällskapets förlag, 2021).

Eldebo, Runar, *Den ensamma tron: En studie i Frank Mangs predikan* (Örebro: Libris, 1997).

Ellis, Christopher J., *Gathering. A Theology and Spirituality of Worship in Free Church Tradition* (London: SCM Press 2004).

Engemann, Wilfried, *Homiletics: Principles and Patterns of Reasoning* (Berlin: De Gruyter, 2019).

Evolvi, Giulia and Giorda, Maria Chiara, "Introduction: Islam, Space, and the Internet." *Journal of Religion, Media and Digital Culture* 10:2 (2021), 1–11.

Fahlgren, Sune, *Predikantskap och församling: Sex fallstudier av en ecclesial baspraktik inom svensk frikyrklighet fram till 1960-talet* (Örebro: ÖTH rapport, 2006).

— "Preaching and Preachership as Fundamental Expression of Being Church." *International Journal for the Study of the Christian Church* 6:2 (2006), 180–199.

— "Studying Fundamental Ecclesial Practices." In *Ecclesiology in the Trenches: Theory and Method under Construction*, eds. Sune Fahlgren and Jonas Ideström (Eugene, Oregon: Pickwick Publications, 2015), 102–105.

Farrow, Douglas, *Ascension Theology* (London: T&T Clark International, 2011).

Flick, Uwe, *An Introduction to Qualitative Research*, 4th ed. (London: Sage, 2009).

Foley, John Miles, *Oral Tradition and the Internet: Pathways of the Mind* (Urbana, Chicago, and Springfield: University of Illinois Press, 2012).

Ford, Dennis, *A Theology for a Mediated God: How Media Shapes our Notions About Divinity* (London: Routledge, 2016).

Sveriges kristna råd, *Frikyrkor*, https://www.skr.org [Accessed 13 March 2023].

Gaarden Marianne and Lorensen, Marlene R., "Listeners as Authors in Preaching: Empirical and Theoretical Perspectives." *Homiletic* 38:1 (2013), 28–45.

— *Prædikenen som det tredje rum* (Köpenhamn: Anis, 2015).

— *The Third Room of Preaching: A New Empirical Approach* (Eugene, Oregon: Pickwick publications, 2021).

Garner, Stephen, "Theology and New Media." In *Digital Religion: Understanding Religious Practice in Digital Media*, eds. Heidi Campbell and Ruth Tsuria, 2nd ed. (London & New York: Routledge), 266–281.

Garpe, Sara, Ideström, Jonas and Mannerfelt, Frida, "Att vara kyrka i digitala rum." In *Kyrka i digitala rum: Ett aktionsforskningsprojekt om församlingsliv online*, eds. Sara Garpe and Jonas Ideström (Uppsala: Svenska kyrkan, 2022), 6–18.

Gerdmar, Anders, *HBTQ och Bibeln: Svärdet genom svensk kristenhet* (Uppsala: STH Academic, 2023).

The Worlds of the Preacher: Navigating Biblical, Cultural, and Personal Contexts, ed. Scott Gibson (Grand Rapids, MI: Baker Academic, 2018).

Gregersen, Niels Henrik, Kristensson Uggla, Bengt and Wyller, Tryggve, "Reconfiguring Reformation Theology: The Program of Scandinavian Creation Theology." In *Reformation Theology for a Post-Secular Age: Lögstrup, Prenter, Wingren, and the Future of Scandinavian Creation Theology*, eds. Niels Henrik Gregersen, Bengt Kristensson Uggla, and Tryggve Wyller (Göttingen: Vandenhoeck & Ruprecht, 2017).

Gustavsson, Caroline, *Delaktighetens kris: Gudstjänstens pedagogiska utmaning* (Skellefteå: Artos, 2016).

Halldorf, Joel and Wenell, Fredrik, "Introduction." In *Between the State and the Eucharist: Free Church Theology in Conversation with William T. Cavanaugh*, eds. Joel Halldorf and Fredrik Wenell (Eugene, Oregon: Pickwick Publications 2014), 1–12.

— *Biskop Lewi Pethrus: Biografi över ett ledarskap. Religion och mångfald i det svenska folkhemmet* (Skellefteå: Artos, 2017).

— "Mötet i frikyrklighet och väckelse." In *Kristen Gudstjänst – en introduktion*, ed. Stina Fallberg Sundmark (Skellefteå: Artos, 2018), 137–169.

Hallingberg, Gunnar, *Läsarna: 1800-talets folkväckelse och det moderna genombrottet* (Stockholm: Atlantis bokförlag, 2011).

— *Moderna läsare: 1900-talets frikyrklighet som kulturbygge* (Stockholm: Atlantis bokförlag, 2016)

Hayes, Ramona, *Digital and Analog Preaching in a Multi-media World*, D.Min. Thesis, (Luther Seminary, 2018).

Helboe Johansen, Kristine and Schmidt, Ulla, *Practice, Practice Theory and Theology. Scandinavian and German Perspectives* (Berlin: De Gruyter, 2022).

Hewson, Claire, "Ethics Issues in Digital Methods Research." In *Digital Methods for Social Science: An Interdisciplinary Guide to Research Innovation*, eds. Helene Snee et al. (London: Palgrave Macmillan 2016), 206–221.137

Hine, Christine, *Ethnography for the Internet: Embedded, Embodied and Everyday* (London: Bloomsbury, 2015).

Holmberg, Andreas, *Kyrka i nytt landskap: En studie av levd ecklesiologi i Svenska kyrkan* (Skellefteå: Artos Academic, 2019).

Holstein, Johanna, "'Snygghetsstudien' i Lund utreds – bilder användes utan vetskap." *SVT Nyheter*, 4 November 2022, https://www.svt.se/nyheter/lokalt/skane/snygghetsstudien-pa-lunds-universitet-utredas-kanns-markligt-att-mitt-utseende-anvants-utan-tillatelse [Accessed 19 March 2023].

Hoover, Stewart M. and Echchaibi, Nabil, *Media Theory and the Third Spaces of Digital Religion*, 2014, https://www.researchgate.net/publication [Accessed 13 October 2022].

— *The Third Spaces of Digital Religion* (London & New York: Routledge, 2023).

Horsfield, Peter, *From Jesus to the Internet: A History of Christianity and Media* (Chichester, West Sussex: Wiley Blackwell, 2015).

Hudgins, Tripp, "Preaching Online." *Anglican Theological Review* 101:1 (2019), 78–89.

Hutchings, Tim, "Ethnography, Representation, and Digital Media." In *What Really Matters: Scandinavian Perspectives in Ecclesiology and Ethnography*, eds. Jonas Ideström and Tone Stangeland Kaufman (Eugene, Oregon: Pickwick Publications, 2015), 227–246.

— "Augmented Graves and Virtual Bibles: Digital Media and Material Religion." In *Materiality and the Study of Religion: The Stuff of the Sacred*, eds. Tim Hutchings and Joanne McKenzie (London & New York: Routledge, 2017), 85–99.

Härdelin, Alf, "Homiletik: Ordet och orden." In *Kyrkans liv: Introduktion till kyrkovetenskapen*, ed. Stephan Borgehammar, 2nd ed. (Stockholm: Verbum, 1993), 203–220.

Hörsch, Daniel, *Digitale Verkündigungsformate während der Corona-Kris: Eine Ad-hoc-Studie im Auftrag der Evangelischen Kirche in Deutchland*, 2020, https://www.mi-di.de/materialien/digitale-verkuendigungsformate-waehrend-der-corona-krise [Accessed 9 January 2022].

Ideström, Jonas, *Folkkyrkotanken – innehåll och utmaningar: En översikt av studier under 2000-talet* (Uppsala: Svenska kyrkan, 2012).

— "Implicit Ecclesiology and Local Church Identity. Dealing With Dilemmas of Empirical Ecclesiology." In *Ecclesiology in the Trenches: Theory and Method under Construction*, eds. Sune Fahlgren and Jonas Ideström (Eugene OR: Pickwick Publications, 2015), 121–138.

— *Ikoniska kartor: Att göra teologi i kyrkans vardag* (Stockholm: Verbum, 2021).

Ideström, Jonas and Stangeland Kaufman, Tone, "The Researcher as a Gamemaker – Response." In *What Really Matters: Scandinavian Perspectives on Ecclesiology and Ethnography,* eds. Jonas Ideström and Tone Stangeland Kaufman (Eugene, Oregon: Pickwick Publications, 2018), 173–179.

— "Hur framträder kyrkan i de digitala rummen? – kommunikation, teologi och folkkyrko-tankar." In *Kyrka i digitala rum: Ett aktionsforskningsprojekt om församlingsliv online*, eds. Sara Garpe and Jonas Ideström (Uppsala: enheten för forskning och analys, 2022), 31–43.

Jackelén, Antje, "Ärkebiskopen: Twitter domstol och avrättningsplats." *Svenska Dagbladet* (SvD) 9 September 2016, https://www.svd.se/a/OPgKl/arkebiskopen-twitter-domstol-och-avrattningsplats [Accessed 12 December 2019].

Jones, Mark D., "Ethical Issues in the Study of Religion and New Media." In *Digital Religion: Understanding Religious Practice in Digital Media*, eds. Heidi Campbell and Ruth Tsuri, 2nd ed. (New York: Routledge 2022), 250–265.

Josefsson, Ulrik, "Bilder av församlingen: Frikyrklig ecklesiologi under och genom pandemin." In *Svensk frikyrklighet i pandemin: En studie av församlingen i corona och corona i församlingen*, eds. Ulrik Josefsson and Magnus Wahlström (Forskningsrapporter från Institutet för Pentekostala Studier, No. 9, 2021), 60–89.

Journal of Religion, Media and Culture, https://brill.com/view/journals/rmdc/rmdc-overview.xml [Accessed 6 January 2023].

Kasselstrand, Isabella, "Nonbelievers in the Church: A Study of Cultural Religion in Sweden." *Sociology of Religion* 76:3 (2015), 275–294.

Klassen, Pamela E. and Lofton, Karen, "Material Witnesses: Women and the Mediation of Christianity." In *Media, Religion and Gender: Key Issues and New Challenges*, ed. Mia Lövheim (New York: Routledge, 2013), 53–63.

Knowles, Michael P, "E-word? McLuhan, Baudrillard, and Verisimilitude in Preaching" *Religions* 13:1131 (2022), 1–16.

Knox, Jeremy, "What's the Matter with MOOCs? Socio-material Methodologies for Educational Research." In *Digital Methods for Social Science: An Interdisciplinary Guide to Research Innovation*, eds. Helene Snee et al. (London: Palgrave Macmillan, 2016), 175–189.

Kraske Cressman, Lisa S., "B.C. and A.C: Preaching and Worship Before COVID and After COVID." *Journal for Preachers* 44:2 (2021), 46–52.

Kurlberg, Jonas, "Introduction." In *Missio Dei in a Digital Age*, eds. Jonas Kurlberg and Peter M. Phillips (London: SCM Press, 2020), 1–20.

Kurlberg, Jonas, Challenges Facing Digital Theology Today, October 2022, https://medium.com/@jonas.kurlberg/challenges-facing-digital-theology-today-dd93d27e238 [Accessed 9 December 2022].

Kusmiertz, Katrin, Predigt als Unterhaltung 2.0, 2020, https://www.liturgik.unibe.ch/ueber_uns/liturgie_in_virtuellen_raeumen/index_ger.html [Accessed 1 September 2022].

Kvale, Steinar and Brinkman, Svend, *Den kvalitativa forskningsintervjun* (Lund: Studentlitteratur, 2014).

Kwabena, Asamoah-Gyadu, "'Get on the Internet!' Says the LORD': Religion, Cyberspace and Christianity in Contemporary Africa." *Studies in World Christianity* 13:3 (2012), 225–242.

Kyrkoordning för Svenska kyrkan (Verbum: Stockholm, 2023).

Lagen om Svenska kyrkan (1998:1591).

Lagerkvist, Amanda, *Existential Media: A Media Theory of the Limit Situation* (Oxford: Oxford University Press, 2022).

Leavy, Patricia, *Research Design: Quantitative, Qualitative, Mixed Methods, Arts-based, and Community-based Participatory Research Approaches* (New York/London: The Guilford Press, 2017).

Lenhammar, Harry, "Tryckpressarna i kyrkans och väckelsens tjänst." In *Sveriges Kyrkohistoria: Folkväckelsens och kyrkoförnyelsens tid*, ed. Oloph Bexell (Stockholm: Verbum, 2003), 306–315.

Anna-Katharina Lienau, "Kommunikation des Evangeliums in social media." *ZThK* 117 (2020), 489–522.

Lincoln, Yvonna and Guba, Egon, Naturalistic *Inquiry* (Beverly Hills, CA: Sage, 1985).

Lorensen, Marlene R., *Preaching as a Carnivalesque Dialogue – between the 'Wholly Other' and 'Other-Wise' Listeners*, Ph.D. thesis (Copenhagen: Copenhagen University, 2012).

— *Dialogical Preaching: Bakhtin, Otherness and Homiletics* (Göttingen: Vanderhoeck & Ruprecht, 2014).

— "Homiletik i den praktiske teologi." In *Den praktiske teologi i Danmark 1973-2018: Festskrift til Hans Raun Iversen*, eds. I. L. Christoffersen, N. H. Gregersen, and K. M. S. Leth-Nissen (København: Anis, 2019), 111–119.

— "Nyere nordisk homiletik: Empirisk vending, fremmedhed og resonans." *Nordic Journal of Practical Theology* 37:1 (2020), 42–53.

Lorensen, Marlene R. and Buch-Hansen, Gitte, "Listening to the Voices: Refugees as Co-authors of Practical Theology." *Practical Theology* 11:1 (2018), 29–41.

Lose, David J., *Preaching at the Crossroads: How the World and our Preaching is Changing* (Minneapolis: Fortress Press, 2013).

Lundby, Knut and Evolvi, Giulia, "Theoretical Frameworks for Approaching Religion and New Media." In *Digital Religion: Understanding Religious Practice in Digital Media*, ed. Heidi Campbell and Ruth Tsuria, 2nd ed. (London & New York: Routledge, 2022), 233–249.

Löhr, Miriam, *Gottesdienst im digitalen Raum*, 2020, https://www.liturgik.unibe.chGottesdienstimvirtuellenRaum_ger.pdf [Accessed 26 August 2022].

Lövheim, Mia, "Introduction: Gender – a Blind Spot in Media, Religion and Culture?" In *Media, Gender and Religion: Key Issues and New Challenges*, ed. Mia Lövheim (London & New York: Routledge, 2013), 1–14.

— "Comments by Mia Lövheim." *Religion and Society: Advances in Research* 7 (2016), 97–115.

Lövheim, Mia and Lundmark, Evelina, "Gender, Religion and Authority in Digital Media." *ESSACHESS, Journal for Communication Studies* 12:2 (2019), 23–38.

Löwegren, Mikael, "Gudstjänst i Svenska kyrkan." In *Kristen Gudstjänst - en introduktion*, ed. Stina Fallberg Sundmark (Skellefteå: Artos, 2018), 103–130.

Mannerfelt, Frida, "Hör ni som har öron: En studie av samtalets funktion för nutida predikan." Master thesis (Lund: Lunds universitet, 2017).

— "Hör ni som har öron!" *Svensk Kyrkotidning* 114:11 (2018), 324–327.

— "Kontrast och kontinuitet: Predikoideal i Svenska kyrkans prästutbildning 1903-2017." *Årsbok för svenskt gudstjänstliv* 93, ed. Stephan Borgehammar (Skellefteå: Artos, 2018), 123–158.

— "Back to the Roots or Growing New Branches: Preaching, Orality and Mission in a Digital Age." In *Missio Dei in a Digital Age*, eds. Jonas Kurlberg and Peter M. Phillips (London: SCM Press, 2020), 195– 220.

— "Människa och kristen 3.0: teologisk ontologi för en digital kultur och det digitala rummet." In *Människa och kristen idag: Skapelseteologiska perspektiv på samtiden*, eds. Johanna Gustafsson Lundberg and Frida Mannerfelt (Stockholm: Verbum, 2021), 207–234.

— "Kan vi tala om trötthetsskulden." *Dagen* 13 August 2021.

— "From the Amphitheatre to Twitter: Cultivating Secondary Orality in Dialogue with Female Preachers." *Studies in World Christianity* 28:1 (2022), 6–27.

— "Between Ritual and 'Advertisement': Theological Negotiation in the Development of Digitally-mediated Worship Services at the End of the COVID-19 Pandemic." Paper presented at the Global Network of Digital Theology conference "How Theology and Faith Practices shape Digital Culture," online conference 7 July 2022, https://gonedigital [Accessed 10 July 2022].

— "Old and New Habits: The Transition to Digitally-Mediated Worship in Four Swedish Free Church Denominations during COVID-19." In *Svensk frikyrklighet i pandemin: En studie av församlingen i corona och corona i församlingen*, eds. Ulrik Josefsson and Magnus Wahlström (Forskningsrapporter från Institutet för Pentekostala Studier, No. 9, 2022b), 90–119.

— "Preaching Online: Developing Homiletics for a Digital Culture." In Oxford Handbook of Digital Theology, eds. Alexander Chow, Jonas Kurlberg, and Peter M. Phillips (Oxford: Oxford University Publications, forthcoming).

Mannerfelt, Frida and Maurits, Alexander, *Kallelse och erkännande: Berättelser från de första prästvigda kvinnorna i Svenska kyrkan* (Stockholm & Göteborg: Makadam, 2021).

Mannerfelt, Frida and Roitto, Rikard, "Mellan rit och reklam del 1: Berättelsen om två församlingars utveckling." In *Kyrka i digitala rum: Ett aktionsforskningsprojekt om församlingsliv online*, eds. Sara Garpe and Jonas Ideström (Uppsala: Svenska kyrkan, 2022a), 47–60.

— "Mellan rit och reklam del 2: Interaktion, synkronicitet och integritet i förinspelade digitalt förmedlade andakter." In *Kyrka i digitala rum: Ett aktionsforskningsprojekt om församlingsliv online*, eds. Sara Garpe and Jonas Ideström (Uppsala: Svenska kyrkan, 2022b), 61–79.

Mannerfelt, Frida and Stangeland Kaufman, Tone, "Understanding the Paradox of (Im)perfection: A Socio-material Approach to Digitally-Mediated Preaching" (forthcoming).

Carl Henrik Martling, *Fädernas kyrka och folkets: Svenska kyrkan i kyrkovetenskapligt perspektiv* (Stockholm: Verbum, 1992).

Masoga, Mogomme Alpheus, "Effectiveness of WhatsApp Homiletics in the Era of COVID-19 in South Africa." *Pharos Journal of Theology* 101 (2020), 1–16.

McLuhan, Marshall, *Understanding Media: The Extensions of Man* (Corte Madera, CA: Gingko Press, 2003).

Meireis, Torsten, "Jesus in the eShop. A Christian Perspective on Power in the Digital World." *Cursor_*, 21 April 2021, https://cursor.pubpub.org/pub/meireis-jesus-in-the-eshop/relea se/4 [Accessed 10 May 2022].

Menzel, Kerstin, "More than the Argument of Experience? Preaching with Episodes from Everyday Life on Instagram." Paper at the *Societas Homiletica* 2022 conference "Preaching towards truth." Budapest, 12–17 August 2022.

Meyer, Birgit, "Religion as Mediation." *Entangled Religions* 11:3 (2020), 1–15.

Michaels, David H., "Dipping Into a Shallow Pool or Beginning a Deeper Conversation: A Case Study of a Minister's Engagement With the Internet for Preaching." *Journal of Religious & Theological Information* 8:3–4 (2009), 164–178.

Mjaaland, Marius Timman, "Prekenen som hendelse: Analyse av fire prekener på Mariabudskapsdag." *Teologisk tidsskrift*, 9:2 (2020), 22–37.

Moberg, Jessica, *Piety, Intimacy and Mobility: A Case Study of Charismatic Christianity in Present-day Stockholm*, Ph.D. thesis (Södertörn College 2013).

Müller, Sabrina, *Lived Theology: Impulses for a Pastoral Theology of Empowerment* (Eugene, Oregon: Cascade Books, 2021).

Nicolini, Davide, *Practice Theory, Work, and Organization: An Introduction* (Oxford: Oxford University Press, 2012).

Nord, Ilona, *Realitäten des Glaubens: Zur virtuellen Dimension christlicher Religiosität* (Berlin: De Gruyter, 2008).

Nord, Ilona, "Experiment with Freedom Every Day: Regarding the Virtual Dimension of Homiletics." *Homiletic* 36:2 (2011), 31–37.

Nystrand, Clara, "Nöd och nåd i aktuell svensk predikan." In *Årsbok för svenskt gudstjänstliv* 93, ed. Stephan Borgehammar (Skellefteå: Artos, 2018), 163–185.

Nystrand, Clara, "Predikans ärende i tider av pandemi: Lidande, hopp och evighetens horisont under corona och spanska sjukan." In *Corona och kyrkorna: Lärdomar, digitala möten och beredskap för nästa kris*, eds. Sune Fahlgren, Elin Lockneus and Daniel Strömner (Stockholm: Libris, 2021), 235–256.

Når folkekirken skal spille efter reglerne – men uden for banen: Folkekirkens håndtering af coronaperioden i foråret 2020 (Aarhus: Folkekirkens Uddannelses- og videnscenter, 2020).

O'Lynn, Rob, "Digital Jazz, Man: The Intersection of Preaching and Media in the Era of COVID (and After)." In *Academy of Homiletics 2021 Workgroup Papers and Abstracts*, 5–15. Dare We Dream – A Preaching Renaissance, 2–4 December 2021, Online Conference.

Ong, Walter, *The Presence of the Word* (New Haven: Yale University Press, 1967).

— *Orality and Literacy: The Technologizing of the Word* (London: Methuen, 1982).

Orr, Peter C., *Exalted Above the Heavens: The Risen and Ascended Christ* (Downers Grove: InterVaristy Press, 2018).

Peters, John D., *The Marvellous Clouds: Toward a Philosophy of Elemental Media* (Chicago: University of Chicago Press, 2015).

Pettit, Tom, "Media Dynamics and the Lessons of History: The Gutenberg Parenthesis as Restoration Topos." In *A Companion to New Media Dynamics*, eds. J. Hartley Burgess and A. Brund (Chichester: Wiley Blackwell, 2013), 53–72.

Phillips, Peter M., Kurlberg, Jonas and Schiefelbein-Guerrero, Kyle, "Defining Digital Theology: Digital Humanities, Digital Religion and the Particular Work of the CODEC Research Centre and Network." *Open Theology* 5 (2019), 29–43.

— *The Bible, Social Media and Digital Culture* (London & New York: Routledge 2019).

— "Conclusion." In *Missio Dei in a Digital Age*, eds. Jonas Kurlberg and Peter M. Phillips (London: SCM Press, 2020), 259–268.

— *Hybrid Church: Blending Online and Offline Community* (Cambridge: Groove Books Limited, 2020).

— "Digital Being." *Crucible: The Journal of Christian Social Ethics* (2023), 22–31.

— "Digital Theology and a Potential Theological Approach to a Metaphysics of Information." *Zygon, Journal of Religion & Science* 59:2 (2023), 1–19.

Pink, Sarah, et al., *Digital Ethnography: Principles and Practice* (London: Sage, 2016).

Pleizier, Theo, *Religious Involvement in Hearing Sermons* (Delft: Eburon Academic Publisher, 2010).

— "Studying the Listener? The Paradox of the Individual in Sermon Reception Research and a Reassessment of Preaching as Caring for the Community of Faith." In *Preaching Promise within the Paradoxes of Life*, eds. Johan Cilliers and Len Hansen (Stellenbosch: African Sun Media, 2018), 161–168.

Plüss, David, "The Dialogue Form of Online Preaching. Case Studies." Paper at the *Societas Homiletica* 2022 conference "Preaching towards Truth." Budapest, 12–17 August 2022.

Powery, Luke A., "Preaching and Technology." In *Ways of the Word: Learning to Preach for Your Time and Place*, eds. Luke A. Powery and Sally A. Brown (Minneapolis: Fortress Press, 2016), 209–234.

Price Grieves, Gregory, "Religion." In *Digital Religion: Understanding Practice in Digital Media*, eds. Heidi A. Campbell and Ruth Tsuria, 2nd ed. (New York & London: Routledge 2022), 25–39.

Reckwitz, Andreas, "Toward a Theory of Social Practices: A Development in Culturalist Theorizing." *European Journal of Social Theory* 5: 2 (2002), 243–263.

— *The Society of Singularities* (Cambridge: Polity Press, 2020).

Regeringskansliet, *För ett hållbart digitaliserat Sverige – en digitaliseringsstrategi*, chrome-extension://efaidnbmnnnibpcajpcglclefindmkaj/https://digitaliseringsradet.se/media/1191/digitaliseringsstrategin_slutlig_170518-2.pdf [Accessed 22 April 2023]

Rystad, Linn S., *Overestimated and Underestimated: A Case Study of the Practice of Preaching for Children with an Emphasis on Children's Role as Listeners*, Ph.D. Thesis (Oslo: MF Norwegian School of Theology, 2020).

Sauerberg, Lars Ole, "The Gutenberg Parenthesis: Print, Book and Cognition." *Orbis Litterarum* 64:2 (2009), 79–80.

Schatzki, Theodore, *The Site of the Social: A Philosophical Account of the Constitution of Social Life and Change* (University Park, Pennsylvania: The Pennsylvania State University Press, 2002).

— *The Timespace of Human Activity: On Performance, Society, and History as Indeterminate Teleological Events* (Plymouth: Lexington Books, 2010).

— "Sayings, Texts and Discursive Formation." In *The Nexus of Practices: Connections, Constellations, Practitioners*, eds. Allison Hui, Theodore Schatzki, and Elizabeth Shove (London & New York: Routledge, 2017), 126–140.

— *Social Change in a Material World* (London & New York: Routledge 2019).

Schmidt, Katherine G., "Digital Inculturation." In *Missio Dei in a Digital Age*, eds. Jonas Kurlberg and Peter M. Phillips (London: SCM Press, 2020), 23–35.

— *Virtual Communion: Theology of the Internet and the Catholic Sacramental Imagination* (Lanham, Maryland: Lexington Books/Fortress Academic, 2020).

Schmidt, Ulla, "Practice, Practice Theory and Theology." In *Practice, Practice Theory and Theology: Scandinavian and German Perspectives*, eds. Kristin Helboe Johansen and Ulla Schmidt (Berlin: De Gruyter, 2022), 35–55.

Sigmon, Casey T., *Engaging the Gadfly: Homilecclesiology for a Digital Age*, Ph.D. Thesis, (Austin: Vanderbilt University, 2017).

Silverman, David, *Interpreting Qualitative Data*, 5th ed. (London: Sage, 2014).

Simons, Helen, "Case Study Research: In-depth Understanding in context." In *The Oxford Handbook of Qualitative Research*, ed. Patricia Leavy, 2nd ed. (New York: Oxford University Press, 2020), 676–703.

Sleeman, Matthew, "The Ascension and Spatial Theory." In *Ascent into Heaven in Luke-Acts: New Explorations of Luke's Narrative Hinge,* eds. David K. Bryan and David W. Pao (Minneapolis: Fortress Press, 2016).

Snee, Helene, et al., "Digital Methods as Mainstream Methodology: An Introduction." In *Digital Methods for Social Science: An Interdisciplinary Guide to Research Innovation,* eds. Helene Snee et al. (London: Palgrave Macmillan, 2016), 1–11.

Stake, Robert E., *The Art of Case Study Research* (Thousand Oaks: Sage 1995).

— *Multiple Case Study Analysis* (New York, London: The Guilford Press, 2006).

Stangeland Kaufman, Tone, "From the Outside, Within, or in Between? Normativity at Work in Empirical Practical Theological Research." In *Conundrums in Practical Theology,* eds. Joyce Ann Mercer and Bonnie Miller McLemore (Boston: Brill, 2017), 134–162.

— *Forkynnelse for barn og voksne,* ed. Tone Stangeland Kaufman (Oslo: Prismet bok, 2021).

— "Forkunnelse for barn og voksne." In *Forkunnelse for barn og voksne,* ed. Tone Stangeland Kaufman (Oslo: Iko-Forlaget, 2021), 7–18.

— "The Scandinavian Contribution?" Keynote lecture at the symposium and book release of *The Wiley Blackwell Companion to Theology and Qualitative Research.* Oslo, 6 December 2022.

Stangeland Kaufman, Tone and Mosdøl, H.O., "More than Words: A Multimodal and Socio-material Approach to Understanding the Preaching Event." In *Preaching Promises within the Paradoxes of Life,* eds. Johan Cilliers and Len Hansen (Stellenbosch: African Sun Media, 2018), 123–132.

— "Forskjellen som (ut)gjør en forskjell: En analyse av prekenhendelsen i to gudstjenester med utdeling av fireårsbok med vekt på materialitet." In *Forkunnelse for barn og voksne,* ed. Tone Stangeland Kaufman (Oslo: Iko-Forlaget, 2021), 91–112.

Stangeland Kaufman, Tone and Danbolt, Lars Johan, "Hva er praktisk teologi?" *Nordic Journal of Practical Theology* 37:1 (2020), 6–18.

Svenska kyrkan, *Statistik,* www.svenskakyrkan.se/statistik [Accessed 2 January 2023]

Statistiska Centralbyrån, https://www.scb.se [Accessed 2 January 2023].

Stiernstedt, Fredrik, "Free Churches of the Air: the History of Community Radio in Sweden." *Historical Journal of Film, Radio and Television* 41:2 (2021), 317–337.

Stirling, Eve, "'I'm Always on Facebook!': Exploring Facebook as a Mainstream Research Tool and Ethnographic Site." In *Digital Methods for Social Science: An Interdisciplinary Guide to Research Innovation,* eds. Helene Snee et al. (London: Palgrave Macmillan, 2016), 51–66.

Stückelberger, Johannes, *Liturgie in Virtuellen Räumen: Der Raum in Online-Gottesdiensten https://www.liturgik.unibe.ch* [Accessed 26 August 2022].

Tholvesen, Øyvind, *Frikyrkoundersökningen: En rapport on frikyrkornas utveckling i Sverige 2000–2020* (Örebro: Frikyrkosamrådets styrelse, 2021).

Text Messages: Preaching God's Word in a Smartphone World, ed. John Tucker (Eugene, OR: Wipf and Stock, 2017).

Tveitereid, Knut, "Making Data Speak – The Shortage of Theory for the Analysis of Qualitative Data in Practical Theology." In *What Really Matters: Scandinavian Perspectives on Ecclesiology and Ethnography,* eds. Jonas Ideström and Tone Stangeland Kaufman (Eugene, Oregon: Pickwick Publications, 2018), 41–57.

Tveito Johnsen, Elisabeth and Afdal, Geir, "Practice Theory in Empirical Practical Theological Research: The Scientific Contribution of LETRA" *Nordic Journal of Practical Theology* 37:2 (2020), 58–76.

Vägmärken för baptister: Tro frihet gemenskap: Svenska baptistsamfundet 1848–2012 (Karlstad: Votum Media, 2016).

Ward, Mark, "The PowerPoint and the Glory: An Ethnography of Pulpit Media and Its Organizational Impacts." *Journal of Media and Religion* 14:4 (2015), 175–195.

Ward, Pete, "Is Theology What Really Matters?" In *What Really Matters: Scandinavian Perspectives on Ecclesiology and Ethnography*, eds. Jonas Ideström and Tone Stangeland Kaufman (Eugene, Oregon: Pickwick Publications, 2018), 157–172.

— "Theology and Qualitative Research: An Uneasy Relationship." In *The Wiley Blackwell Companion to Theology and Qualitative Research*, eds. Pete Ward and Knut Tveitereid (Oxford: Wiley Blackwell, 2022), 7–15.

Ward, Pete and Tveitereid, Knut, "Introduction." In *The Wiley Blackwell Companion to Theology and Qualitative Research*, eds. Pete Ward and Knut Tveitereid (Oxford: Wiley Blackwell, 2022), 1–4.

Watkins, Clare, *Disclosing Church: An Ecclesiology Learned from Conversations in Practice* (London & New York: Routledge, 2020).

Westhelle, Vitor, *Eschatology and Space: The Lost Dimension in Theology Past and Present* (London: Palgrave MacMillan, 2012).

Widdersheim, Michael M., "Historical Case Study: A Research Strategy for Diachronic Analysis." *Library and Information Science Research* 40:2 (2018), 144–152.

Wigg-Stevenson, Natalie, *Ethnographic Theology: An Inquiry into the Production of Theological Knowledge* (New York: Palgrave Macmillan, 2014).

Wilson, Paul S., *The Practice of Preaching* (Nashville, Tennessee: Abingdon, 2007).

Witte, Alison, *Preaching and Technology: A Study of Attitudes and Practices*, Ph.D. thesis (Bowling Green: Bowling Green State University, 2013).

Wormbs, Nina, *Det digitalas materialitet* (Göteborg & Stockholm: Makadam, 2022).

Yang, Sunggu A., "The Word Digitized: A Techno-Theological Reflection on Online Preaching and Its Types." *Homiletic* 46:1 (2021), 75–90.

— "Preaching / Hermeneutics and Rhetoric / Religious Speech." In *International Handbook of Practical Theology*, eds. Birgit Weyel et al. (Berlin: De Gruyter, 2022), 445–456.

FRIDA MANNERFELT

From the Amphitheatre to Twitter: Cultivating Secondary Orality in Dialogue with Female Preachers

ABSTRACT

Ever since the theory of orality and literacy was introduced, it has provided scholars with a deeper understanding of the intertwined nature of culture and communication, as well as an appreciated tool for analysis. This is true also for the field of World Christianity. As the era of digital media emerged, the theory was developed as a tool to interpret digital culture as a 'secondary orality'. This article critiques and cultivates this theory, by showing how the analytical tool of orality, literacy and secondary orality might be sharpened. This is done in dialogue with the practice of female preachers. Preaching thus serves as an example for a wider discussion on the development of the theory. The sharpening of the tool is done through letting the complexity of practices inform the theory. Through historical case studies of three strategically chosen female preachers, four questions are identified that would be important to consider when the theory and its developments are used in analysis: genre of communication, the categories of body and space, and how authority is construed. Finally, the cultivated theory is applied in the analysis of a female preacher in a digital culture and space.

Keywords: orality, literacy, secondary orality, digital culture, preaching

Studies in World Christianity 28.1 (2022): 6–27
DOI: 10.3366/swc.2022.0368
© Edinburgh University Press
www.euppublishing.com/swc

INTRODUCTION

Ever since it was introduced in the middle of the twentieth century, with the professor of literature Walter J. Ong as one of its most renowned advocates, the theory of orality and literacy has provided scholars with a deeper understanding of the intertwined nature of communication and culture – not least in the field of World Christianity.

A prominent example is Andrew Walls, who in his discussion of how Christianity is transmitted through culture used the theory to shed light on how Christians have interacted with scripture. He stressed that the early church interacted with the Bible as an oral culture. It was not until the invention of the printing press that Western society found itself 'moving from an oral to a literary relationship with Scripture'. According to Walls, this has implications for both historical and contemporary study of Christianity (Walls 1996: 41–2; Walls 2002: 3–26).

Another World Christianity scholar who has engaged with the theory is Lamin Sanneh, who argues that the Bible in the vernacular provides 'written authority for the force of oral tradition' (Sanneh 1989: 185). It prompts oral tradition by encouraging narrative storytelling, fresh theological thought, and 'faith, active subject of life'. This is in contrast to Western Christianity which, as part of a literate culture, put too much focus on belief as a passive construct of thought (Sanneh 1989: 172–3). This is discussed also by Kwame Bediako, who contrasts 'written theology' with 'oral theology' that stems from the living experience of Christians. However, oral theology is for Bediako not a phase towards written theology, where the written becomes the 'real' theology, but a foundation for and partner in written theology (Bediako 1993, 1996).

A more recent example is found in Aminta Arrrington's study of the Lisu Christians, where the interplay between orality and literacy enables understanding of the focus on lived/practised faith instead of reading the Bible in solitude (Arrington 2015), and of Lisu Christians doing their theologising in relation to practice and experience in contrast to a Western culture where literacy is idealised (Arrington 2019).

The era of digital media has in no way diminished the importance of the theory – not least since digital culture may be interpreted as a 'secondary orality', a kind of restoration of an orality blended with literacy. Although the phrase 'secondary orality' originally was coined by Ong to describe the effects of radio and television, it has been developed in various ways to describe the effects of digitally mediated communication on human culture and cognition. Among theologians and church historians who have used developments of the theory are

Soukup (2003), Horsfield (2015), Ford (2016) and Mannerfelt (2020). However, this approach is not as common in the field of World Christianity. There are only a few scholars in the field who have discussed the connection between orality, literacy and digital culture, like J. Kwabena Asamoah-Gyadu in his study of digital media in different Christian denominations in Ghana (Asamoah-Gyadu 2007). In the light of the theory's importance for discussion in the field, further exploration of digital culture as secondary orality could hold potential for World Christianity. This article is an invitation to such exploration.

But the article also urges a deeper engagement with the critique against the theory. One major problem, for which it has been duly criticised, is that it describes the progressive history of communication from the perspective of a white, male, privileged and Western individual. This runs the risk of obscuring the role of women and those from cultures that are not as text-based as Western culture (Bassi 1997).

Critics have also pointed out that orality/literacy suffers from the same problems as all binary categories: they tend to provide a nice point of departure for abstract discussion, but as soon as they are applied to the complexity of real-life practices, the categories collapse (Ames and Himsel 2011: 3–4). Moreover, they tend to align themselves with other binaries and their inherent power structures. For example, you easily end up with a notion of the written word as accurate, enduring, truthful, nuanced and – since women historically have been excluded from education and thus from literacy – associated with the male, and the oral as less in all aspects and associated with femininity and the female (Ames and Himsel 2011: 1–2). As suggested above, these problems are partially addressed in the field of World Christianity, in particular in connection with the idea of progression and the idealisation of literacy, but an extensive discussion of critique against the theory is lacking.

Unfortunately, the expanded theory of secondary orality has inherited some of these problems. With few exceptions (for example, Nayar 2013), discussions on these issues are scarce. Therefore, if this theory, in original or expanded form, is to be used for scholarly discussion in any field – World Christianity included – it needs to be cultivated, that is, further clarified and qualified. The aim of this article is to give an example of how such cultivation can be done. In other words, to provide a method to sharpen the theoretical tool.

In this article I will, first, provide an overview of the concept of secondary orality. Ong's original concept will be presented along with some prominent examples of how it has been used and developed.

Secondly, I will give some examples of the problems mentioned above in Ong's reasoning, and how they could be said to have transferred into the developed frameworks of secondary orality, and thus call for cultivation.

I then move on to give an example of how such clarification and qualification could be achieved. This is done through 'test pit digging' in church history. The method of using strategically chosen historical individuals as 'samples' to shed light on a general phenomenon is discussed, for example, by Sune Fahlgren (2006: 19–27) and Peter M. Phillips (2017: 88–108).

As Andrew Walls points out, 'diversity exists not only in a *horizontal* form across the contemporary scene, but also in a *vertical* form across history' (Walls 1996: xvii). In this case, the discussion will be limited to the question of gender. Three strategically chosen preachers will be discussed in relation to the communication discourse of each period: within the orality paradigm, from the early church, Saint Perpetua and from the medieval church, Saint Birgitta of Sweden, and from the literacy paradigm, the Swedish nineteenth-century evangelist Nelly Hall. How do these preachers relate to the discursive rules of communication in their time? In this way, some relevant questions will be identified that would be important to consider when the theory is used as a tool for analysis. As the article focuses only on the perspective of gender, the list of questions will of course not be complete. It will, however, provide *some* relevant areas along with an invitation to, and a method for, further cultivation.

Finally, the article will discuss these questions in relation to secondary orality and apply the sharpened tool of the cultivated theory to the practice of a female preacher in a digital culture and space: the Archbishop of ELCS, Antje Jackelén.

EXAMINING THE TOOL

Below I will present a brief overview of the concept of secondary orality. For a comprehensive presentation of the development of the field from the 1990s up until 2005, see Soukup (2007). The overview will also give some examples of the problems addressed in the critique against Ong, and how some of these issues are at work in the developed frameworks.

Secondary Orality in Ong's Work

In his works Ong identifies different stages of cultural evolution based on shifts in communication: primary oral culture, manuscript culture, print culture and secondary oral culture. These stages are part of a progressive development where each stage is a prerequisite for the next (Ong 1967: 17–110).

The primarily oral culture is described as embodied and relational. Since it consists of one person's sound to another person's ear it is an interpersonal event, performed in the here-and-now. Knowledge and communication are therefore structured to promote memorisation: it is rigid, typical, thematic, formulaic, metric. Authority is connected to being a person who can tell a convincing story, through practice, and the ability to combine what is already known into content that fits the present situation. Oral culture fosters community, since it unites people in groups and requires interaction with other persons (Ong 1967: 22–35; Ong 1982: 136–44).

With the development of writing, the word becomes a fixed thing, closed off in time and space, a body of its own. It is that *corpus* the writer and reader meet, not each other. Reading and writing are therefore activities carried out in solitude and silence. This makes the visual more important than the aural, which also enhances isolation. Since the author is not present with his or her body to convey meaning, there is a need for more words to avoid misunderstanding. This is also possible since writing provides means for external memory (Ong 1967: 31–67; Ong 1982: 77–113). Printing changes the patterns of communication and thought. Symbolic thinking is enhanced. Language is conceived of as something that can be 'correct', and there are dictionaries to check spelling. Introducing new original ideas and complicated plots in narrative is encouraged. The notion of independent authors who can claim ideas as their own is promoted (Ong 1982: 116–35).

Orality and literacy are thus presented as two distinct and contrasting categories. To mitigate the clear-cut boundaries, Ong describes the change over time as a 'progression' where features of oral culture linger on as 'oral residue'. However, in doing this Ong enforces the binary. In all his works, Ong writes the history of the progression in similar ways. For example, in *Presence of the Word* (1967), where Ong explicitly deals with the question of orality and literacy in relation to religion, he traces the development of the word.

Ong points to the fact that witnesses from primarily oral cultures cannot be directly accessed since they left no traces. Instead, he discusses at length the oral residue found in written records. For example, during Antiquity, philosophers and politicians remained committed to the spoken word despite their ability to read and write. They learned by listening, read out aloud, and the oration and recitation of epic were appreciated art forms. In the Middle Ages, academic education contained a high degree of oral residue (Ong 1967: 17–114).

Although writing was subordinated to the oral, Ong describes the Middle Ages as a far more text-centred era than Antiquity, where reading became a status symbol for the medieval man. During the Renaissance (the Early Modern Age), the text becomes even more important, and Ong states that it 'had discernibly altered man's feeling for the world in which he lived and for his way of relating to his surroundings' (Ong 1967: 63). In short, the history of orality and literacy, in Ong's version, is the history of the communication of the privileged, European man and his transformation into a literate intellectual. Thus, the historiography of a progression designed to solve the problem of clear-cut categories, instead reinforces them.

When it comes to secondary orality in Ong's work, the concept is not as thoroughly developed as orality and literacy. Ong usually includes it in his historiographies as the turning point that makes it possible to discern the differences between orality and literacy (Ong 1967: 17–18; Ong 1982: 2–3). He describes it as an 'electronic age' where media like telephones, radio and television bring back the oral–aural. He stresses that this is a succession that in no way cancels out the printed book, but at the same time shares many features of orality: hence, 'secondary orality'.

Development of Secondary Orality

Various kinds of developments of the theory and the notion of secondary orality in relation to digital media that draw on Ong are circulating in the media history discourse. For an extensive overview of scholars, thinkers and authors who have contributed, see Pettitt (2013a). Secondary orality has been a tool to analyse the character of digitally mediated communication practices, like social media or higher education (Bounegru 2008; Soffer 2010; Sligo 2015), but as mentioned above, a tool also in the fields of church history and theology.

In addition, there are two more thoroughly elaborated developments of the theory. Firstly, 'the Pathway project', presented by the professor of classical studies and English John Miles Foley. His main idea is that oral tradition (OT) and internet technology (IT) operate similarly by navigating through networks. These networks are not linear but flexible, structured around nodes. Neither operates by spatialising, sequencing or objectifying. Instead, they emerge in interpersonal activity as they both invite and require participation. Both forms of communication offer variation within limits in the practice of remix and reuse. They promote open sharing among a community and distributed authorship and lack the concept of a complete-in-itself item (like a journal). Foley carefully points out that this 'homology does not mean absolute equivalence' but that they share 'a fundamental functionality: navigating through linked networks of potentials' (Foley 2012: 7–8, 17–19, 62–3, 189, 256–7, 265).

The second framework is called 'the Gutenberg parenthesis', hereafter GT (Sauerberg 2009; Pettitt 2013b). In this approach, the era of print is seen as an anomaly in human history that is coming to an end. The closing of the parenthesis comes with digital media, which resembles the era before print. Sauerberg's collegue, professor in medieval studies Tom Pettitt, has continued to develop the theory (Pettitt 2013a, 2013b).

The concept of closure is central to both Sauerberg and Pettitt, as they consistently argue that one of the defining features of the GT is an emphasis on boundaries and containment. Words are bound in books or confined to authorial canons and the ownership of the copyright holder. However, outside of the parenthesis content functions as in medieval times: it belongs to everyone. Like Sanneh, they note that this affects the content. When a story is retold in a new situation, it changes. Outside the communication paradigm of the GT, a story is always incomplete, and therefore there are only better and worse versions of it. Pettitt and Sauerberg also claim that in the digital era, the word is again characterised by 'here-and-now'. Websites disappear, platforms are replaced, media storages quickly become outdated, search algorithms 'hide' information, and so on (Pettitt 2013a, 2013b; Starkman 2012).

The notion of closure also affects the construal of authority. Within the parenthesis, authority is placed in books, and individuals get authority from writing and reading the facts and referring to them. Outside the parenthesis, authority seeks other points of orientation, which according to Sauerberg and Pettitt poses a bit of a problem for the digital end of the parenthesis. Where medieval people found it in hierarchy of family and/or professional networks and the notion of a God, the digital era finds authority in networks and narrative. Authority is gained from being able to tell the most credible story (Starkman 2012).

Closure is also central in Pettitt's argument of the connection between books and bodies. Combining the GT theory with ideas from the 'corporeal turn' in literary history and cultural studies, he argues that there is a relation between the dominant media form and how a culture conceives of the human body. He uses the fairy tale *Red Riding Hood* as an example to point to a shift from body and space as connected, to body and space as confined areas. Pettitt refers to other studies which show that in the Modern Era, the female body is portrayed as ideally enclosed and avoiding both intrusion (male penetration) or extrusion (female verbal or physical outgoing) (Pettitt 2009a, 2009b, 2013c).

When elaborating on this, Pettitt describes two ways of perceiving the human body and space: *homo conexus* and *homo clausus*. *Homo clausus* thinks of his body as separated and enclosed, and his identity something innate. He worries about threats from outside and holds high the individual's autonomy. He perceives of his surroundings as delimited areas, as rooms, houses, regions and nations. *Homo conexus* thinks of his identity as connected to others in social networks like family, friends and professional or societal groups. Likewise, he perceives of his body as connected, and he worries about his place within the network (his honour or status). He views his surroundings in terms of junctions in a network, as roads, paths, doors, bridges and crossings. With digital media, *homo conexus* is re-entering the world (Pettitt 2013c, 2013d).

Although Pettitt's discussion of the enclosed and networked body provides important tools for understanding how body and space can be conceived of in a digital-media culture, unfortunately it discloses similar problems as Ong's above. Human comes across as a homogenous category. There is no appreciation of the diversity of human experience of bodies and spaces. Furthermore, there is no discussion of what it means to be part of a network in relation to power structures and hierarchies. With few exceptions, this is the case in all the developments of the theory. Besides that, they have in common that the binary categories only work on a theoretical level, as a discourse. As soon as it is used to analyse the complexity of practice, they appear 'far too wooden for our contemporary cultural landscape' (Nayar 2013: 226) and need further development.

SHARPENING THE TOOL

How, then, can this theoretical tool be sharpened? In the following, I will discuss this in relation to the practice of preaching, where practices will be allowed to inform the theory. Considering the theory's chronological character, the practices are chosen from a chronological, rather than geographical, perspective. Here, three preachers will be discussed in relation to the communicative discourses of orality and literacy of their time: two from periods characterised by oral communication (Antiquity and the medieval period): Saint Perpetua (181–203) and Saint Birgitta of

Sweden (1303–73); and one from Late Modernity, when literacy and print dominated: Nelly Hall (1848–1916), one of the earliest female evangelists in Sweden. In this way, I will identify relevant questions that would be important to consider when the theory is applied.

The preachers in question are strategically chosen. As one of the problems of the theory is its homogenous understanding of human, they are chosen to include the perspective of 'the other', in this case the non-male. In relation to the World Christianity discourse, there are of course several other perspectives that would be equally important to consider, like non-Western, non-white or non-Christian. However, due to the limited space of the article format, only the gender perspective will be highlighted – in the hope that it will inspire further discussion.

Perpetua during Antiquity

As Ong himself states, the public speech of the rhetor is one of the most important forms of communication during Antiquity. Mary Beard, professor of classics, points out that it was considered the business of men, and closely associated with masculinity. According to Beard, there were only two exceptions in the classical world: women could speak out either as victims, or as advocates of their own sectional interests, like home and children (Beard 2015). The professor in literature Karen Bassi argues that the distinction orality/literacy is too artificial for the analysis of text from Antiquity, like Greek epic. It makes us blind to the fact that 'gender-specific codes and hierarchies operate in every aspect of Greek cultural production' (Bassi 1997: 316). Oral communication is not a unitary category. In Greek culture, the ideal oral communication takes place face-to-face and conveys masculinity and military strength. It stands in contrast to oral communication that is mediated, like gossip (associated primarily with women and slaves) or written down (Bassi 1997).

At first glance, Perpetua would fall into the category of victim. However, when one takes a closer look a more complex picture emerges. Perpetua is one of three authors of the *Passio Perpetuae et Felicitatis*, in which she recounts her experiences and visions in prison. Paul Scott Wilson, professor of homiletics, argues that these texts in relation to her martyrdom, could be understood as autobiographical and apocalyptical preaching (Scott Wilson 1992: 31–2).

As contributors to the volume *Perpetua's Passions: Multidisciplinary Approaches* point out, Perpetua was aware of and shaped by the cultural and literary tradition and the gender patterns of her own time

(Williams 2012). This is shown not least in how she adjusts her style of writing to ensure maximum authority, and make sure that there is an eyewitness account from the male editor who can vouch for the accuracy of her visions (Waldner 2012). In addition to the written body, Perpetua's own body – marked by her gender – is a fundamental element in the narration (Bremmer 2012: 2–6). It is the 'body' of the written account in combination with the actions of her body in martyrdom that create her sainthood. Both bodies, tied together by the male witness, are the foundation of her authority (Weigel 2012).

According to Pamela E. Klassen and Kathryn Lofton (2013), authority from the body is the hallmark of a religion centred around divine incarnation. This has been a common strategy to gain authority for Christians throughout history, especially those who were closed off from the other two sources of authority: educational and ecclesial (ordained). However, there is a paradox here. The body is not just a source of authority for women, it is also the very thing that puts their authority in question since a female body per definition is the 'wrong' body, implying that women simultaneously achieve *and* lose authority because of their bodies. The authority is fragile and only to be had if certain bodily conditions are fulfilled (Klassen and Lofton 2013: 53–63).

The control of body and sexuality as a source of authority for women is also discussed by the professor of ecclesial history Karen L. King (1998). King argues that it is a matter of space too. Although women have preached in practice throughout two millennia of Christianity as witnesses, teachers and prophets, they were preaching from the margins and not from the sanctioned, sacred space. Both these things could be said to apply to Perpetua: she was allowed to preach as a visionary and witness in prison and the arena, but not from the pulpit inside a church. And, as language professor Julia Weitbrecht states, since women at the time were given authority only as widows or virgins, Perpetua had to reject motherhood (Weitbrecht 2012).

To sum up: one important question to consider in the cultivation of the theory would be the genre of communication. Oral communication can be a wide range of things, and these genres are connected to gender and power structures. Another important question would be the category of body. In an oral culture, the body is a vital part of communication. But bodies differ too, and what kind of body it is that is involved in communication has great significance. This is especially pressing in relation to the third question: how authority is construed. In a Christian context the body could be a source of authority that allows the preacher to break the rules of the dominating communication discourse. However, it is an unstable and conditioned authority, in particular for women whose bodies are the very thing that put their authority in question in the first place. Finally, the category of space is relevant. What is tolerated in one space may be prohibited in another.

Birgitta of Sweden during the Medieval Period

In the medieval period, there was a significant shift in the attitude towards orality and literacy. Christine Marie Neufeld, professor of literature, describes a public discourse that juxtaposed oral gossip with the textual scribe. Since orality was associated with women, this communication form was subordinated. In addition, this gendering of communication limited women's access to authority (Neufeld 2001: 55–73). In other words, communication forms would be tied to gender and power structures where some forms were more valued than others.

In her study of Birgitta, theologian Päivi Salmesvuori presents a more complex picture. Again, authority from the body could be said to allow exception that proves the rule. Salmesvuori describes Birgitta's authority as performed, and thus in constant need of renegotiation and confirmation (Salmesvuori 2014: 1–8). Just as in the case with Perpetua, the written body of a text validated by men was crucial in the negotiation of authority. In the fourteenth century this process was regulated. If a woman had a vision, her oral proclamation would be written down by a male confessor, who would give her the 'home of literacy' (Salmesvuori 2014: 15). Salmesvuori also notes that '[t]he more respected the confessor was, the more secure the position of the woman he approved would be' (2014: 102). Birgitta was able to enrol two suitable confessors, the subprior Peter in Alvastra Monastery, who recorded the revelations in Latin (as the language of the learned it gave authority), and Master Mathias, theologian and canon of Linköping. He was a well-regarded preacher who verified and spread her revelations.

Authority of the body also took precedence over other kinds of authority. Salmesvuori argues that Birgitta's authority, even though she was from one of the wealthiest families in Sweden and a close friend of the king, was dependant on practice. An important part of that was ascetic practices to compensate for her bodily shortcomings – she was a mother of eight. Despite this, Birgitta's authority was constantly questioned by those who thought she had stepped outside of 'the women's sphere' (Salmesvuori 2014: 72–3, 91–2, 102, 167–73).

Nelly Hall during Modernity

Moving into the era of print, the associations male–written and female–oral remain. In the introduction to *Oral Traditions and Gender in Early Modern Literary Texts* (2008: xvii–xxv), professor of English Mary Ellen Lamb discusses another binary: creative individuality–passive community. In this paradigm the individual male authorship of a written, printed book emerges as an ideal. Oral narrative, like tales, ballads and gossip, was considered a passive passing on and associated with illiterate women. However, this discourse was not upheld in practice. Lamb writes, 'while the associations between gender and oral traditions are pervasive and long-lasting, their expressions in early modern literature suggest their complexity and unpredictability' (2008: xix).

An example of this tension about how women's writing is portrayed in the Late Modern Era is found in Louisa M. Alcott's *Little Women* (1868). In a close reading, Bernstein (1993) suggests genres like poetry and short stories for recreational purposes were deemed suitable for women, whereas novels and research ought to be written by men. Furthermore, the heroine Jo's writing serves both to support the constructs of family and as a means to independence.

The novel was published in 1868, when the Swedish evangelist Nelly Hall (1848–1916) was in her twenties. Hall was a schoolteacher and travelling preacher who preached at revival meetings held in barns, tents, mission houses or occasionally other large assembly halls that the hosts of the meetings could find. Although there is a source that indicates that Hall at least on one occasion preached in a local church building in 1885 (*Svenska Dagbladet* 19 June 1911), this was an exception to the rule. Again, place stands out as an important category to consider.

It is also interesting to see how her authority as a preacher was construed. As Sune Fahlgren (2006: 155–200) points out, Hall was not ordained or officially sent by a community. Instead, her authority was tied to her person and practices, and as such continuously negotiated. In addition to the fact that Hall never married, her authority as a preacher was 'based on personal alliance', and it was the 'fruits' of her preaching that gave her a right to speak. In other words, she was welcome to preach if it led people to Jesus, and as long as the right people validated her authority. As church historian Joel Halldorf has shown, numerical success as a foundation of authority for preachers was common in the modern era, especially in the revival movements (Halldorf 2020: 32).

How far this kind of personal, embodied authority could extend in a Christian context is shown in the fact that Hall in 1887 – thirty-three years before women were allowed to vote in Sweden – was one of the founding members of the board when the Swedish Holiness Union (SHU), a missionary society inspired by Methodism and the holiness movement, was formally established. (For a historical overview of SHU, see Halldorf 2012: 159–73.) However, the instability of her negotiated authority is discussed by, for example, church historian Gunilla Gunner. In 1901 Nelly Hall was voted out from the board by her twelve male colleagues. According to Gunner, the protocols hint that the reason was doctrinal disagreement, yet without any indication of the error. There are, however, plenty of historical sources that recount the massive criticism that SHU suffered for allowing female preachers. This leads Gunner to argue that SHU was pressured to conform to the societal norms of their time and that Hall's last published text, from 1914, may reflect the experience of being silenced (Gunner 2003: 211–12).

Here we may also note the importance of genre. Hall published a great number of written texts. She wrote for the SHU publication *Trons Segrar*, translated theological literature and edited and published reports from the missionaries in the field without anyone raising an eyebrow. It was her oral performances that were the problem. A review of one of her sermons clearly shows how preaching is associated with the male:

> Apart from the female voice and appearance she conducted herself in a way that distinguishes the accomplished preacher. Confident and calm, she led the large gathering of people and was not interrupted, not even when a woman in the crowd fainted in the heat ... Despite the fact that she spoke entirely free ... the lecture flowed with an ease and coherence that would have made any male speaker proud of himself. She was obviously led – and this ought to be the most unusual thing – more by the calm and reasoning operation of intelligence, than by fantasy and profuse emotions. (Fahlgren 2006: 181)

The quote also exemplifies the practice of calling women's preaching something else. Here, her sermon is called 'lecture'. This was a strategy that Hall herself employed: throughout the years, when she defended her right to preach, she repeatedly called it 'prophesising'.

In summary, through this test-pit digging in church history in relation to female preaching, important questions have been identified that would be important to consider when the theory of orality and literacy and its developments are to be used for analysis.

Firstly, genre is an important question. There is not just orality and literacy. Within all the communication paradigms there are different kinds of orality and literacy. Furthermore, these genres are associated with gender and power structures. Some genres are considered more important, and it is generally the communication forms that are associated with the male. For an analysis of digital culture, it would be important to discuss it not just as secondary orality, but to consider what kind of orality blended with literacy is at play, and if that genre (platform) is associated with a certain gender.

This points to the second and third questions, body and authority. As this article has shown, the body of the communicator plays an important part in Ong's argument as well as in the developments of the theory – especially in oral culture, where it not only conveys meaning, but also contributes to the construal of authority. The *ethos* of the communicator is connected not just to the ability to remix and reuse common knowledge and tell a convincing story, but also to practices. But bodies differ as well as genres, and the ability to communicate in a certain cultural setting is greatly affected if the communicator's body deviates from the norm. In a Christian context, the rules of the dominant communication discourse are partly set aside by the weight that incarnation theology gives to bodily practices as a source of authority. This is a key aspect in understanding orality and literacy in a Christian context. But for women there is a paradox: the same body that can provide authority is the very thing that causes loss of authority. In an analysis of Christian practices in the secondary orality of digital culture, it would be important not just to discuss the importance of the body in communication, but also to ask the question, 'What kind of body and authority?'

Finally, the category of space. Where does the communication take place? The three female preachers were able to transcend the rules of the orality/literacy discourse of their time, but only in certain spaces. Preaching was allowed as long as it took place from the margins, from a prison, execution place, confessional, barn or tent, and as long as it is called lecture, witness, prophecy or teaching. The pulpit was out of the question.

With the analytical tool sharpened by an attention to these questions, the article now turns to the final section in which the cultivated theory will be put to use in the analysis of a preacher in the secondary orality of digital culture.

USING THE TOOL

Digital media is often heralded as a space of equality and democracy where everybody can participate in communication (Cheong 2013: 74–8). As previously shown, the expanded theory characterises digital space as defined by connectivity, relationality, interactivity and sharing. The digital space as enabler for democracy is, for example, elaborated by Briana Wong. In her study of the impact of COVID-19 on Cambodian Evangelical life, Wong argues that the enforced transition from 'the physical to the technological realm' led to a democratisation of spiritual leadership as lay leaders, especially women who were already used to ministry in digital space, played an important role in the digitally mediated Easter celebration (Wong 2020: 281–97).

But if the category of space is scrutinised, a more complex picture emerges. Majid Khosravinik and Eleonora Esposito, who specialise in digital-media discourse research, point to the widespread idea that digital space is male space. This is due to the social norm that technology is typically male and the typical agent in the digital space is a man. Accordingly, women are seen as precarious subjects (Khosravinik and Esposito 2018).

When the question of genre is added, there seem to be certain kinds of digital communication that are less gender-differentiated. According to Mary E. Hess, a professor of educational leadership, one of the least gender-differentiated areas in the digital space is digital storytelling in social media (Hess 2013). In relation to authority, this oral genre could even be seen to be favoured by women. As Klassen and Lofton point out, women tend to do their digital storytelling about religion with the authority from their bodies and practices, not from educational or ecclesial authority. Women tend to focus on what they *do* as Christians and communicate their Christian faith as mothers, lovers, prophets, wives and celebrities (Klassen and Lofton 2013). In relation to the GT, this is beneficial since authority in secondary orality is not found in books, but in networks and narrative.

But this should also be problematised. As discussed earlier, this kind of authority tends to be unstable and conditioned. According to Klassen and Lofton, this feature is enhanced in the digital space. Referring to a study by Mia Lövheim, they notice that the ethical space for female bloggers is highly unstable. This is because all materiality, including bodies, is questioned in the digital space, and to the fact that the authority of a blogger always needs validation from the followers (Lövheim 2011). This would mean that in secondary orality, the embodied authority is even more unstable and conditioned. But there is a difference in relation to earlier oral culture. In the secondary orality of digital culture, the validation of authority from the body is not restricted to a select few.

Klassen and Lofton discuss this in relation to space. Women tend to write and speak from platforms they built themselves on blogs or social media, not from the ecclesially sanctioned space of the official church website (Klassen and Lofton 2013). This is also the case in the study by Wong mentioned earlier, who states that 'for the women broadcasting their devotional activities online and over the phone, their informal predications typically served as an unsanctioned supplement or alternative to the official pulpit preaching that remained within the purview of male pastors' (Wong 2021: 289). Along these lines, women could be said to preach from the margins also in digital space.

There are also other problems with the kind of authority favoured in the secondary orality of digital culture. This is discussed by Khosravinik and Esposito (2018), who state that online hatred is the flipside of the democratisation of public discourse. Mary Beard makes similar observations about online hatred and relates it to the aspect of genre. Beard claims that the contemporary communication discourse has much in common with the ancient, because the communicative ideals that were formed in the Early Modern Era were drawn explicitly from ancient speeches and handbooks. Therefore, there is a 'powerful template for thinking about public speech, and for deciding what counts as good oratory or bad, persuasive or not, and whose speech is to be given space to be heard. And gender is obviously an important part of that mix' (Beard 2015: 812). In social media, it is expressed as online hatred and fits right into the ancient patterns of silencing women (Beard 2015).

Khosravinik and Esposito agree that online hatred affects women in a special way. They find it reasonable to assume that digital social networks function as any other social network, where deviators from the norm are often questioned and silenced. In the digital space, women are deviators and accordingly more likely to be subjected to online hatred. Would not, then, the fact that you can keep your gender identity hidden in the digital space be an advantage for women? The authors say no, because it is in fact part of the problem. Due to anonymity, you cannot see how many women inhabit the space, so the idea of digital space as male space is rarely questioned (Khosravinik and Esposito 2018).

This discussion of space, body, authority and genre enriches our understanding as we turn to the case of a preacher within the paradigm of secondary orality. The preacher in question in Antje Jackelén (1955-), former professor in systematic theology and since 2013 the first female Lutheran Archbishop in Sweden, elected in the first round – an indicator of remarkably strong support. Jackelén is known as the tweeting bishop. She often takes part in public debate, but most notably she tweets 'Sunday words', a short sermon, every Sunday. She also regularly appears in short videos, for example before Easter and Christmas, and runs a Podcast.

In relation to the theory of orality, literacy and secondary orality, she would be expected to be a well-regarded preacher. A closer look reveals a more complex picture, especially in relation to a digital culture and space. When she was elected in 2013, there was a massive wave of online hatred, even multiple death threats (Larsson and Degréus 2013). Jackelén has addressed the problem several times since then. In 2016 she evaluated her first five years on Twitter and characterised it as a place of execution. She wrote:

> When several hundred people in one day take away your honour and righteousness and kick the truth with their feet, it feels like an invasion in your body. You need to mobilize an enormous energy to push back and maintain your integrity. For a pastor, who is supposed to be open, understanding and attentive, it clashes with your pastoral identity. To survive you need to steel yourself and develop thick skin. At the same time, your pastoral duty is to constantly practice attentiveness and empathy. (Jackelén 2016)

In an interview during the spring of 2020, she mentioned that the hateful tone on the internet makes her think twice before she tweets. When speaking of her own reactions, she mentioned two pitfalls that she wants to avoid: silence, and looking for conflict to prove that she will not be silenced. However, in the spring of 2021, the Archbishop announced that she would leave Twitter. She could no longer accept that her words were twisted around and misinterpreted to intentionally harm the church (Habul 2020).

The cultivated theory brings understanding to these reactions to Jackelén's presence and preaching in the secondary orality of digital culture. It can be seen as a matter of space. While the ELCS has accepted women in the sacred space of the pulpit since 1958, the digital space is still associated with the male. It does not matter that she communicates from officially sanctioned digital platforms of the church websites and official social media channels: Jackelén is still the wrong body in the wrong space.

It could also be interpreted as a matter of communication genre. Public speech and the short, doctrinal statements of the 'Sunday words' sermons – the hallmark of Twitter – is understood as a male genre. That could explain the online hatred and her feeling that people are trying to silence her. In relation to genre, when the Archbishop left Twitter, she instead chose Instagram. In her first post, she wrote that she would share pictures and 'give glimpses from the everyday life as an Archbishop'. The gospel is therefore not proclaimed in short doctrinal statements, but through personal narrative, and hateful comments are rare. Could a contributing reason be that she conformed to the rules of communication genre and chose the more gender-differentiated genre of digital storytelling?

Finally, it could be understood as a matter of how authority functions in a digital space. As Archbishop and former professor, Jackelén is the epigone of ecclesial and educational authority. However, in secondary orality a networked and narrated authority is favoured, in particular from a woman. As shown in the quotes, it is Jackelén's bodily authority, her 'honour and righteousness' that is put in question. The drawbacks of the networked and narrated authority are painfully clear, as Jackelén states that the only way to survive is to close herself off from others.

The analysis of Jackelén's preaching points to the importance and usefulness of the sharpened tool of a cultivated theory, not least in relation to the secondary orality of digital culture. Furthermore, a cultivated theory could also indicate how change could come about in relation to the problems and drawbacks of secondary orality.

Firstly, it points to the importance of women being not only present but also visible in the digital space, in order to question the idea that it is a male space. This is applicable in relation to communication genres as well. Secondly, this relates to the networked and narrated authority of secondary orality. There are drawbacks to this feature of secondary orality, but the same feature also carries potential. In the historical perspective, the connections needed to sanction authority were provided by the right group of men. But in the secondary orality of digital culture the sanctioning of authority is democratised. This is not just an opportunity to express online hatred, but also support and recognition for women – as well as other deviators from the norm – who make their voices heard and their bodies visible in digital space.

SUMMARY

This article discusses the theory of orality and literacy and its developments in relation to digital media, where digital culture is understood as a 'secondary orality'. Studies in World Christianity have discussed orality and literacy among cultures which are much less text-based than European cultures, and scholars are aware of the diveristy of bodies, spaces and expressions. However, the field has yet to engage with the theories of literacy/orality and secondary orality as established by Ong and others. The article acts as a point of information and consideration for studies in World Christianity. It provides an explanation and critique of current theory in dialogue with the practice of female preaching over history, and offers a method that might also be used to examine the lived experience of different Christian cultures across the globe.

Frida Mannerfelt is a Ph.D. candidate in Practical Theology with Church History at University College, Stockholm, and a teacher at Lund University, Sweden. Her Ph.D. research examines various aspects of preaching in a digital culture and space. Together with the Church historian Dr Alexander Maurits she is co-author of *Kallelse och erkännande: berättelser från de första prästvigda kvinnorna i Svenska kyrkan* (2021), the result of a research project that collected and analysed narratives of vocation from the first women to be ordained as pastors in the Evangelical Lutheran Church of Sweden, 1960–1970.

REFERENCES

Ames, M., and Burcon S. Himsel. 2011. 'Introduction: Women and Oral Culture.' In *Women and Language: Essays on Gendered Communication Across Media*, edited by Ames and Himsel, 1–16. London: McFarland.

Arrington, A. 2015. 'Orality, Literacy, and the Lisu Linguistic Borderlands.' *Missiology* 43.4: 398–412.

———. 2019. 'From Missionary Translation to Local Theological Inquiry: A Narrative History of the Lisu Bible.' *Studies in World Christianity* 25.2: 202–19.

Asamoah-Gyadu, J. K. 2007. '"Get on the Internet!" Says the LORD': Religion, Cyberspace and Christianity in Contemporary Africa.' *Studies in World Christianity* 13.3: 225–42.

Bassi, K. 1997. 'Orality, Masculinity, and the Greek Epic.' *Arethusa* 30.3: 315–40.

Beard, M. 2015. 'The Public Voice of Women.' *Women's History Review* 24.5: 809–18.

Bediako, K. 1993. 'Cry Jesus! Christian Theology and Presence in Modern Africa.' *Vox Evangelica* 23: 7–26.

———. 1996. 'The Significance of Modern African Christianity – A Manifesto.' *Transformation* 13.1: 20–9.

Bernstein, S. N. 1993. 'Writing and Little Women: Alcott's Rhetoric of Subversion.' *American Transcendental Quarterly* 7.1: 25–43.

Bounegru, L. 2008. 'Secondary Orality in Microblogging.' Available at https://mastersofmedia.hum.uva.nl/blog/2008/10/13/secondary-orality-in-microblogging/ (accessed 11 March 2020).

Bremmer, J. N. 2012. 'Perpetua's Passions: A Brief Introduction.' In *Perpetua's Passions. Multidisciplinary Approaches to the Passio Perpetuae et Felicitatis*, edited by J. N. Bremmer and M. Formisano, 1–13. Oxford: Oxford University Press.

Cheong, P. 2013. 'Authority.' In *Digital Religion: Understanding Religious Practice in New Media Worlds*, edited by H. A. Campbell, 72–87. London: Routledge.

Fahlgren, S. 2006. *Predikantskap och församling: Sex fallstudier av en ecklesial baspraktik inom svensk frikyrklighet fram till 1960-talet.* Örebro: ÖTHrapport.

Foley, J. M. 2012. *Oral Tradition and the Internet: Pathways of the Mind.* Chicago: University of Illinois Press.

Ford, D. 2016. *A Theology for a Mediated God: How Media Shapes Our Notions About Divinity.* London: Routledge.

Gunner, G. 2003. *Nelly Hall: Uppburen och ifrågasatt: Predikant och missionär i Europa och USA 1882–1901.* Uppsala: Uppsala Universitet.

Halldorf, J. 2012. *Av denna världen: Emil Gustafson, Moderniteten och den evangelikala väckelsen.* Skellefteå: Artos.

———. 2020. *Pentecostal Politics in a Secular World: The Life and Leadership of Lewi Pethrus.* London: Palgrave Macmillan.

Habul, K. 2020. 'Ärkebiskopen: "Vi ska inte vara en front mot islam"'. *Sydsvenska Dagbladet* 23 February.

Hess, M. E. 2013. 'Digital Storytelling: Empowering Feminist and Womanist Faith Formation with Young Women.' In *Religion and Gender: Key Issues and New Challenges*, edited by M. Lövheim, 169–82. Abingdon, Oxon.: Routledge.

Horsefield, P. 2015. *From Jesus to the Internet. A History of Christianity and Media.* Chichester, West Sussex: Wiley Blackwell.

Jackelén, A. 2019. 'Ärkebiskopen: Twitter domstol och avrättningsplats.' *Svenska Dagbladet* 4 September.

Khosravinik, M., and E. Esposito. 2018. 'Online Hate, Digital Discourse and Critique: Exploring Digitally-mediated Discursive Practices of Gender-based Hostility.' *Lodz Papers in Pragmatics* 14.11: 45–68.

King, K. L. 1998. 'Afterword: Voices of the Spirit – Exercising Power, Embracing Reaponsability.' In *Women Preachers and Prophets through Two Millennia of Christianity*, edited by B. M. Kienzle and P. J. Walker, 335–44. Berkley: University of California Press.

Klassen, P. E., and K. Lofton. 2013. 'Material Witnesses: Women and the Mediation of Christianity.' In *Media, Religion and Gender: Key Issues and New Challenges*, edited by M. Lövheim, 53–63. New York: Routledge.

Lamb, M. E. 2008. 'Introduction.' In *Oral Traditions and Gender in Early Modern Literacy Texts*, edited by K. Bemford and M. E. Lamb, xvii–xxv. Aldershot: Ashgate.

Larsson, S., and A. Degréus. 2013. 'Våg av näthat mot Antje Jackelen.' *Sveriges radio* 30 November.

Lövheim, M. 2011. 'Young Women's Blogs as Ethical Spaces.' *Information, Communication & Society* 14.3: 338–54.

Nayar, S. J. 2013. 'Primary Issues with Secondary Orality.' *Explorations in Media Ecology* 11.3: 219–29.

Neufeld, C. M. 2001. *Xanthippe's Sisters: Orality and Femininity in the Late Middle Ages.* Montreal: McGill University.

Ong, W. J. 1967. *The Presence of the Word.* New Haven: Yale University Press.

—— 1982. *Orality and Literacy: The Technologizing of the Word.* London: Methuen.

Pettitt, T. 2009a. 'Book and Bodies, Bound and Unbound.' *Orbis Litterarum* 64.2: 104–26.

—— 2009b. 'Containment and Articulation: Media, Cultural Production, and the Perception of the Material World.' Paper presented to *Media in Transition 6*: 'Stone and Papyrus, Storeage and Transmission'. Available at web.mit.edu/comm-forum/legacy/mit6/papers/Pettitt.pdf (accessed 16 November 2021).

—— 2013a. 'Media Dynamics and the Lessons of History: The "Gutenberg Parenthesis" as Restoration Topos.' In *A Companion to New Media Dynamics*, edited by J. Hartley, J. Burgess and A. Bruns, 53–72. Chicester: Wiley-Blackwell.

—— 2013b. 'Bracketing the Gutenberg Parenthesis.' *Explorations in Media Ecology* 11.2: 95–114.

—— 2013c. 'The Privacy Parenthesis: Gutenberg, Homo Clausus and the Networked Self.' Paper presented to *Media in Transition 8*: 'Public Media, Private Media'. Available at https://www.academia.edu/4169829/The_Privacy_Parenthesis_Gutenberg_ Homo_ Clausus_and_the_Networked_Self (accessed 16 November 2021).

—— 2013d. 'Books and Bodies: A Gutenberg (Paren)thesis. An Inaugural Lecture.' Available at https://www.academia.edu/5317420/Books_and_Bodies_A_Gutenberg_ Paren_thesis (accessed 16 November 2021).

Phillips, P. M. 2017. *Engaging the Word: Biblical Literacy and Christian Discipleship.* Abingdon: Bible Reading Fellowship.

Salmesvuori, P. 2014. *Power and Sainthood: The Case of Birgitta of Sweden.* New York: Palgrave Macmillan.

Sanneh, L. 1989. *Translating the Message: The Missionary Impact on Culture.* Maryknoll, NY: Orbis.

Sauerberg, L. O. 2009. 'The Gutenberg Parenthesis – Print, Book and Cognition.' *Orbis Litterarum* 64.2: 79–80.

Sligo, F. 2015. 'Rethinking Oral and Literate Identities in Tertiary Study at the Closing of the Gutenberg Parenthesis.' *Communication Research and Practice* 1.4: 362–74.

Soffer, O. 2010. '"Silent Orality": Toward a Conceptualization of the Digital Oral Features in CMC and SMS Texts.' *Communication Theory* 20.4: 387–404.

Soukup, P. A. 2003. 'The Structure of Communication as a Challenge for Theology.' *Teología y Vida* 44.1: 102–22.

—— 2007. 'Orality and Literacy 25 Years Later.' *Communication Research Trends* 26.4: 3–21.

Starkman, D. 2012. 'The Future is Medieval.' *Columbia Journalism Review* 6 June: 20.

Waldner, K. 2012. 'Visions, Prophecy, and Authority in the Passio Perpetuae.' In *Perpetua's Passions. Multidisciplinary Approaches to the Passio Perpetuae et Felicitatis*, edited by J. N. Bremmer and M. Formisano, 201–23. Oxford: Oxford University Press.

Weigel, S. 2012. 'Exemplum and Sacrifice, Blood Testimony and Written Testimony.' In *Perpetua's Passions. Multidisciplinary Approaches to the Passio Perpetuae et Felicitatis*, edited by J. N. Bremmer and M. Formisano, 180–206. Oxford: Oxford University Press.

Weitbrecht, J. 2012. 'Maternity and Sainthood in the Medieval Perpetua Legend.' In *Perpetua's Passions. Multidisciplinary Approaches to the Passio Perpetuae et Felicitatis*, edited by J. N. Bremmer and M. Formisano, 150–68. Oxford: Oxford University Press.

Williams, C. 2012. 'Perpetua's Gender: A Latinist Reads the Passio Perpetuae et Felicitatis.' In *Perpetua's Passions. Multidisciplinary Approaches to the Passio Perpetuae et Felicitatis*, edited by J. N. Bremmer and M. Formisano, 54–77. Oxford: Oxford University Press.

Wilson, P. S. 1992. *A Concise History of Preaching*. Nashville: Abingdon Press.

Closer Away from Us: Theologizing in the Intersection Between Ascension Theology and Experiences of a Pandemic and Digital Space

Abstract: This article aims to discuss the theology that has been done and what kind of theology could be done in relation to experiences of the COVID-19 pandemic and digital space. For this purpose, it is guided by two questions. First: How do preachers theologize in the intersection between these experiences and Ascension theology? This is discussed in relation to an analysis of 32 sermons from Ascension 2020, held by Swedish protestant preachers in Stockholm, Gothenburg, and Malmö. Second: How could theology continue to be done in a digital culture? Drawing from the resources of Ascension theology, several suggestions are made. I argue for maintaining the absence in presence, the possibility of preaching about the mediated nature of presence, sacramental participation in salvation history, and the importance of including the category of place. This could promote a deeper understanding of the nature of Christ, human bodies, and creation for the present time as well as the *eschaton* of time. Furthermore, I argue that it is a re-actualization of theological themes already present in Christian Scripture and doctrine. Finally, I claim that there are indications in the sermons that this kind of theology has already begun being done, prompted by the experience of digital space and the pandemic.

Original publication: Mannerfelt, Frida, "Closer Away from Us: Theologizing in the Intersection Between Theology and Experiences of a Pandemic and Digital Space". Accepted for publication in *Words in Times of Crisis: Conference Proceedings Societas Homiletica 2020* (Berlin: LIT Verlag, forthcoming). Published with permission.

Introduction

How is theology done in relation to the experience of a pandemic? Practical theological Jonas Ideström draws on the work of Gordon Lathrop to describe the process of theologizing as a "juxtaposition" of the sacred and everyday life that creates and expands meaning. The practice of theologizing is characterized by being related to the Gospel, being an integrated form of learning that presupposes faith, and always being situated in a specific place, space, and time. According to Ideström, the situation of the covid19 pandemic (not least the transition to digital space) has caused a need for renewed theologizing. There is a "pedagogy of the situation" that prompts a "theology of the situation" (Ideström 2021, 18–21).

What kind of theology is promoted, then? Studies of preaching in the initial stages of the pandemic indicate that it activates reflection on the presence of God (Steyn et al. 2021; Nystrand 2021). Scholars of digital theology have made similar observations concerning digital space. There seems to be a "pedagogy of absence" (Schmidt 2020, 145) where the experience of digitally mediated liturgical practices, for example, "forces one to acknowledge that there is no unmediated [...] bodily presence at worship, online or offline" (Berger 2018, 20). This article aims to take a closer look at the theology that has been done and discuss what kind of theology could be done in relation to the experience of the pandemic and digital space.

For this purpose, I analyzed sermons from Ascension in May 2020. By that time, the initial stage of the pandemic was over, and reflections on the experiences would have deepened. In addition, the liturgical year activated scriptural and doctrinal reflection on presence and absence. Blogposts written early in the pandemic by theologians that engage with digital culture (for example, Thompson 2020) proposed Ascension theology as a resource, and theologians that engage with Ascension theology suggest that it could be used to inform a theory of digital spaces (see for example Sleeman 2016, 171-172). With this article, I want to contribute to such a discussion.

This is done by analyzing 32 sermons held during Ascension 2020 in Swedish protestant churches. How did the preachers theologize in the intersection of the pandemic experience, digital spaces, Scripture, and doctrines concerning the Ascension of Christ?

The sermons were held on either Ascension Day or the Sunday before Pentecost 2020 by preachers serving in congregations in the Uniting Church of Sweden (henceforth UC) and the (Lutheran) Church of Sweden (henceforth CoS) in the country's three largest cities, Stockholm, Gothenburg, and Malmö. Due to governmental restrictions, only up to fifty people were allowed to gather in the local church space. This caused the lion's part of the sermons to be digitally mediated, but six were delivered locally only. In most cases, the Scripture passages the preachers engaged with were chosen from the lectionary that both church traditions use. For Ascension Day, the assigned texts were the vision of the man coming on the clouds of heaven in Dan 7:13-14, a part of Christ's intercession in John 17:1-8 and, of course, Acts 1:1-11, the Lukan narrative of the ascension of Christ. Three days later, on Sunday before Pentecost, the readings from Acts continued with verses 12-14, along with the narrative of Elijah's theophany on Mount Horeb in 1 King 19 and John 16:12-15 about the Spirit of truth.

In addition to analyzing what kind of theologizing that has been done, the article also wants to discuss how theologizing could be further developed. Pandemics eventually go away, but digital technology will not. The need to continuously do theology in relation to digital culture and space is indisputable. In this pursuit, Ascension theology could provide a viable and creative source.

Presence and Absence

The dominating characteristic of the 32 sermons is that theology was done in relation to a perceived situation of distance and fear. All preachers referred, explicitly or implicitly, to the pandemic as a situation of distance, isolation, loneliness, and uncertainty.

The most common way to address the situation caused by the pandemic and/or digital space was through narratives. Many of the sermons from Sunday before Pentecost were structured on the Elijah narrative, whose experience was repeatedly described as loneliness, despair, and feeling abandoned by God. The situation changes as God eventually provides Elijah with the presence of friends and/or the God he longed for and needed. Presence was also said to be "the point of Ascension." Most preachers stated that since it is not possible to understand the physics of the Ascension, the important thing is the meaning of the event: the ubiquity of Christ. Because of his ascension, Christ is present everywhere, also with the listeners.

The findings correspond with Clara Nystrand's study of preaching in the CoS during the initial stages of the pandemic, where the dominant depiction of God was that God is present and with us in our suffering (Nystrand, 2021). This means that the strategy of preaching identified by Steyn et al. in the South African context was also at work in the Swedish context. In their study of sermons held in a reformed church in South Africa during Easter, Steyn et al. found that the preachers commonly spoke of the contrast between the "experienced reality" that everyone is far and fear is near and the "proclaimed reality" that death is far, and God is near. To enable the listeners to discern this proclaimed reality, the preachers encouraged habits of faith. This enticed actions like celebrating the Eucharist at home or lamenting, particularly "serviceability." In other words: care for others (Steyn et al., 2020).

Bible scholar Peter C. Orr points to some theological problems with this way of understanding God's presence in relation to the Ascension. According to Orr, there is a risk of preaching "unqualified ubiquity," where the presence of Christ is collapsed into either the Spirit or the church. Therefore, he argues for the importance of proclaiming that there is an absence in the divine presence. Especially since it is presented in Scripture, expressing both the eschatological future and the congregation's experiences. (Orr 2018, 1, 37–75, 115–131). Theologian Katherine G. Schmidt also argues that absence is a crucial category that needs to be reclaimed by theologians, particularly in relation to ecclesiology and sacramental theology. Schmidt claims that the notion that Christ is present without any absence could lead to an idealization or even idolatry of the local congregation, sacraments and/or the people administrating them (Schmidt 91-104, 128-135).

Due to the contrasting strategy identified by Steyn et al., the sermons leaned considerably towards unqualified ubiquity. Absence in presence was seldom expressed, although there were occasional exceptions, like the preacher who, in their digitally mediated sermon, pointed out that Christ is not here precisely in the same ways as we read about in the gospels. The closeness we long for must be done at a distance, just like in the situation "right now" (DSvM5). The experience of the pandemic and digital worship thus seems to have prompted this insight.

Moreover, it is interesting to see how unqualified ubiquity was expressed. As both church traditions heavily emphasize the local gathering in their ecclesiology, one might expect the preachers to stress that Christ after the Ascension is present through the body of Christ as in church and/or the Eucharist. Indeed, six sermons elaborated on the church now being the body of Christ on earth. Like this UC preacher, they were often dangerously close to equalling Christ's presence with the church: "The meaning of ascension is that Jesus' visible presence on earth is replaced by his disciples, of his followers." (DEqG3). However, mentions of the Eucharist were scarce. This was probably because Eucharist was not celebrated because of the risk of contagion. Only one preacher elaborated on it, but not in relation to the presence of Christ here and now, but to eschatological hope:

> The distance we experience now can remind us of the distance between our reality and eternity. The longing we might have experienced in the interruption to worship together because of the risk of contagion is similar to the longing after community with

God – without obstruction and limitations. [...] This can remind us of the feast together with God in what we call heaven. [...] We can be reminded of the hope that there is a time after Corona but also a time after the limitations of our lives. A time with God, a time when Jesus returns in glory (LSvMI).

Instead, many preachers chose to speak of Christ being present through the Spirit. Here we may observe that although Christ's presence usually was unqualified (as in no mention of absence), the preachers spoke of it as coming *through* the Spirit, thus avoiding a total collapse of Christ into the Spirit.

Most preachers in this study related the presence of the Holy Spirit to everyday life and the qualities of individuals (like strength, patience, and love). This strong tendency to talk about the Holy Spirit in relation to individuals, not community or congregation, sprung forth in interpreting the words "the spirit of truth that will guide with the whole truth." This was rarely interpreted collectively but as the personal growth of the individual. Regarding the Elijah narrative, the standard Swedish translation of the Bible invites an interpretation of *qol demamah daqqah* – the quiet whisper of God's presence – as the wind of the Holy Spirit. Several preachers connected this to the notion that through the Holy Spirit, God is present in the "quiet whisper of everyday life" of the individual.

Is the individualized interpretation of God's presence caused by the experience of the pandemic and/or digital space? According to digital theologian Peter M. Phillips, it is not. However, while digital media do not *cause* the tendencies towards individualized, practice-oriented Bible content and interpretation, they could be said to *amplify* them by the logic of digital media (Phillips 2018, 91-111). A contributing cause is reasonably also that the idea of God's presence in everyday life is emphasized in a dominant Lutheran theological tradition in CoS (Gregersen et al. 2017).

How can theology be done in the future? One important thing would be to maintain the absence in the divine presence when theologizing in, for example, sermons. As previously discussed, Orr and Schmidt emphasize the importance of keeping the tension between presence and absence together in theology and spirituality. In relation to this, they both discuss the mediated nature of presence. According to Schmidt, the digital space is a powerful reminder of the conditions of presence. Presence is always mediated by a medium of some kind, and accordingly, there is always an absence in presence. This is, in fact, what the church always has taught in its ecclesiology (the presence of the local congregation always points to the absent church universal) and sacramental theology (Christ's presence in the Eucharist always points to a more complete presence at the end of time) (Schmidt 2020, 134-148). From the vantage point of Ascension theology, Orr, too, finds

God's presence mediated. He identifies three modes of presence. Christ is active on earth through the church, in heaven through his intercession, and finally through what Orr calls his "epiphanic presence" as mediated, for instance, through preaching. (Orr 2018, 133–152). Orr and Schmidt's arguments show that this is not something new under the sun but a re-actualization of teachings already existing in Scripture and doctrine.

Presence, Absence, and Time

As discussed above, Ideström states that theologizing is done in relation to time, space, and place. My study confirms and illustrates this statement. While digital space was explicitly mentioned only five times in the sermons, it was regularly theologized at the beginning of the worship services. In both sermons and introduction, presence and absence were similarly discussed in relation to time, space, and place. The congregation was described as present to each other since "neither time nor space nor isolation or distance can limit God's presence" (DSvM4). However, there were significant differences in how time and space were elaborated in the sermons.

Although God's presence was generally described as unqualified, several preachers did discuss God's absence. This was done in relation to time. Time was an essential trope for many preachers and was discussed both in relation to God's presence and absence.

When it came to absence in relation to time, this was expressed in the narratives about the disciples. These narratives were not as elaborated as the Elijah story but concentrated on the two actions mentioned in the gospel reading: praying and waiting.

This inspired teaching on prayer and a significant amount of teaching on waiting. It could be expressed as follows: "You could say that waiting is the center of this time between the ascension and Pentecost. [...] And such waiting is important. It is a time of grace, a timing for what God is about to do" (DSvG4). Waiting was also expressed in relation to digital space. One preacher spelled out the advantages of the digital space for preaching. It allows the preacher to sit down and lower the voice, which mediates an attitude of equality and conversation – like Jesus when he taught his disciples. It also teaches the preacher "more thoughtfulness, waiting." (DEqM1) Again, the experience of the digital and the pandemic seem to serve as a "pedagogy of absence" – it even teaches you how to be more present as a preacher!

When it comes to presence in relation to time, several preachers described this as a sort of upheaval of the time. "And suddenly [...] we are drawn into a holy context, and we are standing on holy ground because God is there." (DEqS3) According to the preachers, this could occur in everyday life and in relation to the digital space. On two of the occasions when preachers spoke explicitly about the experience of digital space, they stressed the fact that even if the listener were not participating in the service at the same time as it was recorded, "we are gathered here right now. Together we can sing God's praise, hear God's word, pray together." (DSvG6) The preacher and the listener may not be present to each other in chronological time (*chronos*) but in God's time (*kairos*).

A potential resource for continued theologizing is found in the roots of Ascension theology. According to church historian Joris Geldhof, this way of conceiving time as a *locus* for God's presence was expressed in the preaching of the Early Church. In his discussion of a quote from an Ascension sermon by Leo the Great in 445 ("What was seen of our redeemer has passed over into the sacraments"), he argues that the interpretation of this quote by the liturgical movement has given it more ecclesiological and liturgical meaning than it originally had. According to Geldhof, Leo the Great was not talking about how Christ is made visible in the *sacramentum* of the Eucharist, but through time – as in the practice of making Christ present here and now through immersing yourself and joyfully participating in the *sacramentum* of salvation history. (Geldhof 2016, 386-405).

In the sermon material in my study, there are a few examples of this. Again, they are articulated in relation to the pandemic and the digital space. One preacher pointed to a painting of the ascended Christ surrounded by the heavenly hosts and invited the listeners to join in the joy that comes from remembering and integrating the event of Ascension in their own lives, claiming that this could be done both from the local space and the digital space (DSvG3). A preacher who spoke on the topic "Everything you fought your whole life to reach is already yours" made a similar invitation stating that through the experience of joy in the present, we may be connected to the joy of eternity. However, this preacher suggests another event in salvation history for the listeners to participate in; creation. The listeners are invited to remember and actualize to themselves the gift of life, an act through which they will experience the presence of God (DEqG4). Once again, this could be described as a rediscovery of theology activated when the preachers theologized in the intersection between Ascension theology and the experience of the pandemic and digital space. In doing this, the preachers seemingly discovered time as a theological resource to speak about God's presence and absence.

Presence, Absence, and Space

While time was an important trope, the preachers rarely referred to space. This tendency among theologians to focus on time at the expense of space is discussed by theologian Vitor Westhelle. According to Westhelle, eschatology has always been a problematic issue in Christian dogmatics, and since Modernity, increasingly so. Theologians tend to avoid the topic of eschatology since it is difficult and even a bit embarrassing to talk about the return of Christ. Nevertheless, it is a central part of Christian dogmatics, so theologians developed a strategy. The solution was to separate time and space and focus on the temporal dimension of eschatology, either in terms of *telos* (a temporal event waiting to be fully realized) or as *axios* (an experience an eternal now).

This strong inclination towards time, especially in Western 20th Century theological reflection, is problematic since it makes theology blind to the fact that eschatology also concerns creation. Therefore, Westhelle argues for the importance of understanding the *eschaton* in spatial terms and introduces the concept of "tangential space" to describe the liminal space of the borderlands that ought to be the starting point for reflection. In other words: theologizing should be done from the experience of being on the margins, like in liberation theology. Awareness of spatial dimension fosters the ability to see that there is an outside and, accordingly, the marginalized other (Westhelle 2016, 1-2, 13-20, 73-83). The lack of reflection on space in the sermons is, thus, typical for a traditional Western theological context.

Westhelle's argument could also shed light on other observations in the sermon analysis. The first is the absence of encouragement of what Steyn et al. called "serviceability," or care for others. In the South African sermons, "habits of faith" were preached as a means to discern the proclaimed reality of God's presence. This was also done in the Swedish sermons, where listeners were encouraged to cling to habits of faith like praying and waiting. However, while serviceability was the most encouraged habit of faith in the South African context, the Swedish preachers almost entirely omitted it. While three preachers encouraged neighborly love and solidarity in general wording, only one gave concrete examples and elaborated on this in relation to Scripture (LSvG2).

The second is the scarcity of eschatology. It is a topic given in Scripture and doctrine through the narrative of the Ascension, in which Jesus promises to return. Moreover, eschatology is integral to the theological heritage of the founding churches of UC (see, for example, Gunner 1996). This is related to a third observation in relation to how the preachers theologized on the concept of "the kingdom of God." The kingdom is commonly mentioned in sermons that narrate the story

of the disciples. This is no surprise; Scripture mentions it, and it is an essential concept in the founding churches of UC (Gunner 1996, 52 and *Trons Grund*, 1-9).
However, while almost all UC preachers mentioned the concept, they rarely developed its meaning. Among the CoS preachers, only a few mentioned "the kingdom of God." Most used the same vague expressions as their UC colleagues, but
three of them developed the concept. It is noteworthy that all three occurrences
are done in relation to experiences caused by the pandemic. One preacher focused
on its eschatological meaning and placed the kingdom of God in a time to come in
relation to the experience of reaching one's limits in this life. Two preachers developed an understanding of the kingdom of God here and now.

Notably, these two are among the few preachers who encouraged the care of
others. One of them stated that a Christian should live in the kingdom of God and
gave examples of how in relation to the situation caused by the pandemic
(DSvG2). The other compared the kingdom of God with the Coronavirus: "It is
invisible in many places, it affects people in various degrees, and its consequences
go far beyond the already infected." In this kingdom, Jesus reigns with love, and
the congregation is invited to participate and give others what they have received
(LSvG1).

In the light of Westhelle, the lack of eschatology and vague conceptualization
of the kingdom of God is no surprise and due to tendencies to avoid the topic of
eschatology in general and its spatial dimensions in particular. If that is the case,
this lack is not caused by the experience of the pandemic and/or the digital space.
On the contrary, finding examples of it at all is rather remarkable. Judging from
the few occurrences in the sermon material, it seems that these experiences bring
eschatological reflection. Again, already existing theological themes and doctrines
could be said to be rediscovered or re-actualized through theologizing on experiences of the pandemic and the digital space.

Westhelle's argument could also explain the connection between space and
care for others in the sermon material. Where spatial dimension is lacking, so is an
encouragement to serviceability. Without a notion of space, the suffering people
"outside" are eclipsed. On the other hand, in the two sermons that elaborate on
the kingdom of God as manifested on earth, the care of others is addressed.

Theologians that reflect on Ascension theology often point to the importance
of space for a correct understanding of the presence of Christ. Some valuable insights can be found here in the continuing task of theologizing in digital culture.
Theologian Douglas Farrow argues that it is important to understand the Ascension of Christ as a "transformative relocation" where his physical body went to a

particular space – the right hand of God. Here, there are clear parallels to Westhelle's thoughts on eschatology since Farrow states that without the notion of space, ascension might be conceived of as something that exists only in time or the mind, not affecting human bodies or creation. Moreover, it may cause a collapse of Christ into the local church or the sacraments. Like Schmidt, Farrow emphasizes that the tension between presence and absence in the view of the sacraments must stay intact to avoid "the tendency to fetishize pure presence through liturgical and devotional practices" (Farrow 2011, 2-47; 65-69).

To Farrow, this is related to eschatology. The eschatological perspective clarifies that the Eucharist is not just Christ coming down to the altar, but humans lifted up to see what they will become since what happened to Jesus will eventually happen to the human bodies through the grace of God. (Farrow 2011, 70-74)

According to Farrow, it has been common among theologians throughout the church's history to describe the physical body of Christ as gone. (Farrow 2011, 10-40). In this aspect, the preachers in my study are not unique, as most of them vaguely state that Jesus is "taken away" or "disappearing into the air."

Like Farrow, biblical scholar Matthew Sleeman stresses that Ascension relates to space as well as time. Drawing on Edward Soja's work on the concept of "third space," he argues for a way of conceiving space that resembles Westhelle's notion of "tangential space" that encourages serviceability. Through the Ascension of Christ, "Heaven and earth, as a dichotomous division between humanity and God, is breached and reformed – in and by and for the ascended and exalted Jesus. This previously neat and tidy demarcation of spaces is replaced; it is "thirded" by a new configuration of spatial relations" (Sleeman 2016, 161). When Christ's physical body is imagined in a place, it not only transforms the view of what is possible for earthly bodies, it changes how earthly spaces are regarded. It triggers an inherently theological "thirding" of earth that goes beyond dichotomies and affects how believers produce space. In other words, it encourages sharing and caring. According to Sleeman, "third space" also "helps facilitate widening the kinds of spaces in which Jesus's ascension has an impact. One obvious example is the rise of digital space." (Sleeman 2016, 162-164, 171-172.)

Strictly speaking, the concept of third space offers a fruitful way of thinking about space that encourages serviceability. It also draws our attention from dichotomies like real/virtual and digital/physical to the potential of all space as a third space where we may be involved in acts of serviceability. In a digital culture, where the experience of a pandemic increased the importance of digital space for the life of the church, this could contribute to a continued theologizing beyond the black-

and-white one-way-street of digital as body-less, space-less, and unreal where theologians often too quickly end up (see for example Berger 2018, 16-17 and Schmidt 2020, 15-18). In particular, since this way of conceiving space, bodies, and creation is already firmly rooted in Scripture and doctrine. The only thing needed is to rediscover and re-actualize it. As I have shown, there is reason to believe this process has already begun.

Summary

In this article, I have studied how Swedish protestant preachers theologize in the intersection between Ascension theology and the experience of a pandemic and digital space. Thirty-two sermons from the celebration of Ascension 2020 have been analyzed regarding this. Although the pandemic is passing, digital culture will remain. Therefore, I have also discussed how such theologizing could be further developed about Ascension theology.

The analysis showed that the preachers emphasized the presence of God in their sermons. Digital and Ascension theology scholars cautioned against this since the proclamation of an unqualified ubiquity (presence without absence) tends to collapse the presence of Christ into either church/Eucharist of the Spirit. In several of the sermons, this was indeed the case. In the continued theologizing of digital space, the mediated nature of presence with its tension between presence and absence needs to be maintained.

Time was an important trope in the sermons of the study. It was elaborated on in relation to both the absence and presence of God, pointing to the notion of God's *kairos*. Ascension theology pointed to the further development of that notion of synchronicity through the example of Early church preaching where the presence of Christ was understood to be mediated through the sacrament of time, in the joyful participation in salvation history when "then" merges with "now."

While time was a recurring theme in the sermons, the category of place was almost entirely omitted. According to theologian Vitor Westhelle, that would be expected in a Western church context. Westhelle argues that this is a problem since the notion of space is important for a proper understanding of eschatology and the ability to see end engage with the people who exist in the spatial *eschaton*: the marginalized other. Westhelle's argument shed light on the scarcity of eschatological themes, reflections on place, and encouragement of care for others in the sermons. Again, Ascension theology holds resources for continued theologizing on this, in its insistence on the category of space as the foundation for a correct understanding of the body of Christ. This is, in turn, crucial for an understanding of human bodies and creation, both here and now and in a time to come, that encourages care for others and the world and goes beyond the limitations of binary thinking. Moreover, these resources are not new inventions but a rediscovery or re-actualization of theology already present in Scripture and doctrine.

Finally, the study of the 32 sermons indicated that a developed theologizing has already begun. There were examples of a few preachers who did talk about absence in presence, the act of being present in God's *Kairos* through the joyful participation in the sacrament of salvation history, eschatology, place, and the care of others. Notably, this was done in relation to experiences of pandemic and/or digital space.

Literature

Berger, Teresa. @Worship: Liturgical Practices in Digital Worlds. Abingdon: Routledge, 2018.

Farrow, Douglas. Ascension Theology. London: T&T Clark International, 2011.

Geldhof, Joris. "Paschal Joy Continued: Exploring Leo the Great's Theology of Christ's Ascension into Heaven" in Preaching after Easter: MidPentecost, Ascension, and Pentecost in Late Antiquity, edited by Richard W. Bishop, Johan Leemans, and Hajnalka Tamas, 386–405. Boston: Brill, 2016

Gregersen, Niels Henrik, Kristensson Uggla Bengt, and Tryggve Wyller (eds.). Reformation Theology for a Post-Secular Age: Løgstrup, Prenter, Wingren, and the Future of Scandinavian Creation Theology. Göttingen: Vandenhoeck & Ruprecht, 2017.

Gunner, Göran. *När tiden tar slut: motivförskjutningar i frikyrklig apokalyptisk tolkning av det judiska folket och staten Israel*. PhD Uppsala University, 1996.

Ideström, Jonas. Ikoniska kartor: Att göra teologi i kyrkans vardag. Stockholm: Verbum, 2021.

Nystrand, Clara. "Predikans ärende i tider av pandemi: Lidande, hopp och evighetens horisont under corona och spanska sjukan" i Corona och kyrkorna: Lärdomar, digitala möten och beredskap för nästa kris, edited by Sune Fahlgren, Elin Lockneus and Daniel Strömner, 235–266. Stockholm: Libris bokförlag, 2021.

Orr, Peter C. Exalted Above the Heavens: The Risen and Ascended Christ. Downers Grove: InterVarsity Press, 2018.

Phillips, Peter M. The Bible, Social Media and Digital Culture. Abingdon: Routledge, 2021.

Schmidt, Katherine G. Virtual Communion: Theology of the Internet and the Catholic Sacramental Imagination. London: Fortress Academic, 2020.

Sleeman, Matthew. "The Ascension and Spatial Theory." In Ascent into Heaven in Luke-Acts: New Explorations of Luke's Narrative Hinge edited by David K. Bryan and David W. Pao. Minneapolis: Fortress Press, 2016.

Steyn, Marileen, Wepener, Cas and Pieterse Hennie. "Preaching During the COVID-19 Pandemic in South Africa: A Grounded Theoretical Exploration." International Journal of Homiletics 4 (2020): 1-20.

Thompson, Deanna. "Christ is really present virtually: a proposal for virtual communion" (March 26, 2020). Accessed October 14, 2020. https://wp.stolaf.edu/lutherancenter/2020/03/christ-is-really-present-virtually-a-proposal-for-virtual-communion/

Westhelle, Vitor. Eschatology and Space: The Lost Dimension in Theology Past and Present, London: Palgrave Macmillan, 2012.

Listening to Listeners in a Digital Culture: The Practice of Listening to Digitally-mediated Sermons

Abstract: This study examines digitally-mediated listening practices by listening to twenty-nine listeners from Swedish Protestant congregations. The analysis draws on Theodore Schatzki's practice theory, focusing on the entanglement of human activity, material arrangements, and the ends of practices—including how changes to any or all of the above impact the practice in question. The study found that listeners strove to uphold the listening practices they were used to from their respective churches and attempted to carry these over into the digitally-mediated preaching event. To a large extent, they succeeded in opening and managing a "third room of preaching." Furthermore, the study highlighted the importance of knowing the ends of these listening practices. The study also demonstrated the significance of material arrangements and how changes in these arrangements sometimes led to the obstruction—or even breakdown—of listening practices. However, changes in material arrangements also inspired new practices—pointing to the need to rethink listening practices that are merely borrowed from in-church services.

Keywords: online preaching; sermon listeners; Theodore Schatzki; homiletics; digital mediation.

Original publication: Mannerfelt, Frida, "Listening to Listeners in a Digital Culture: The practice of listening to digitally-mediated sermons. Accepted for publication in *Homiletic* 48:1 (2023). Published with permission.

Introduction

During the last few decades, homiletics has seen a turn to listeners.[1] An exemplary work of scholarship is the 2004 landmark study *Listening to listeners*.[2] In recent years, homileticians have begun to describe the practice of listening in more detail—for example, Theo Pleizier's empirical study of religious involvement in hearing sermons.[3] The turn to listeners has also affected the field of homiletics in Scandinavia, with several recent qualitative studies. Marianne Gaarden interviewed listeners about their interaction with sermons and their meaning-making processes in her *Third room of preaching*.[4] Together with Marlene Ringgaard Lorensen, Gaarden has argued that, in a sense, listeners function as primary authors of their own sermons as they interact with the preacher's words.[5] Another notable Scandinavian example is Linn Sæbø Rystad's work on children as listeners.[6]

These Scandinavian homileticians emphasize the importance of materiality in the meaning-making process of listeners. Gaarden shows how the preacher's person and physicality are essential for meaning-making.[7] Lorensen and Gitte Buch-Hansen observe that the presence of other listeners affects how the sermons are heard.[8] Furthermore, Rystad uses practice theory to show how "mediational means," such as artifacts, clothing, and narratives, play an integral part in the

---

[1] For overviews of empirical research with focus on the listener, see David Rietvield, "A Survey of the Phenomenological Research of Listening to Preaching", Homiletic 38, no. 2 (2013) and Marianne Gaarden, Third Room of Preaching: A New Empirical Approach (Eugene, Oregon: Pickwick Publications 2021), 7–21.

[2] John S. McClure, Ronald J. Allen, Dale P. Andrews, L. Susan Bond, Dan P. Mosely, and G. Lee Ramsey, *Listening to Listeners: Homiletical Case Studies* (St. Louis: Chalice Press, 2004). See also Ronald J. Allen and Mary Alice Mulligan, "Listening to listeners: five years later", *Homiletic* 34, no 2 (2009), 4–17.

[3] Theo Pleizier, Religious Involvement in Hearing Sermons: A Grounded Theory Study in Empirical Theology and Homiletics (Delft: Ebmon Academic Publishers, 2010).

[4] Gaarden, The Third Room of Preaching, 55–106.

[5] Gaarden, Marianne & Lorensen Ringgaard, Marlene, "Listeners as Authors in Preaching: Empirical and Theoretical Perspectives", *Homiletic* 38, no 2 (2013), 28–45.

[6] Linn Sæbø Rystad, "I Wish We Could Fast Forward it – Negotiating the Practice of Preaching", *Homiletic* 44, no 2 (2019), 18–42.

[7] Gaarden, The Third Room of Preaching, 51–68.

[8] Marlene Ringgaard Lorensen and Gitte Buch-Hansen, "Listening to the voices: refugees as co-authors of practical theology", *Practical Theology* 11 (2018), 29–41.

preaching event. She concludes that it is essential to include perspectives that consider the materiality of the preaching event.[9]

What happens, then, when the material conditions for the practice of listening are radically altered? What happens when the preaching event is digitally mediated? What would we homileticians discover if we listened to listeners in digital cultures?

While the number of online and/or digitally-mediated preaching studies is rapidly increasing, these studies focus solely on the preacher and/or the specific digital medium involved.[10] In-depth analyses of the *listeners'* perspectives on digitally-mediated preaching are virtually non-existent.[11] This article aims to examine the practice of listening to digitally-mediated sermons and, since there is a lacuna in research, suggest some areas in which this research can be further developed.

I will argue that listeners are able to uphold their listening practices in the digitally-mediated preaching event, which supports the hypothesis that listeners are interactive co-authors of the sermon, and preachers have limited control over their meaning-making. Yet important differences between the local preaching event and the digitally-mediated service can also make it difficult for listeners to uphold what they think are the proper ends to the listening practice. Changes in material arrangements may lead to the obstruction, or even the destruction, of listening practices. However, new material arrangements may also inspire new listening practices.

An analysis of group interviews with twenty-nine active members from Protestant congregations in the South of Sweden, drawing on the practice theory of Theodore Schatzki, serves as the foundation for this work. The results will be discussed in light of recent homiletical studies about the practice of listening to sermons.

---

[9] Linn Sæbø Rystad, "Preaching at the thresholds – Bakhtinian polyphony in preaching for Children", in *Practice, Practice Theory and Theology: Scandinavian and German Perspectives*, eds. Kristine Helboe Johansen and Ulla Schmidt (Berlin/Boston: De Gruyter, 2022), 165–184.

[10] See for example Sunggu A. Yang, "The Word Digitalized: A Techno-Theological Reflection on Online Preaching and Its Types", *Homiletic* 46, no 1 (2020), 75–89; Anna-Katharina Lienau "Kommunikation des Evangeliums in social media", *ZThK* (2019) 117: 489–522, Michael P. Knowles "E-Word? McLuhan, Baudrillard, and Verisimilitude in Preaching", *Religions* 13, no. 12:1131 (2022), 1–16.

[11] I stand to be corrected, but I have not found anyone.

Concepts, Material, and Methods

This is a study of digitally-mediated practices of listening to a sermon. Accordingly, two key concepts are essential for this article: "digitally mediated" and "practices." As I present the two key concepts, I will also describe the source material and the theoretical approach used in the analysis.

A Digitally-mediated Source Material

For this article, I have chosen the "digitally-mediated" concept instead of the more frequently used "online preaching." "Digitally-mediated" discloses important assumptions that impact how the source material is created and understood. As the editors of *Digital Religion* point out, digital media and technology are intertwined with everyday life, including religious practices. There are no clear distinctions between online and offline anymore.[12] The term "online" may also imply that "unmediated" preaching exists. But as Teresa Berger, for instance, has acknowledged: all religion is mediated in some way.[13]

As scholars in digital ethnography highlight, digital mediation is characterized by multiplicity, and can be experienced in a million different ways, depending on the software, hardware, context, and how a person chooses to interact with them.[14] This insight has prompted attempts to categorize digitally-mediated sermons.[15] For example, Tripp Hudgins offers three categories: *the social media platform sermon*, where the preaching event in the local church is recorded and disseminated afterward in social media; *the live from the pulpit sermon*, where the preaching is live-streamed from the local church; and *the online sermon for the online church*, in which there is no congregation gathered in a local church.[16] The listeners in this study have engaged in all three categories—on occasion, even experiencing all of them within the same community, as their digitally-mediated practices and those of their local congregation changed during different stages of the pandemic.

---

[12] Heidi Campbell and Ruth Tsuria, "Introduction to the Study of Digital Religion", in *Digital Religion: Understanding Religion in a Digital Age* (2nd edition), ed. Heidi Campbell and Ruth Tsuria, (London/New York: Routledge, 2021), 1–22.

[13] Teresa Berger, *@Worship: Liturgical Practices in Digital Worlds* (London/New York: Routledge, 2018), 7.

[14] Sarah Pink, Heather Horst, John Postill, Larissa Hjorth, Tania Lewis and Jo Tacchi, *Digital Ethnography: Principles and Practices* (Thousand Oaks: Sage, 2016), 10; Christine Hine, *Ethnography for the Internet: Embedded, Embodied and Everyday* (London & New York: Bloomsbury Academic, 2015), 26–30.

[15] Yang, "The Word Digitalized", 83.

[16] Tripp Hudgins, "Preaching Online", *Anglican Theological Review* 101, no 1 (2019), 79–88.

As discussed by Jonas Kurlberg and Alexander Chow, the development of digital transition strategies on the part of churches was influenced by governmental restrictions at the local level.[17] Unlike many other countries, a complete lockdown was never imposed in Sweden. Instead, there were fluctuating and varied restrictions on the number of people allowed to gather for local events, including worship services. These changed from five hundred people on March 12th, 2020, to fifty people two weeks later, to eight in November 2020. In June 2021, the restrictions were lifted—only to be lowered back to fifty in December 2021. As a result of these shifting limitations, congregations generally moved from *social media platforms* and *live from the pulpit* sermons, with up to fifty people present in the local church, to *online sermon for the online church* when the restrictions hardened.

However, format was not the only change. There are many ways to be a digitally-mediated church. John Dyer makes a distinction between "broadcast church" (via one-way mediums like Youtube) and "interactive church" (which use two-way interactive mediums like Zoom).[18] In Swedish Protestant congregations, the transition from digital platforms that only utilized one-way broadcasting to the adoption of platforms that allowed for a higher degree of interaction was quite common.[19] Some of the listeners in this study reported that their congregations made such a change.

The fourteen interviews analyzed here are part of the source material that was created in the framework for a larger research project, in which four researchers followed twenty-four local congregations from five Protestant denominations in the region of Småland (in the south of Sweden) during the first year of the COVID-19 pandemic (April 2020-June 2021). The interviews were conducted at the end of this period, in the spring of 2021.[20] To protect the identity of the

---

[17] Jonas Kurlberg and Alexander Chow, "Two or Three Gathered Online: Asian and European Responses to COVID-19 and the Digital Church", *Studies in World Christianity* 26, no 3 (2020), 299–318.

[18] John Dyer, "Exploring Mediated *Ekklesia*: How We Talk about Church in the Digital Age", in *Ecclesiology for a Digital Church: Theological Reflections on a New Normal*, ed. Heidi Campbell and John Dyer (London: SCM Press, 2022), 5–8.

[19] Frida Mannerfelt, "Old and New Habits The Transition to Digitally-Mediated Worship in Four Swedish Free Church Denominations during COVID-19", in *Svensk frikyrklighet i pandemin: En studie av församlingen i corona och corona i församlingen*, eds. Ulrik Josefsson and Magnus Wahlström, (Research report from the Institute of Pentecostal Studies No. 9, 2022), 81–82.

[20] The author of this article was responsible for conducting interviews with employees and members of the congregations; in total 40 interviews with 64 persons. The employees served as

participants, listeners were interviewed in groups of 2–3 people and are subsequently referred to as a group.[21]

A total of twenty-nine persons were interviewed. Half of the interviewees (15) belong to the Lutheran majority church, the Church of Sweden (CoS), and half (14) belong to four so-called Free church denominations.[22] These are the Uniting Church (UC, a merger of the Mission Covenant Church of Sweden, the United Methodist Church of Sweden, and the Baptist Union of Sweden); the Swedish Pentecostal Movement (PM); Interact; and the Swedish Mission Alliance (SMA). The sampling was made within the overarching research project's framework, which dealt with comparisons between the CoS and the Free churches. While such a comparison may also be relevant here, it is, however, not the main focus of the discussion in this article.

The interviews covered a wide range of topics related to the entire life of the congregation during the first year of the pandemic, not just digitally-mediated preaching. This context affects what they say in their responses. Like Theo Pleizier, I found that "there is some *vagueness* in how listeners distinguish between the worship service as a whole and the sermon in particular."[23] According to Pleizier, this is because listeners often experience the service and sermon as an inseparable whole.[24] Because of this, the analysis also necessarily includes what listeners say about the worship considered in its entirety.

Listening Practices

The second key concept is "listening practice." Here, I follow the lead of several Scandinavian homileticians who draw on practice theories in the analysis. As previously stated, practice theories may be useful in the homiletics field as they draw

---

gatekeepers who provided names of active members who might be suitable participants. Each person was contacted individually, and 2–3 persons were selected for participation. The project has been approved by the Swedish Ethical Review Authority (SERA). Dnr. 2020-06823, approved 2021-02-16.

[21] Throughout the article, the groups are referred to as groups, the letter "S" (for Church of Sweden) or "F" (for Free churches), and a number.

[22] In Sweden, these protestant churches are often referred to – and self-identify – as "Free churches", where free" signal an emphasis on freedom in structure, leadership, and liturgical forms, as opposed to the structures in CoS. For a discussion of the concept "Free churches", see Joel Halldorf and Fredrik Wenell, *Between the State and the Eucharist: Free Church Theology in Conversation with William T. Cavanaugh* (Eugene, Oregon: Pickwick Publications, 2014), 6.

[23] Pleizier, Theo, *Religious Involvement in Hearing Sermons* (Delft: Eburon Academic Publishers, 2010)165.

[24] Ibid., 165.

attention to how materiality plays an essential role in the complex process of inter-pretation and communication of the preaching event.[25]

Practice theories are not only advocated by homileticians but are often also re-ferred to in handbooks on digital ethnography as beneficial for empirical studies. Since digital technology is embedded in human life, it tends to become invisible and therefore ignored in analysis. Practice theories draw attention to the material-ity of digitality and its implications, while at the same time enabling an approach that acknowledges but does not overemphasize the significance of media.[26] In other words, practice theories provide a productive approach to the study of the practice of listening to digitally-mediated sermons.

In the analysis put forth in this article, the practice theory of Theodore Schatzki has informed the analytical questions explored throughout. According to Schatzki, the social consist of *nexuses* of *bundles of practices*. These "bundles" con-sist of the entanglement of *human activity* and *material entities*, often as a se-quence of actions (*chain of events*) in relationship to entities grouped as *material arrangements*. Schatzki underlines the importance of not overlooking material en-tities' part in practices.[27] Accordingly, an analysis of listening practices must pay careful attention to both human activity and the material arrangements involved.

The bundles of practice are *organized* through *rules, pools of understanding*, and *teleoaffective structures*. Rules are explicit directives and instructions, often written down. Pools of understanding are a combination of practical and general understandings—for example, the practical knowledge of where to tap your finger on the mobile phone to download and launch Zoom, as well as the more general-ized knowledge that it is possible in the first place to participate in worship via Zoom.[28] Teleoaffective structures are an important concept in Schatzki's thinking. According to Schatzki, human activity is teleological, that is, directed toward an

---

[25] Rystad, "I Wish We Could Fast Forward it", 18–42; Marlene Ringgaard Lorensen, *Dialog-ical Preaching: Bakhtin, Otherness and Homiletics* (Göttingen: Vanderhoeck & Ruprecht, 2014), 21–40; Tone Stangeland Kaufman and H.O. Mosdøl, "More than Words: A Multimodal and Socio-material Approach to Understanding the Preaching Event", in *Preaching Promises within the Paradoxes of Life*, eds. Johan Cilliers and Len Hansen (Stellenbosch: African Sun Media, 2018), 123–132; Linn Sæbø Rystad, *Overestimated and underestimated: A Case Study of the prac-tice of Preaching for Children with an Emphasis on Children's Role as Listeners*, PhD Thesis (Oslo: MF Norwegian School of Theology, 2020); Tone Stangeland Kaufman (ed.), *Forkynnelse for barn og voksne* (Oslo: Prismet bok, 2021).

[26] Pink et al., *Digital Ethnography*, 41–58.

[27] Theodore Schatzki, *Social Change in a Material World* (London & New York: Routledge, 2019) 26-27.

[28] Schatzki, Social Change in a Material World, 30–32.

end. People act for desired *ways of being* or the expectation of a particular *state of affairs*.[29] This means that an analysis of listening practices needs to attend to the organization of the practices, particularly the question of which *ends* the listeners are involved in when they engage in the practice.

Social changes occur when: a) humans engage in *chains of activity*; and/or b) through *material events and processes*. Schatzki underlines that human activity always is the principal generator of social change. A classic example is technological innovation, which comes about foremost through human activity.[30] However, while material entities are intertwined with human activity, they may also sometimes engage in their own events and processes without the involvement of humans, which can also lead to social change. Schatzki's example from his 2019 book seems prophetic in retrospect: a biological infection. Finally, due to the entanglement of human activity and material entities, it is often difficult to decide which factors ultimately brought about the change.[31] Following Schatzki, therefore, any analysis of the practice of listening to digitally-mediated sermons must pay attention to changes in all of the above: chains of activity, material events and processes, and their organization.

With practice theory as a framework, the research questions guiding the analysis in this study are: How do the listeners describe their listening practices? What kind of activities and material arrangements make up that practice? To what ends are they engaging in the practice? Do the listeners describe changes to their listening practices, and if so, what kind of changes? And how might the results be understood in dialogue with recent homiletical research on the practice of listening to sermons? The findings will be discussed through the prism of a final research question: How can the results of this study be informed by recent studies on listening practices?

Results

[Interviewer]: It is Sunday; it is time for a digitally-mediated worship service. What do you do?

[Interviewee 1]: I usually broadcast from the phone to the TV. Often it is just the children and me. And earlier in this period we lit some candles and things like that. I think we have stopped doing that lately, and perhaps we have become less motivated to

---

[29] Theodore Schatzki, The Timespace of Human Activity: On Performance, Society, and History as Indeterminate Teleological Events (Plymouth: Lexington Books, 2010), 111–115.

[30] Schatzki, Social Change in a Material World, 78–104.

[31] Ibid. 106.

participate as time passed. A little less focus and things like that. But otherwise, it has been on the TV, and the hymnbook on the table, and some crafts for my youngest daughter, and my eldest has her own Bible and takes notes. [laughs] Well, the children usually come directly from the bed, and sometimes we eat breakfast at the same time [as the service].

[Interviewer]: What do *you* do?

[Interviewee 2]: Well, I want to participate, so I sit down. I only use my phone, so I sit in a place where I can put it down and still hear and see well. Because now it is worship, and I want to participate, of course the hymnbook is out, and in the beginning, I lit candles too. I even stood up for the creed. But lately—neither candles nor standing. But no crafts or things like that because it is worship, and I want to participate.

[Interviewee 1]: It has become a standing joke in our house when the pastor says *"Please be seated,"* we are already seated! [laughs] And every time it happens, someone says *"Thank you,"* and then we laugh at it. It is not entirely as it used to be.

There are several important things expressed in this quote from group F8. First, the listeners uphold their usual practices for a Sunday morning: attend a worship service. Second, to uphold this practice, they not only engage in their regular activities; they also use material entities and arrangements that they are used to from the local church (candles, hymnbooks, Bibles), or they try to replicate the material arrangements of the church space. Third, they express a clear desired way of being, or state of affairs, with the practice: participation in the worship service. Fourth, they mention new material arrangements. These are primarily digital technologies, but because of the nature of digital mediation, other new material arrangements may be introduced into the practice, like the couch or the breakfast table. These material arrangements vary, depending on the kind of technology the listeners use. And fifth, the practices gradually change in relation to these new material arrangements. Practices like standing up no longer make sense. Instead, they begin to engage in new practices, such as eating breakfast together while listening. These themes run through the fourteen group interviews and will structure the presentation of the results.

Upholding Familiar Listening Practices Through Activities

The practice of attending a worship service and listening to a sermon was considered necessary to the listeners in this study. They were accustomed to doing both and frequently mentioned the importance of upholding these vital routines and habits. Most felt that upholding these practices was best done through digitally-mediated worship services. For example, the listeners in group S1 reported that they had been offered printed orders for home worship on their own but never used them. When asked why they said it was "the power of habit." The digitally-mediated worship felt closer to what they were used to.

Upholding these familiar practices was done in several ways. Listeners commonly mentioned worshipping "at the proper time" on Sunday morning. Although digital mediation often permitted them to listen whenever they wanted, quite a few agreed that gathering at the same time was important. So was the service's order. Listeners expressed a preference for the order typically followed by their local church. Notably, several of the Free Church listeners also expressed this same preference. Typically, they would claim as group F1: "it is important to keep the things we can have the same way as before for everyone to feel at home."

Upholding Familiar Listening Practices through Material Arrangements

When the listeners were asked about their practices, it was striking how frequently material arrangements were mentioned—for example, in their choice of preacher. When asked which preachers they chose to listen to—especially in light of having digital access to all the preachers in the world, more or less—the listeners almost always stated that they preferred listening to their own preacher from their own local church. When asked why, they frequently mentioned the preacher as being part and parcel of a combination of material arrangements that they were used to interacting with. Often, when asked why they chose a particular preacher, listeners answered by talking about their community and church instead. Like the listeners in focus group S8:

> [Interviewee 2]: I have mostly stuck with the community I belong to. That sense of belonging has been important and is important, so it is my choice to listen to the [local service I am used to]. I have listened to other broadcasts too. But to me, it is important to belong to a community.

> [Interviewee 1]: I would probably have done [the same] if the community I belong to had broadcasted [from the church we typically attended]. I would have followed that [broadcast], especially for the sake of the children. I am more flexible myself. But to them, at least for my youngest, it is important to recognize the church. To know that I have been there for real many times, to feel at home.

The quotes above show that the preacher is associated with the community and the church. These things are important to listeners, especially for the listener whose congregation chose to broadcast from only one of the church locations in the denomination, and not from the location the listener typically attended before the pandemic. Earlier in the interview, the listener talked about disappointment and "homelessness." This is a recurring theme in many of the interviews: they choose preachers from their own congregation since they considered that community "family" and "home." Even if their preacher wasn't the "best", they nevertheless felt committed to their community and church. These quotes also show another recurring theme: while some listeners do listen to other preachers, they tend to do it afterward, once their own local digitally-mediated service has concluded.

Notably, one group of listeners also mentioned that they listened to their own preacher because it was the most convenient option. This group consisted of older CoS listeners who found digital technology difficult to navigate. It was more convenient since they knew where to find the link on the community home page, and sometimes even got reminders on their smartphones ("[name of the congregation] has started a live stream. Do you want to join?").

As mentioned earlier, continuing to uphold the practices listeners were used to was sometimes also related to the church building. Listeners mentioned two reasons for this. First, the church building itself was tied to the experience of community. They not only wanted to recognize the people; they wanted to recognize the church too. Second, recognizing the church made falling into the routine of proper practices easier.

Several listeners mentioned that they now realized how important the local church space had been for their ability to listen and participate. It helped them to focus. Furthermore, listeners realized that the material space of the local church also contributed to their meaning-making. Like this listener in group S4:

> I like being able to sit and watch the altarpiece, the cross, the paintings—to sink into them. [...] If my mind strays away, I can watch the altarpiece and Jesus who kneels there, and the focus is [on] something else [than it is at home]. The *words* might be the same, but their experience and strength are stronger in the church space.

This aspect was also mentioned by Free church listeners, who usually have fewer embellishments in their churches. The significance of the church building points to the role that material arrangements play in upholding practices. When listeners did not have access to the material arrangement of their church buildings, they made other material arrangements that were in accordance with what they would normally see and use in a worship service in their local church. They lit candles and put out icons, brought out Bibles and pillows for kneeling (Free church listeners) and hymnbooks (CoS listeners), and in general tried to arrange a space in their home that resembled the conditions found in their local church. Both CoS and the Free church listeners also commonly mentioned changing into Sunday clothes.

Upholding the Familiar Ends of the Listening Practices?

Throughout the interviews, it became clear that listeners engaged in activities related to material arrangements that they were familiar with in order to uphold the familiar ends. Notably, many of them stated that they succeeded. They reached the expected and desired ends of the practice, often expressed as "reacting," "being moved," "getting nourishment," and "being transformed." If this happened, the sermon had "worked."

The fact that preaching "worked" is particularly interesting, since the interviews are replete with statements that digital mediation had caused a massive change. Some interviewees even cried at the thought of what had been lost: a sense of community that came from the constitutive elements of gathering, communal singing, holy communion, the imposition of hands during prayer, and so on. But there were no significant changes regarding the element of preaching. Preaching was the one thing that "worked"—or, at least, listening did. Several Free church interviewees were lay preachers and had experienced preaching "from both ends." While they thought digital mediation led to significant differences in the practice of *delivering* a sermon, they felt the practice of listening to a sermon remained substantially the same.

Notably, when asked why preaching "works," the most common answer was that preaching is—mostly, but not entirely—a one-way communication. But there were some minor differences, and these differences often affected the listeners' ability to uphold the ends they desired. When asked to describe the difference, they typically mentioned three things. First, the presence of other listeners in the room was thought to create a unique atmosphere that impacted their meaning-making. A listener from Group F5 stated: "I think it is different to be in the local church then because you can hear others react even if you do not react yourself." Words were experienced as "stronger" when they saw that others were moved by them too. Listeners mentioned this from both CoS and Free church denominations.

However, there were some differences that seemed to be specific to particular denominations. CoS listeners typically mentioned that they could not be seen by the preacher and/or other congregants. One listener in focus group S5 elaborated on this by stating that if the preacher only sought eye contact with the people in the church and not with the listeners behind the camera, this listener could not "see—feel—that it is given to *me.*"

Like the listeners in focus group F3, listeners from Free churches sometimes debated where there was a difference. When asked if there was a difference when it came to preaching, they stated:

> [Interviewee 1]: No, I do not think so. Because—well, how do I say this [laughs]—it might be for better or worse, but I mean—in reality, the sermon is one-way communication, at least in our church. Not like a conversation in a cell group when you can twist and turn different angles, like in a Bible study. But it is one person who is preaching, and the others sit quietly, no matter if it is digital or not. That is why I do not think that there is a difference.

> [Interviewee 2]: No, I disagree. The difference is smaller, but I would not say it is insignificant. [...] And that is probably connected to the singing, because the element of worship songs that comes afterward is often a moment when you reflect on the sermon and respond in singing or prayer. [...] God is speaking something in the sermon, and I get to respond afterward. But I have not done that in the same way during this period. [...] It becomes slightly more like just a transfer of information.

While the first listener described the sermon as "one-way communication" and saw no differences between digitally-mediated sermons and local preaching, the second thought that *singing* is connected to the preaching event in a special way, as the moment when the listener *responds* to the sermon. The second listener also mentioned "transfer of information" as an undesired end.

The listeners in this study were generally clear on what they thought were the wrong ends of the listening practice. Several of the listeners mentioned watching TV to explain the difference. The purpose of watching TV is to be entertained, which is not the purpose of listening to a sermon. Furthermore, when watching TV, you are a mere spectator. When you listen to a sermon, you are expected to engage on a deeper level, not as a distant onlooker. Some of the listeners found this difficult and stated that they had to consciously decide to listen to a sermon to not slip into the role of a spectator simply looking for entertainment.

The listeners mentioned two things that increased the risk of becoming a spectator. The first was to worship alone. As group F3 puts it: "You easily become a mere spectator when you sit by a screen [...] if you are alone in front of the TV, I think it becomes more difficult." The second reason relates to the medium's degree of interactivity and the platform used in the digitally-mediated service. The listeners who had experiences with both broadcasted and interactive digital platforms stated that the latter makes you less of a spectator. As group S6 stated:

> It works if you run it on Discord, Zoom, Teams, or something like that. But just sitting there and watching on YouTube, it feels like—well, when you do a service, you usually have a congregation. Everyone participates, and we answer and things like that. But if you watch YouTube or something, you become an audience.

Simply put, according to group S6, it is easier to achieve the ends of the practice of listening to a sermon if you are not entirely alone, and if the sermon is mediated from a digital platform that allows for interaction. However, the listener's mindset was also crucial to ensuring that the listening practices were not performed to the wrong ends. As group S5 noted:

> There is a risk that it becomes a performance at home because it is up to *you* what you make of it if you can shut out everything else and make it your own. And if you can, it can be wonderful. But it can also become like any other TV show: something that you watch. It is up to you when you sit there in front of your screen.

Here, the listener thinks that the practice of listening can be performed to different ends—and that it is up to the listener to make sure that they engage with the right approach and mindset.

Upholding Familiar Practices in Relation to New Material Arrangements

As previously mentioned, the differences the listeners experienced also related to a change in material arrangements. Some arrangements (like the church building) were lost, some were reproduced (like candles and hymnbooks), and some were entirely new. In digitally-mediated preaching events, digital technology and media, unsurprisingly, play a prominent role.

The interviews made it apparent that there were various kinds of digital material arrangements, including multiple ways a worship service and sermon might be mediated. The listeners engaged with different hardware and software, using them differently in their various contexts. There was a fascinating interplay between the choice of technology and the social conditions of the listener.

The listeners' descriptions of their practices showed a clear pattern. Generally, if there were more than one listener at the location (often a family), they would broadcast the service on the TV screen in front of the couch in the living room. If the listener were in a single household, they would usually be seated comfortably (for example, in an armchair), using an iPad or a smartphone. Sometimes the listener already had a designated place for prayer in their home, where they would also sit for services. In cases where the listener was part of a larger household in which they were the only Christian, they would sit in their bedrooms with the door closed, using a laptop or a smartphone. As indicated above, listeners who were alone found it more difficult to engage in the practice of listening. Furthermore, the ones who were the only Christians in their family described how the new material arrangements made it impossible to perform the practice to the desired degree. This listener from group S4 describes their difficulty:

> I have been sitting with my laptop in my bed or on the couch [...] and decided to watch this, but it is futile. [...] Or, it is possible, but it is—you try to replicate something irreplaceable, and it always ends with me feeling disappointed and lonely.

Here, new material arrangements caused listening practices to break down. Notably, for one of the listeners in group S6, the breakdown led to the invention of *new practices*. They went out into the garden to pray and listen to music—using songs that functioned as sermons or messages to the listener. Interestingly, since the songs were played on Spotify, the listener still used the same material arrangements as they had before in the digitally-mediated service (a smartphone and headphones). But in the new practices described above they were now being used differently, resulting in the listener reaching the desired end: "I realized this is wonderful. I had found something of the thing that disappeared."

There is an interesting denominational difference in the setup of material arrangements. The Free church listeners mostly belonged to the category of those who worshipped on the couch in front of the TV with the family. There were, of course, exceptions, as in the case of listeners who used Zoom. Because many of those using Zoom felt they needed access to a camera or webcam to share their own video, they used their laptops. The CoS listeners often belonged to the category of listeners who worshipped alone.

The new digital material arrangements did not only impact and reflect the social life of the listeners, they also led to entirely new material arrangements. Most commonly mentioned were the couch and the kitchen table. Notably, several of the listeners reported that they moved from the couch to the kitchen table over time. A few of the listeners who worshipped alone also reported moving to the kitchen or dining table over time. The reason for this transition is a new practice: drinking and eating. In the next section, I will return to these practice changes and explore their relation to the new material arrangements.

Many of the listeners also mentioned how material arrangements that relate to everyday life became included in the practice. Since the listeners were "worshipping amid the chaos of life," as one of them put it, everyday material arrangements such as laundry, plants that need watering, visitors, and the sound of the microwave were all drawn into the listening practice. These were often described as distracting, and contrasted with the features of the local church building. Typically it was these everyday material arrangements that prompted the listeners' insights into how important the church building had been to their listening practices.

New Material Arrangements in Relation to Changes to Listening Practice

As indicated in the previous section, new material arrangements sometimes led to changes in listening practices. One of the new practices relates to the kitchen table. Several listeners stated that, as time passed, they started having coffee, tea, or breakfast during worship services. Listeners in group F4 said:

> In the beginning, we had breakfast before [the service], but after a while, [...] we had "fika." We always set the table. I think we did it partly for our teenagers' sake. It became something extra to sit and eat together in front of the TV; it became a thing that we thought was positive. It is a little different from what you usually do, but it was a way to gather.

This group's quote represents the listeners' positive view of this new practice. This kitchen table-focused practice was seen as connected to the practice of gathering that they were used to from church. Some listeners also made parallels to the practice of having a cup of coffee after the service and stated that the two "rituals"— the worship service and the gathering afterward—had blended into each other. In this quote, the listener also describes how the practice of having breakfast facilitated the participation of teenagers. Other parents of teenagers reported the same phenomenon. Young people, usually characterized as reluctant to go to church, participated more willingly from the kitchen table.

As mentioned earlier, parents of younger children thought that digitally-mediated worship facilitated participation for them too. The children could behave like children—make noises, play, or even throw tantrums—and see the service elements better than they usually would have when seated in the children's corner in the back of the church. However, parents of smaller children whose community offered Sunday school for children were not as keen. They felt that their children missed out on something: learning the practices of the Christian faith.

Another change due to the new material arrangements was the ability to participate on occasions when the listeners would not have been able to otherwise. Two of the listeners described how their chronic pain sometimes made them unable to attend church. One of them cried with joy as they spoke about how they could now access God's comforting word in their suffering. Other listeners described how they were now able to listen afterward to the service on occasions when they would otherwise have missed out entirely. In these cases, it was primarily the sermon they were interested in.

A third change was that the listeners started to listen to more sermons—in addition to the sermon they had already heard. They found it enriching to hear different interpretations of the same biblical text. When asked who these preachers were, several mentioned preachers from congregations with whom they had some other previous relationship. They also chose "famous and skilled" preachers in notable ecclesial leadership positions. Notably, there seemed to be pronounced ecumenical crossover, as denominational borders were frequently breached. One listener was critical of this new practice and wondered if it might not be performed to the right end. Did listening to different sermons and preachers really "make you transform your life," or was it just entertainment?

Interestingly, the listeners that listened to more than one sermon from different sources sometimes reported that they engaged somewhat differently in the practice of listening while doing so. They did not try to copy the practices of the local church at all. Instead, they would listen while engaging in activities that included everyday material arrangements like cleaning, driving, walking, and cooking. They did not think these arrangements disrupted the listening practices in these cases. Instead, they helped facilitate the experience, just as with the practice of eating breakfast and drinking coffee.

Listening to other preachers could be a conscious choice, but it is noteworthy that some listeners reported they sometimes "got stuck" watching YouTube and engaged with new sermons somewhat by happenstance. After the particular service they had decided to watch was finished, they sometimes received further suggestions from the platform's algorithm: "If you liked this video, perhaps you would like to watch another one like this?"—and then a new worship service would start rolling.

Discussion

In this section, I will discuss the findings in light of recent homiletical research on listening practices that I presented at the beginning of the article. This research offers several frameworks for understanding the results and suggests an orientation for research on listeners in a digital culture.

To the listeners in this study, it was essential to uphold the practices of participation in worship and listening to sermons. They upheld these practices through the same activities they were used to from local church services, including gathering at a particular time, following liturgical practices, and using familiar material arrangements such as candles and hymnbooks. They also chose their regular preacher, community, and church building. The listeners could also reach the desired and expected ends of their listening practices: they found that preaching "works" in the digitally-mediated preaching event.

The fact that generally preaching "worked" but nevertheless broke down for some, and that many listeners perceived differences between local services and digitally-mediated services, might be helpfully understood through Theo Pleizier's model of listening religiously to a sermon. Based on his own interviews with listeners, Pleizier describes three listening stages necessary for a sermon to "work": opening up, dwelling in the sermon, and actualizing faith. To Pleizier, the word "dwelling" is essential since his listeners describe their interaction with the sermon as a spatial experience in which they become part of a religious world performed by the preacher in the preaching event. In other words, the sermon is a space in which they can perceive.[32]

According to Pleizier, there is a communal dimension to all three stages of the practice of listening. The presence of the community plays a part in the opening stage when the listeners prepare for listening through liturgy and being in the community; as well as in the dwelling stage, when they sometimes dwell in the sermon on behalf of others; and also finally in the final stage, when faith is actualized in remembrance.[33] As I have shown, the differences the listeners experienced all pertain to this communal dimension. They missed the church building, the preacher's gaze, and the community's reactions. Furthermore, the listening practices tended to break down the most when the listener was alone. A general principle thus emerges: when the communal dimension is weakened, the practices become more fragile and prone to interruption. When the communal aspect is enhanced through actions and arrangements that facilitate greater connection, such as interactive digital platforms, listening together with others, and the entangled triad of their usual preachers, churches, and communities, the practice of listening is easier to uphold.

This study has also pointed to the importance of knowing the ends of listening practices. "It is up to you when you sit there in front of your screen"—that is, the listener must listen with the proper purpose or risk becoming a distanced spectator. These descriptions of the importance of intentionality, of knowing the ends, alongside the fact that listeners reported being able to uphold their listening practices even in a digitally-mediated preaching event, support Gaarden and Marlene Ringgaard Lorensen's claim that listeners can be understood as authors of the sermon, as they interact with the preacher's words to create meaning.[34] Listening to

---

[32] Pleizier, Religious Involvement in Hearing Sermons, 188.

[33] Ibid., 278.

[34] Gaarden & Lorensen, "Listeners as Authors in Preaching: Empirical and Theoretical Perspectives", 28–45.

listeners in a digital culture underlines their insight: listeners are indeed authors of the sermon.

However, the importance of knowing the ends of the practice raises the question: what about people who have not yet learned the *telos* of these listening practices? What about the children mentioned in this study whose parents voiced concern that they might not learn the practices of the Christian faith in a digitally-mediated environment? Linn Sæbø Rystad's study of children's listening practices confirms that these fears may have some basis. Rystad found that children did not always know that the ends of listening were *transformation*, and included the application of what had been said to their own lives. Instead, they connected the activity to an end they were familiar with from school: taking in information. Rystad points to the importance of teaching listeners the practice of listening, including the intended ends.[35] While Rystad agrees with Pleizier that preaching is a social activity involving preachers and listeners, he believes Pleizier is wrong to assume that both of them share an understanding of preaching as a religious event. Her study shows this is not necessarily the case.[36]

However, as Marianne Gaarden has demonstrated in her empirical study, listeners still interact with the sermon even if they do not listen religiously. Like Pleizier, she uses spatial categories to describe what happens when a sermon works: a "third room of preaching" is erected, and meaning-making occurs in the interaction between the preachers' outer words and the listener's inner experience.[37] According to Ilona Nord, there is reason to believe that this spatial feature of the sermon is enhanced by digital mediation. In a discussion on "the virtual dimension of homiletics," Nord makes the case that the experience of living in a digital culture and inhabiting virtual worlds that are entangled with the real world might facilitate this creative function of the sermon. Drawing on Albrecht Grözinger's idea that the sermon's task is to "imagine mankind into God's horizon of possibility," Nord argues that preachers ought to make use of digital mediation to invite listeners to a life that is centered on God's possibilities, and make the sermon a "creative space" where they might imagine these possibilities.[38]

---

[35] Linn Sæbø Rystad, Overestimated and underestimated, 89–90.

[36] Ibid., 88. Gaarden also raises this issue in the Danish version of *The Third Room of Preaching*. Marianne Gaarden, *Prædikenen som det tredje rum*, Köpenhamn: Anis, 2015.

[37] Gaarden, The Third Room of Preaching, 55–106.

[38] Ilona Nord, "Experiment with Freedom Every Day: Regarding the Virtual Dimension of Homiletics", *Homiletic* 36, no 2 (2011), 31–37.

All these points suggest a need for future research into the practices of listeners who are not regular ("religious") church-goers but who listen to digitally-mediated sermons. A digitally-mediated sermon is, in a sense, even more public than a sermon held in a local church due to the nature of digital media. The possibility exists to reach listeners who have never heard a sermon before. Because of this, digitally-mediated sermons are sometimes thought to have a missional potential. But will the sermons fill a missional purpose if the listeners do not know to what ends they are listening? Or will they—as Gaarden and Nord suggest—still know what to do, since they have already been taught by previous experiences of digital spaces to "imagine God's possibilities"?

As I have shown, listeners' statements about the ends of listening also included strong opinions on what they thought were the wrong ends: being a spectator and being entertained. The question arises: why are these ends unacceptable?

I would argue that a contributing reason for the negative view of being a spectator stems from the ideals of interaction and participation that permeate both digital culture and Swedish protestant churches.[39] As for the negative view of entertainment, Katrin Kusmierz offers a clue in her discussion on digitally-mediated preaching during the COVID-19 pandemic. According to Kusmierz, the fear of entertainment stems from a (Reformed/Protestant) ideal that content is the thing that matters most and that preachers should avoid anything that might distract from that.[40]

Kusmierz identifies a recurring theme in debates on online preaching: the fear that preachers will succumb to the shorter form, hyperactive style of new media to attract listeners, and in the process become "just entertainment." By taking on a listener's perspective, Kusmierz problematizes this idea. Drawing on Albrecht Grözinger and Harald Schroter-Wittke, she asks whether it might not in fact be a good thing if preaching was entertainment. Of course, entertainment can be a shallow, brutal, and mere distraction, but it can also be nutritive, offer sustenance, facilitate conversations between equals, and is often delectable. In her argument, Kusmierz identifies a paradox: when the content is the sole focus, the face-to-face sermon-from-the-pulpit often, and perhaps paradoxically, creates distance. On the

---

[39] Mannerfelt, Frida and & Roitto, Rikard, "Mellan rit och reklam del 2: Interaktion, synkronicitet och integritet i digitalt förmedlade förinspelade andakter", in *Kyrka i digitala rum: Ett aktionsforskningsprojekt om församlingsliv online i Svenska kyrkan*, ed. Sara Garpe and Jonas Ideström (Uppsala: enheten för forskning och analys, 2022), 71–73; Mannerfelt, "Old and New Habits", 110–112.

[40] Katrin Kusmiertz, "Predigt als Unterhaltung 2.0", https://www.liturgik.unibe.ch/ueber_uns/liturgie_in_virtuellen_raeumen/index_ger.html [accessed 221219]

other hand, online preaching creates intimacy and closeness that the onsite counterpart often lacks by means of a shorter format and more direct style of speech.[41] Kusmiertz's argument points to how further inquiry into digitally-mediated listening practices could contribute to a discussion on homiletical ideals and paradigms.

As I have shown, materiality is an important part of the practice of listening to digitally-mediated sermons (or any sermon). They contribute to upholding familiar practices, and changes in material arrangements can lead to obstructed or even disrupted listening practices. Listeners themselves acknowledged the importance of material arrangements, including the church building. As I have shown in this study, material arrangements may also contribute to the creation of new practices. The material arrangements of digital technology, for example, allow listeners to listen to more sermons than they would otherwise be able to. In addition, digital mediation leads to the involvement of new material arrangements, for example, the kitchen table. In short: the "third room of preaching" clearly comes into being in relation to material arrangements, not just human activity. The involvement of material arrangements, both in the local and digital settings, would be an interesting field for further investigation—including a phenomenon that the listeners in this study only hinted at: how algorithms affect listening practices.

Finally, this study has shown how digital technology led to the involvement of further new material arrangements: arrangements of everyday life. Depending on which activities listeners engaged in, these everyday arrangements could be experienced as both a distraction and a facilitator. When listeners tried to copy their usual listening practices from church, the new material arrangements were seen as a distraction. But when listeners let go of their notion of "proper" listening practices and incorporated the everyday material arrangements into their experience, listening was facilitated. In light of these findings, I would argue for the need to rethink practices. While it may seem possible to copy-paste the sermon listening practices from the local church setting (such as sitting quietly in a pew) and still reach the same ends, perhaps there are ways to reach these ends by better cooperation with the new material arrangements in which digitally-mediated sermon listeners find themselves. The example of eating and drinking shows how fruitful that approach can be.

---

[41] Ibid.

Summary

This study aimed to examine the practice of listening to digitally-mediated sermons and, since it has rarely been done before, suggest some areas in which this research might be developed. The source material under consideration was 14 group interviews with 29 listeners from Protestant congregations in the south of Sweden, conducted in the spring of 2021, which was one year into the COVID-19 pandemic and the subsequent digital transition of the churches these listeners attended.

The interviews were analyzed with questions inspired by Theodore Schatzki's practice theory in relation to the elements that practices consist of—activities, material arrangements, and ends—as well as any changes to these elements.

I found that the listeners could reach the desired ends of the practice of sermon listening since the digitally-mediated practices were "mostly the same." However, there were slight differences due to changes in material arrangements that impacted the communal aspect of the listening practice. To most listeners, the differences interfered with their listening practices and put them at risk of engaging in the practice to the wrong ends: entertainment and spectatorship. For some, the differences even led to a breakdown of listening practices. However, new material arrangements could also lead to new listening practices. These new practices related both to the material arrangements of digital technology, but also to everyday material arrangements such as the kitchen table, which inspired the listeners to include eating and drinking as part of their listening practices.

Finally, I discussed the results in light of recent homiletical research on the practice of listening to sermons and argued that: a) material arrangements play a pivotal part in listening practices; b) the listening practices may be affected positively by the spatial experiences of digital mediation; c) the differences that obstructed and disrupted the listening practice were due to changes in material arrangements that affected the communal aspect of listening; d) the importance of knowing the ends of the listening practice raises questions about listeners who might not know the proper ends, and points to the importance of learning them— challenging homiletical ideals about the ends of listening; and e) the need to rethink listening practices in relation to new material arrangement, instead of simply trying to copy the listening practices adopted from the material arrangements in the church building.

Literature

Allen, Ronald J. and Mary Alice Mulligan. "Listening to listeners: five years later." *Homiletic* 34, no 2 (2009): 4–17.

Berger, Teresa. *@Worship: Liturgical Practices in Digital Worlds*. London/New York: Routledge, 2018.

Campbell, Heidi A. and Tsuria, Ruth, "Introduction to the Study of Digital Religion," in *Digital Religion: Understanding Religion in a Digital Age* (2nd edition), edited by Heidi Campbell and Ruth Tsuria, 1–22. London/New York: Routledge, 2021.

Dyer, John. "Exploring Mediated *Ekklesia*: How We Talk about Church in the Digital Age" in *Ecclesiology for a Digital Church: Theological Reflections on a New Normal*, edited by Heidi Campbell and John Dyer, 3–16. London: SCM Press, 2022.

Gaarden, Marianne. *Prædikenen som det tredje rum*. Köpenhamn: Anis, 2015.

Gaarden, Marianne. *Third Room of Preaching: A New Empirical Approach*. Eugene, Oregon: Pickwick Publications, 2021.

Gaarden, Marianne & Lorensen Ringgaard, Marlene. "Listeners as Authors in Preaching: Empirical and Theoretical Perspectives." *Homiletic* 38, no 2 (2013): 28–45.

Halldorf, Joel and Wenell, Fredrik. *Between the State and the Eucharist: Free Church Theology in Conversation with William T. Cavanaugh*. Eugene, Oregon: Pickwick Publications, 2014.

Hine, Christine. *Ethnography for the Internet: Embedded, Embodied and Everyday*. London & New York: Bloomsbury Academic, 2015.

Hudgins, Tripp. "Preaching Online," *Anglican Theological Review* 101, no 1 (2019): 79–88.

Knowles, Michael P. "E-Word? McLuhan, Baudrillard, and Verisimilitude in Preaching." *Religions* 13, no 12 (2022): 1–16.

Kurlberg, Jonas and Chow, Alexander. "Two or Three Gathered Online: Asian and European Responses to COVID-19 and the Digital Church", *Studies in World Christianity* 26, no 3 (2020): 299–318.

Kusmiertz, Katrin, "Predigt als Unterhaltung 2.0", https://www.liturgik.unibe.ch/ueber_uns/liturgie_in_virtuellen_raeumen/index_ger.html [accessed 221219]

Lienau, Anna-Katharina. "Kommunikation des Evangeliums in social media." *ZThK* (2019) 117: 489–522.

Lorensen, Marlene Ringgaard. *Dialogical Preaching: Bakhtin, Otherness and Homiletics*. Göttingen: Vanderhoeck & Ruprecht, 2014.

Lorensen, Marlene Ringgaard and Buch-Hansen, Gitte. "Listening to the voices: refugees as co-authors of practical theology." *Practical Theology* 11 (2018): 29–41.

Mannerfelt, Frida. "Old and New Habits The Transition to Digitally-Mediated Worship in Four Swedish Free Church Denominations during COVID-19" in *Svensk frikyrklighet i pandemin: En studie av församlingen i corona och corona i församlingen*, edited by Ulrik Josefsson and Magnus Wahlström, 90–119. Research report from the Institute of Pentecostal Studies No. 9, 2022.

Mannerfelt, Frida and Roitto, Rikard. "Mellan rit och reklam del 2: Interaktion, synkronicitet och integritet i digitalt förmedlade förinspelade andakter" in *Kyrka i digitala rum: Ett aktionsforskningsprojekt om församlingsliv online i Svenska kyrkan*, edited by Sara Garpe and Jonas Ideström, 61–79. Uppsala: enheten för forskning och analys, 2022.

McClure, John S., Ronald J. Allen, Dale P. Andrews, L. Susan Bond, Dan P. Mosely, and G. Lee Ramsey. *Listening to Listeners: Homiletical Case Studies*. St. Louis: Chalice Press, 2004.

Pink, Sarah, Heather Horst, John Postill, Larissa Hjorth, Tania Lewis, and Jo Tacchi. *Digital Ethnography: Principles and Practices*. Thousand Oaks: Sage, 2016.

Nord, Ilona. "Experiment with Freedom Every Day: Regarding the Virtual Dimension of Homiletics." *Homiletic* 36, no 2 (2011): 31–37.

Pleizier, Theo. *Religious Involvement in Hearing Sermons: A Grounded Theory Study in Empirical Theology and Homiletics*. Delft: Ebmon Academic Publishers, 2010.

Rietveld, David, "A Survey of the Phenomenological Research of Listening to Preaching." *Homiletic* 38, no. 2 (2013): 30-47.

Rystad, Linn Sæbø, "I Wish We Could Fast Forward it – Negotiating the Practice of Preaching." *Homiletic* 44, no 2 (2019): 18–42.

Rystad, Linn Sæbø. *Overestimated and underestimated: A Case Study of the practice of Preaching for Children with an Emphasis on Children's Role as Listeners*, Ph.D. Thesis. Oslo: MF Norwegian School of Theology, 2020.

Rystad, Linn Sæbø, "Preaching at the thresholds – Bakhtinian polyphony in preaching for Children", in *Practice, Practice Theory and Theology: Scandinavian and German Perspectives*, edited by Kristine Helboe Johansen and Ulla Schmidt, 165–184. Berlin/Boston: De Gruyter, 2022.

Schatzki, Theodore. *The Timespace of Human Activity: On Performance, Society, and History as Indeterminate Teleological Events*. Plymouth: Lexington Books, 2010.

Schatzki, Theodore. *Social Change in a Material World*. London & New York: Routledge, 2019.

Stangeland Kaufman, Tone and Mosdøl, H.O. "More than Words: A Multimodal and Socio-material Approach to Understanding the Preaching Event" in *Preaching Promises within the Paradoxes of Life*, edited by Johan Cilliers and Len Hansen, 123–132. Stellenbosch: African Sun Media, 2018.

Stangeland Kaufman, Tone (ed.). *Forkynnelse for barn og voksne*. Oslo: Prismet bok, 2021.

Yang, Sunggu A. "The Word Digitalized: A Techno-Theological Reflection on Online Preaching and Its Types." *Homiletic* 46, no 1 (2020), 75–89.

Co-Preaching: The Effects of Religious Digital Creatives' Engagement in the Preaching Event

Abstract: The preaching event is a complex process of communication and interpretation. The aim of this study is to describe and discuss how the preaching event is affected when it is digitally mediated and involves so-called "religious digital creatives" (RDCs). This is achieved through a case study of the preaching event at two Church of Sweden (CoS) congregations that offered pre-recorded, digitally mediated worship services. The research questions guiding the study were: "When and how do the RDCs engage in the preaching event?" and "How can the effects of this engagement be understood in the light of homiletical theory drawing on the works of Mikhail Bakhtin?" The study found that RDCs engaged in the verbalization phase of the preaching event in several ways—including visualization, direction, editing, enhancement, and contextualization of the sermon—and thus contributed significantly to the preaching event. Furthermore, the RDCs exhibited notable relational authority—an authority based on negotiation, interdependence, and interaction. Employing homiletical theory that draws on Mikhail Bakhtin's work, I argue that the RDCs in this case study are best understood as co-preachers who contribute to expanding the polyphony of the preaching event.

Keywords: online preaching; preaching event; homiletics; social media; religious digital creatives; authority; Church of Sweden; Michail Bakhtin; digital mediation.

Original publication: Mannerfelt, Frida. 2022. Co-Preaching: The Effects of Religious Digital Creatives' Engagement in the Preaching Event. *Religions* 13: 1135. https://doi.org/10.3390/rel13121135. Published with permission. N.B. The original journal font was unfit for the dissertation template and was changed. Since this is an open access article, distributed under the terms and conditions of the license CC BY 4.0 (https://creativecommons.org/licenses/by/4.0), it is possible to do so.

1. Introduction

The preaching event is a complex thing.[1] As Wilfrid Engemann (2019, pp. 3–4) has shown, the preaching event is a process of comprehension and communication that consists of several phases of text interpretations and text introductions that involve the interaction between the authors of the Bible text, the Bible, preacher, sermon manuscript, the delivered sermon, listener, and the "auredit" (what the listener has heard), each in their specific context. Therefore, Carina Sundberg (2008, pp. 11–44, 195–99) has argued, the preaching event—as the product of very complex situated interactions between multiple actors[2] like preacher, listener, architecture, liturgy, artifacts and so on —is characterized by "polyagency".

While the preacher, word, and listener are usually the foci of attention in the preaching event, with a few notable exceptions (Kaufman and Mosdøl 2018, pp. 123–32) scant attention has been paid to materiality as an actor in the communication and meaning-making process. However, as practice theorists like Theodore Schatzki has pointed out, all social phenomena are constituted by the entanglement of human practices and material entities, such as bodies and artefacts, and material arrangements like buildings and technology (Schatzki 2019, pp. 19–22).

In her article "Preaching at the thresholds—Bakhtinian polyphony in preaching for children," Linn Sæbø Rystad (2020) argues that materiality is a dimension of preaching that must not be overlooked. She underlines that: "Focusing on materiality might highlight what preaching from a pulpit does or does not do in the communication situation, or which body it is that is preaching" (pp. 122–23). In the article, she discusses the use of "mediational means" (the biblical narrative, costumes, and objects) in preaching for children. Drawing on James Wertsch, Rystad argues that access to the world is always mediated. For this reason, a scholar should not limit her scope to what humans are doing, but must look into how humans interact with mediating materiality (pp. 45–46, 108–25).

This article will explore and analyze what happens when yet another actor is brought into the complexity of the preaching event: digital technology. According to Schatzki (2019, pp. 19–22, 36–37) human practice has become increasingly dependent on material arrangements enabled by technology, in particular digital technology. Clearly, digital devices are deeply embedded in our daily lives, including worship. In a socio-material perspective, digital technology could be said be an actor in its own right. However, this article will focus on the new human actors that digital technology brings into the preaching event. Dubbed religious digital creatives (RDCs), these are the "individuals whose digital media work and skills grant them unique status and influence within their religious communities" (Campbell 2021, pp. 4–5).

In her book *Digital Creatives and the Rethinking of Religious Authority* (2021), Heidi Campbell (2021) argues that religious authority is transformed by digital media and technology. This transformation is due not only to the transition of established religious authorities (like priests and pastors) from physical spaces into digital environments, but also to the occurrence of new actors (like technicians or social media ministers). They present religious content online and have become religious authorities in their own right. The purpose of this article is to explore and discuss what happens when RDCs engage in a preaching event. This is achieved through a case study of the preaching event in pre-recorded digitally mediated worship services in two Stockholm congregations in the Church of Sweden (CoS).

The research questions guiding this article are: (1) When and how do RDCs engage in the preaching event? (2) How can the effects of RDC engagement in the preaching event be understood? I will argue that the RDCs can be understood as "co-preachers," as they all contribute significantly to the sermon and thus to the preaching event. The effects of co-preaching will be discussed in the light of homiletical theory that focuses on the concept of polyphony.

The article is structured as follows: first, I will present the methodology, material, and the theoretical frameworks employed. In doing so, I will discuss both the concept of RDCs—what it is and how it is applied in the analysis of the article's source material—and the concept of polyphonic preaching invoked in the results discussion. Next, I will describe when and how the RDCs engage in the preaching event. Finally, I will conclude with a discussion of the results in the light of polyphonic preaching, an umbrella term for the Scandinavian line of homileticians inspired by the communication theories of Mikhail Bakhtin.

2. Methods, Materials, and Theoretical Frameworks

The case study's source material was gathered within the framework of the action research project *Church in Digital Space*.[3] As part of the project, I collaborated with the New Testament scholar and pastor Rikard Roitto to follow two congregations in the CoS Diocese of Stockholm, Järfälla and Täby, as they developed short, pre-recorded digitally mediated worship services (Mannerfelt and Roitto 2022a, 2022b).

The subject material was created from August 2021 to February 2022, well into the COVID-19 pandemic, and involves six preaching events, three for each congregation. During the period, researchers and practitioners met once a month. The researchers observed the practitioners' preparation for and recording of the worship services, made individual interviews with all practitioners involved, and gathered recordings and screenshots of publication in social media. A month later, practitioners and researchers met for focus group conversations in which the researchers presented an analysis of what they had seen and heard, and theories that could aid the understanding. The researchers also facilitated a discussion in which the practitioners responded to the analysis and reflected on their own practices. Next month, there was a new round of observations and interviews, and so on.

This article, however, uses an ethnographical case study approach to the sources instead of the highly collaborative practices of action research we initially applied.[4] In other words, the practitioners were not involved in the negotiation of research questions or the analysis and presentation of the research except for an opportunity to reflect on the validity of the RDC theory.

The source material thus consists of 6 observation protocols, transcriptions of 18 individual and 6 focus group interviews, 6 edited recordings of the services, and 18 screen shots of how the recordings were presented on the congregation's websites and social media platforms (Youtube, Facebook, and Instagram).[5] In analyzing the source material, I have drawn on Heidi Campbell's work on authority and religious digital creatives.

2.1 Religious Digital Creatives

As Campbell and Tsuria (2021, pp. 7–12) point out in the introduction to Digital Religion: Understanding Religion in a Digital Age, authority is one of the key research areas and questions in the field of digital religion. In one of her recent books, Digital Creatives and the Rethinking of Religious Authority, Campbell pursues the question of what religious authority looks like in an age of digital media. She states that the typical conclusion in scholarly studies of religious authority and new media is that, since digital culture and technology is characterized by features like freedom and a lack of hierarchy, established religious authorities are challenged. In an effort to turn the tables, Campbell (2021, pp. 1–21) asks instead what religious authority looks like and how it is established in a digital context. Her hypothesis is that internet technology and digital culture both facilitate and empower new religious actors, and their wielding of authority creates hybrid structures that over time may change their religious institutions.[6]

To examine how religious authority is structured in a digital culture, Campbell interviewed 120 individuals, all of whom had been active for at least four years and renowned for their digital work for and in Christian churches (ibid., pp. 14, 53). While these interviews took place between 2011–2016, well before the pandemic and the subsequent radical—and rapid—digital transition of churches, they provided a foundational framework for analyzing future digital mediation. Campbell's analysis of the interviews yielded three categories of actors:

1. Digital entrepreneurs, who create digital resources—platforms or content—for their communities in their free time.
2. Digital spokespersons, who are employed to manage a religious community's digital presence.
3. Digital strategists, who already have an official position (e.g., as pastors and deacons), but who use digital media to do their work more effectively.

Common to all three groups is that they possess skills and experience in digital media work—they are "digital creatives"—which gives them unique influence and status in their religious communities. Hence, they are religious digital creatives, RDCs (ibid., pp. 49–53).

The RDCs in question in this study are employed in congregations in Täby and Järfälla, two communities within the CoS's Stockholm diocese. The team in Järfälla consists of a pastor, a religious educator, two technicians (responsible for recording and editing audio and video), and a communications director (responsible for publishing content on digital platforms). The team in Täby consists of a pastor, a deacon, a musician, and a communications director (who records, edits, and publishes content).[7] In other words, the preaching events in this case study included both digital spokespersons (the communications director and tech team) and digital strategists of the online-minister type.

These particular congregations in this study were chosen for several reasons. For starters, the congregations and RDCs are in Sweden, one of the world's most digitalized societies (Digital Economy and Society Index 2022). In addition, the CoS is also one of the world's wealthiest churches, which has allowed congregations to hire employees such as dedicated A/V technicians. In Campbell and Osteen's (2021) study on how churches digitized during the COVID-19 pandemic, the digital transition was often carried out by either a single pastor (i.e., what Campbell would call "digital strategist") or a small group of volunteers ("digital entrepreneurs"). In this study, we get a glimpse of churches' digital transformation through collaboration between different groups of RDCs. Finally, the RDCs in Campbell's study were mainly focused on missional or educational activities in their digital work. The RDCs in this study are engaged in online worship services and digitally mediated preaching events.

The digital team members at both congregations in this study will be analyzed as RDCs, i.e., people wielding religious authority through their use of digital technology. The analysis will focus on describing what they do, how they understand their work in relation to the digitally mediated preaching event, and what kind of authority they perform through their words and actions.

According to Campbell (2021, pp. 18–37), RDCs use of authority may be described through four categories:

1. *Authority as role based* (as in the works of Weber)
2. *Authority as power struggle* (as in the works of Foucault)
3. *Authority as relational*—where authority is seen as negotiated and mutually beneficial, as described by for example by Mia Lövheim in her study on the authority of bloggers.
4. *Algorithmic authority*—where algorithms "tells us what voices to listen to, which topics are important and which structures to give weight to in evaluating credibility". (Campbell 2021, p. 31) Algorithmic authority comes from statistics and figures like number of followers, hits and rankings from search engines, or—in an academic setting—the number of publications.

Digital spokespersons tend to describe themselves as institutional identity curators whose task is to present and represent the identity of the community in media, particularly on digital platforms. Sometimes they relate to algorithmic authority, but more often on role-based authority, in particular what Weber called rational-legal authority. In other words, they see themselves as part of a structure with particular rules that they support. Within churches, they do their job to serve church's greater mission. However, in this service they are often caught in something of a contradiction: the same institutions that hired them to do digital media work are reluctant about the use of digital technology. When these digital strategists are called upon by the church's leadership to contribute with their expertise, the shift in power dynamic is not always welcome. Therefore, they tend to be very cautious, and emphasize that their work is not about theological interpretation but about making the message of the church accessible. (Campbell 2021, pp. 110–29, 157–62).

Digital strategists view themselves as missional media negotiators. They work in institutions that claim that they do not need digital technology, but the strategists believe the institutions can do their work more efficiently and creatively with the aid of digital media. They continuously blend online and offline ministry, and see digital platforms as an extension of their local work. In this position, they are bridge-builders who often negotiate. This means that they tend to view authority as relational, as something that is created and negotiated between different parties through communicative interaction. Or, as Campbell summarizes it, "Authority comes to the leader through creating a balanced or interdependent relationship" (Campbell 2021, pp. 133–53, 162–66).

It is worth noting that the digital strategists in this case study differ slightly from Campbell's category because they have not chosen the hybrid role themselves. That is, they were given the task to provide digitally mediated worship services during the COVID-19 pandemic, and they state that they would not have taken on this task if they could avoid it. Over time, however, they have grown into the role as bridge builders between onsite and online church. The fact that their work was sanctioned by the leadership and necessitated by the pandemic might explain why stories of "technological apologetics," the justification narratives that were such a prominent feature of Campbell's pre-pandemic RDCs, are virtually absent from the narratives of these CoS strategists.

These conditions also affect the digital spokespersons in this study. Absent are the narratives so common to digital spokespersons in Campbell's study, namely that the same leadership that hired them to do digital work is also suspicious of digital technology. Also missing are Campbell's accounts of grudges stemming from the shift in authority when the spokespeople are called upon to work as media mentors to for example pastors.

Instead, the strategists in this study express a profound gratitude and trust towards the spokespersons. For example, when asked about one of the recording sessions in which the spokesperson (communications director) clearly was in charge of what, when, and how every part of the worship service should be recorded, the strategist (pastor) said that "in that case, it is [the communications director] who does his thing, he is completely in charge. I gladly let him decide what is best". When asked about this, the communications director himself compared it to the local worship service:

> (Interviewee): "[Laughs] If I were to participate in a physical worship service, I would turn to the pastor and musician and ask: "What should I do? Is this right? In what order should this be done?" In the same way, I think they give me more responsibility because they are not at home in this area, even if they have been involved in planning the order of the worship. [...]

(Interviewer): All right. So in this church space, your "sixth church" [an expression frequently used by the team in Täby about online church as an addition to their five local churches], you are more in charge?

(Interviewee): Yes, you could say that. [Smiles] It is quite exiting that I should know more about a church space in that way.

These quotes are not just examples of how the shifting power dynamics between the usual leaders and the digital spokespersons do not seem to cause unease. They are also examples of the spokespersons' use of relational authority. In Campbell's study, her spokespersons often downplayed their autonomy and personal contribution to the messages and underlined their loyalty towards the theological message of their institutions. In other words, they favored a role-based authority. While the spokespersons in this study in some instances did relate to role-based authority, they also commonly performed and spoke about relational authority.

2.2 Polyphonic Preaching

The discussion this study's results builds on the Scandinavian homiletical discussion that draws on the theories of the Russian philosopher and literary critic Mikhail Bakhtin to describe and understand the communication going on in the preaching event. Since the concept of polyphony is central in several of these discussions, I will use the shorthand term "polyphonic preaching" to refer to them.

A landmark volume in the discussion on polyphonic preaching is Marlene Ringgaard Lorensen's *Dialogical Preaching: Bakhtin, Otherness and Homiletics* (Lorensen 2014) in which she explores how preachers expose their preaching to interactions with various 'others' of preaching, and how a Bakhtinian understanding of communication might be incorporated into homiletical theories.[8] While Lorensen herself mainly focuses on Bakhtin's theories of dialogue and carnivalization, the concept of polyphony is intrinsically related to them, and she introduces the concept to offer a theological model of communication for the homiletical strand of "Other-wise preaching" (McClure 2001).

Bakhtin developed the concept of polyphony in his work on Dostoevsky and Rabelais. According to Bakhtin, their novels are dialogical since the characters possess and interact with their own consciousness and voices. As such, the reader does not just hear the author's voice, she also hears the characters' voices and is thus drawn into her own dialogue with them, creating a polyphony. This dialogical polyphony is contrasted with a monological authorship in which the author is omniscient and has the final word on interpretation. To Lorensen (2014, pp. 66–67), "the role of the preacher in contemporary preaching practices has striking similarities to the polyphonic author-position".

In Bakhtin's thinking, communication is thus relational and collaborative. Conversation partners (local and distant) always play a constitutive part in how the speaker develops and shape his or her utterance. With the aid of Bakhtin's theories, Lorensen pleads for a collaborative preaching practice, in which preachers act as hosts who invite others into the conversation and, in the process, become guests themselves. (Lorensen 2011, pp. 26–45; 2014, pp. 66–67). She underlines the importance of the preacher not ventriloquizing different voices, arguing that "If preaching, in spite of its monological appearance, is to function as a dialogical encounter, one of the most important tasks for the preacher, from a Bakhtinian perspective, is to avoid conflating the voices of the listener, preacher, and scripture into one and instead let the polyphony of voices interact in a way that let them transform and enrich each other mutually". To Lorensen, this means that Bakhtin may provide the homiletical movement with "the beginnings of a polyphonic theology of communication" (Lorensen 2011, p. 44).

In the article "Listeners as Authors in Preaching," Gaarden and Lorensen (2013, pp. 28–45) use Bakhtinian perspectives to discuss the empirical findings in Gaarden's study of the listener's meaning-making processes. They argue for a reversed perspective in the analysis of preaching, and challenges fellow homileticians to understand listeners as primary authors of the sermon. They make this rather surprising move in relation to Bakthin's idea that meaning emerges in interaction with dialogue partners. According to Bakhtin, the addressees of an oral or written discourse always play an implicit and explicit part as co-authors, and in this sense the "listener becomes the speaker" (Gaarden and Lorensen 2013, p. 32). Instead of discussing how preachers invite listeners as co-authors in sermon preparation, they want to discuss how listeners invite preachers to be co-authors of their inner reflections during the preaching event. Lorensen elaborates further on this idea in an article written with Gitte Buch-Hansen (Lorensen and Buch-Hansen 2018, pp. 29–41). They argue that the refugees in a Danish church acted as co-authors of practical theology, since they provoked adjustments to the traditional theory of human capital. Furthermore, the refugees' understanding of the ritual challenged traditional Danish Lutheran understandings of the Eucharist and the church. It is this notion of interplay between authors/co-authors that has inspired the concept of "co-preacher" that is found in this study.

In her previously mentioned article, Rystad employs Bahktin's concept of polyphony to analyze two sermons directed to children. Through her discussion about analytical concepts, it becomes clear how communication is tied to authority in Bakhtin's thinking. In delineating both the monological and dialogical, Bakthin makes a distinction between scaffolding (words that are used to build up a monological discourse) and architectonic whole (words that are allowed to influence a dialogical discourse in a way that may lead to transformation and new perspectives). He also makes a distinction between, on the one hand, words that are part of an authoritative discourse that creates monologue, and, on the other, words that are part of and internally persuasive discourse that creates dialogue. In Rystad's interpretation of Bakhtin, authoritative words are words spoken from a distance, which gives an impression of their being more important than our own words, possessing a meaning that must either be accepted or rejected. An inner persuasive word "does not have status or authority and is tightly interwoven with our own words" (Rystad 2020, p. 111). It is creative and interacts with other inner discourses to cause change.

However, Rystad (2020) draws on Olga Dysthe to nuance Bakhtin's notion of authority. Alongside both an authoritarian discourse based on power and tradition, and an inner persuasive discourse free from authority, there is a third discourse of authority based on trust and respect. According to Rystad, preachers often aim for the latter. In her case study, Rystad found that while the sermons started out as polyphonic—particularly through the aid of the mediational means—both sermons ended up as monologues when the preacher stepped in at the end with authoritative words and proclaimed the message of what "all of this truly meant" (p. 45). Rystad concludes that "Polyphony is the most important consideration when laying the groundwork for dialogical interaction with a preaching event. Polyphony helps create a threshold space in which authoritarian discourses are challenged and narratives re-interpreted" (Rystad 2020, p. 124).

It is no wonder that Rystad makes this move. Authority is not just a key research area in the field of digital religion. Ever since Fred B. Craddock's *As One without Authority* (1971), the question of authority has been at the forefront of homiletics.[9] The issue of authority has been particularly important to homileticians who argue for conversational and/or dialogical approaches, like polyphonic preaching. These scholars tend to trace the development of homiletics and build their argument in relation to authority. As for example the homiletical contribution of John McClure (2001) in his landmark book *Other-wise Preaching* According to McClure,

> preaching is exiting itself through the doors of many deconstructions or gradual otherings. Among these are deconstructions of self, culture, scripture, reason, language, metaphysics, tradition, even of the word itself. Most specifically [...] preaching is exiting

through the deconstructions of the four overlapping authorities that have bequeathed preaching to us: the authority of the Bible, the authority of tradition, the authority of experience, and the authority of reason. (p. 2)

McClure not only launches his homiletical theory in relation to changes in the understanding of authority, but he also writes his overview of the development of the homiletical field to show how homileticians over the years have tried to grapple with the deconstruction of authority. His own solution, which draws on Emmanuel Levinas's idea of "the human other as a site for the revelation of the Holy other," argues for a conversational approach (pp. 47–59).

Authority is also at the center of discussion in Casey Thornburgh Sigmon's thesis "Engaging the Gadfly: A Process Homilecclesiology for a Digital Age" (Sigmon 2017), one of the few longer, in-depth contributions to the homiletical field that specifically engages with preaching in digital culture. According to Sigmon, digital media sheds light on how preaching has been caught in a "pulpit-pew binary," where the pulpit represents the locus of authority and the pew the attentive, silent audience. Sigmon points out that the pulpit and pew easily fall into the dualistic framework in the Western Christian tradition, which justifies one part's dominance over the other. Furthermore, the binary hinges on static, substance-oriented categories often regarded as unchangeable truth (ibid., pp. 5–6).

According to Sigmon, homileticians have tried to solve the problem of the pulpit-pew binary since the 1960's, and she describes a movement towards more relationality and mutuality. However, since the homileticians have not had a clear understanding of the problem, they have not completely solved the problem. In an overview of different approaches to the problem of authority and asymmetric power relations, Sigmon discusses both the New homiletic movement and Otherwise homiletics, as well as feminist, post-colonial, and postmodern perspectives, and while she acknowledges the different tactics to handle the pulpit-pew binary problem, she claims that none of them have actually solved the problem.

She hopes that digital culture will prompt homileticians and preachers to create a preaching event that takes an "exit from the house of the sanctuary," and thus will avoid being delimited by liturgy, architecture, and strictly oral-aural relations. Sigmon underlines that this change does not come about by itself, since digital culture is an algorithmic, capitalist system that can be every bit as problematic as the classic Western binary schema. To avoid the negative effects of digital culture, there need to be "theo-ethical norms" to guide its development. Sigmon draws on process theology to describe such a theology of preaching, calling it a "homilecclesiology" (pp. 16–33).

Especially important to Sigmon in her vision of homilecclesiology is the preaching priesthood of all believers. The contribution of unordained laypeople who lack theological training should define the work of the ordained preachers, whose task it is toto build up the laypeople for the task of interpreting and communicating God's words and actions. The preachers are to model the interpretation of sacred texts and traditioned dogmas in relation to culture through their own words and actions, in particular from the pulpit. Authority ought to be relational, no one should assume power over others, and there can be no imposition of truths and timeless statements (pp. 169–87). Sigmon concludes:

> Rather than seeking to become the authority on everything for the church, we seek to cultivate in the laity a sense of their own authority and capacity to challenge the grasp of unidirectional authorities on their life. [...] They [preachers] cultivate the ability to affirm, embrace, and expect ever-growing complexity and beauty without losing Christianity's spiritual center and identity among different realities. (p. 185)

She also offers a few suggestions of how this could be done in practice, both on digital platforms (social media) and in hybrid engagement when technology serve to disrupt the monologue from the pulpit (pp. 200–15).

Though Sigmon does not discuss Bakhtinian approaches to preaching in her overview of different homiletical approaches to the "problem" of authority, I would argue that her vision of authority seems to share traits the polyphonic preaching discussion. with Bakhtin's thoughts on a relational authority. The notion of authority described by Lorensen and Rystad seems quite similar, not only to Sigmon's vision of a homilecclesiology suited for a digital culture, but also to the notion of relational authority as described by Campbell's digital strategists and the participants in this case study. In other words, polyphonic preaching is well-suited as a tool for homiletical discussion of the results from exploration of RDCs' engagement in the preaching event.

3. When Do the RDCs Engage in the Preaching Event?

In order to envision when the RDCs engage in the preaching event, I will use Engemann's (2019, pp. 1–13) description of the communication and comprehensions processes involved in the preaching event. Engemann divides the preaching event into several phases of text interpretation and text production. First, there is the Phase of Tradition, in which the authors of the Bible interpreted the biblical events and produced the Bible text. Next comes the Phase of Preparation, when the preacher, as author, interprets the Bible texts and produces a sermon manuscript. Then comes the Phase of Verbalization, when the preacher, as sender, interprets his or her sermon manuscript and produces the delivery of the sermon. The final stage, according to Engemann, is the Phase of Realization, in which the listener interprets the delivery of the sermon and produces the auredit (Latin for "what is heard). All these phases takes place in a specific context that contributes to the processed of interpretation and communication. Below is visualization of that process (Figure 1):

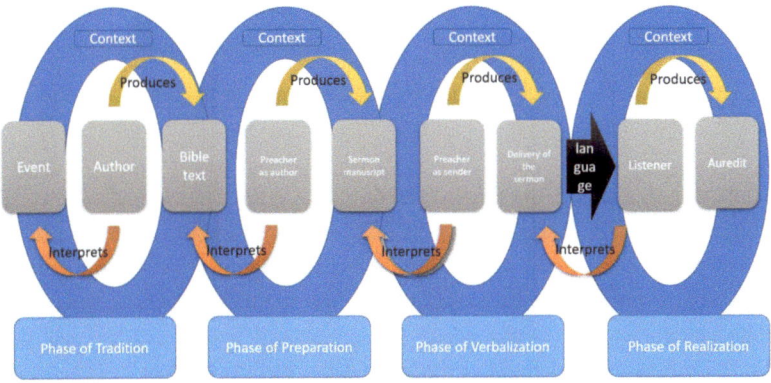

Figure 1. Engemann's diagram of the preaching event.

When the RDCs come into the interpretation and production process of the digitally mediated preaching event, the process is affected in several ways. One important factor that decides how the preaching event is affected is which kind of digital technology—the mediational means—is involved. In this study, the sermons were pre-recorded on Tuesdays, edited during the following days, and published at a certain time later in the week (1 PM on Fridays in Järfälla and 10 AM on Sundays in Täby). Both communities published the sermons on the congregation's website and on Facebook, Youtube, and Instagram. When this study's RDCs, with their particular use of digital technology, are inserted into Engemann's diagram (Figure 2), the processes of interpretation and production changes.

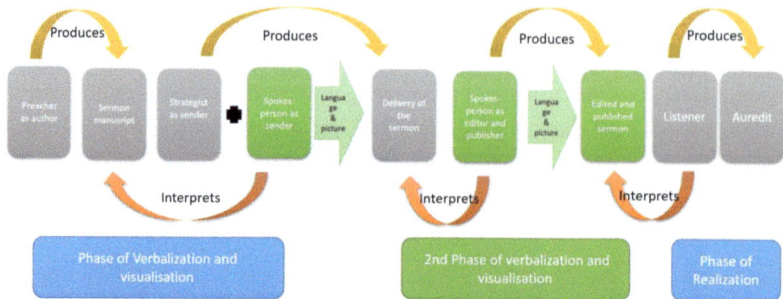

Figure 2. The Religious Digital Creatives (RDCs) involvement in the digitally mediated preaching event.

While the phases of tradition, preparation, and realization remain the same in many ways, the phase of verbalization changes. The strategist is no longer the sole interpreter of the sermon manuscript. She is accompanied by the spokespersons who record the sermon. As mentioned above, the technicians are intensely involved in the worship service where the sermon is delivered and, as I will show, directly influence the delivery of the sermon as well as its content.

This change draws attention to how the verbalization phase is not just a phase of the spoken word. It is a phase of verbalization *and* visualization. While it in one sense always has been[10], the visual character of the preaching event is emphasized.

This is in line with an increased emphasis on the visual in contemporary culture. In their overview of visual culture studies, Promey and Brisman (2010, pp. 188–91) show that the notion of contemporary culture as "hypervisual" has grown in importance. They refer to the work by Nicholas Mirzoeff, who argues that contemporary culture has a tendency to picture or visualize experience and create meaning through pictures rather than written words, a tendency linked to the development of digital technology.

Furthermore, in these two cases, a second phase of verbalization and visualization is introduced through the churches' particular use of digital technology. The listeners no longer interpret the delivery of the sermon; instead, they interpret the *edited* version of the sermon. If the listeners access the sermon from a social media platform, they get yet another additional layer of interpretation: the spokespeople's description of the sermon that accompanies and frames the recording. In the following section, how the strategists and spokespeople engage through each phase will be described in detail.

4. How Do the RDCs Engage in the Preaching Event?

4.1 Engagement in the First Phase of Verbalization and Visualization

The two categories of RDCs considered here engaged in several ways during the first phase of verbalization: through visualization and mediational means, through direction, and through changes to the sermon's content.

As mentioned earlier, during the recording sessions the spokespersons were in charge. They arrived early to the recording location to set up cameras, microphones, lights, and other technical equipment. If the recording took place inside a church, they would adapt the space in different ways to suit their needs. The spokespersons in Järfälla stated that "Everything visual is our responsibility". When asked if they ever discuss the visual with the strategists, they said:

> Some preachers have very clear ideas and thoughts and wishes, and we try to incorporate that if it is possible, suitable, and looks good. But most, in particular pastors, just want to get up and do their thing and do not think about how they stand and how it looks.[11]

They continued to explain how they strive to include the atmosphere from the location, and not just from the preacher's perspective. This was confirmed in the observations. The setting of the recording space varied every time in relation to what the spokesperson thought would catch the atmosphere of, for example, the liturgical year, the theme of the Sunday, or the theme of the sermon (if they had been told what it was in advance). They could also choose a location inside the church that showcased something they thought the participants/viewers would appreciate and meditate on, like a painting or an artifact. Sometimes they chose locations or artifacts that the worshippers would not normally see were they listening from the pew. In other words, the spokespeople were deeply engaged in choosing mediational means intended to interact with the strategists' words.

The spokespersons in Järfälla could also choose a location outside of the church, for example a garden, a square, the cemetery, the children's corner in the parish hall. In those cases, the choice often made in consultation with the strategist. This kind of collaboration with strategists was much appreciated by the spokespersons, since it allowed for creative work and mutual exchange. The spokespersons got inspiration for how the sermon could be visualized, and they were also able to inspire the strategists. It is worth noting that the authority emerging here, both in words and action, is relational authority.

The spokesperson—the communications director—in Täby, who also doubled as technician during the recording sessions, worked in the same way. He came early to prepare and chose the location, camera angles, and mediational means and to set the scene for what he called "the right atmosphere". During one of the observations, there was a slight dissonance between the spokesperson's choice of location and visualization, and the words of the strategist's sermon. The worship service was to be published on All Saint's Day, and the strategist—who had assumed the recording would take place in the old 13th Century church—had chosen to talk about the life of one of the saints depicted in the medieval paintings in the roof of the church. When the team met on the morning of the recording session, she found out that the spokesperson had chosen a modern church that possessed a very large, beautiful globe for lighting candles. During All Saint's weekend, it is very common for people in Sweden to light candles on graves and in churches, and the spokesperson wanted to feature that in the video. He also wanted to include something about the possibility for people to light a digital candle at the CoS's website. After some negotiation, they agreed that the recording session would take place in the modern church after all, but the picture in question would be added during the editing of the recording. The preacher added a paragraph to the sermon about lighting candles.

Just like his counterparts in Järfälla, the spokesperson in Täby reported that most of the strategists let him take full responsibility for the visualization, but a few strategist's wanted to partake in planning how the sermon and worship service should be envisioned. Likewise, he preferred collaboration since it enabled a creative working environment. He mentioned an example that he was particularly pleased with: a worship service with a pilgrimage theme in which they walked during the recording session. This had required a lot of discussion and negotiation on how he could envision the strategists' words along the path, and how his choice of imagery could be verbalized by the strategist.

The spokespersons also engaged through directions. In both churches, they directed the delivery of the sermon in detail. They told the strategists where to stand, look, how to talk, how to interact with the technology, and even what to wear (for example avoid liturgical clothing in certain situations). When asked about this, the spokesperson in Täby commented that he, in addition to the directions we had observed, often also had to instruct the strategist on style, tone of voice, facial expressions and so on.

When the strategist (pastor) in Täby was asked about her thoughts on these directions (in particular, being told not to wear liturgical clothes), she commented:

> If we are a team and we need to make decisions as a team, and then no one's opinion can be superior. And [the communications director] obviously has a reason for it. Even if I do not understand exactly what it is, I have to let this process grow and see if it turns out well. Perhaps he will say: it turned out the way I wanted, and then I will understand.

Both here and in the example of the negotiation about sermon location, the authority that emerges in words and actions is relational. That authority is negotiated through communicative interaction in an interdependent relationship.

This strategist was not the only one who appreciated directions. On the contrary, according to the spokespeople in both Järfälla and Täby, the strategists often asked for them, especially in the beginning of the transition to digital worship services during the pandemic. The Järfälla spokespeople were sometimes even asked to review the sermon manuscript beforehand. Here, there is a slight difference between the two congregations. As earlier mentioned, the spokesperson in Täby suggested changes to the sermon manuscript that the strategist accepted, an example of relational authority. In Järfälla, the spokespeople stated that they tried to be careful not to control the content of the sermon manuscripts and that they thought it was "very strange to poke around in someone's sermon". They would only weigh in when they were asked to do so.

In other words, the spokespersons' starting point was a role-based authority, one that they were accustomed to from their lengthy service as wardens in the local worship services. However, in the digitally mediated service, they were invited to wield relational authority and consequently did. The Järfälla spokespersons stated that the invitations had been more common in the beginning of the pandemic. They thought the preachers had listened to their feedback and had improved the content of their sermons over time. The spokespersons felt that the strategists had learned to compress their sermons, keeping them short and to the point and delivering them with a personal and casual style.

In sum: the digital spokespersons engaged in the preaching event through visualization of the sermon manuscript, the choice of mediational means, the giving of direction, and the occasional advising on the content of the sermon. In this engagement, there are traces of role-based authority emerging in the spokespeople's narratives, but a relational authority is prominent and emerges in practices and narratives, as enabled and encouraged by the digital mediation.

4.2 RDC Engagement in the Second Phase of Verbalization and Visualization: Editing

The engagement of the RDCs in the preaching event created a second phase of verbalization and visualization: editing. In the editing process, it was mainly the spokespersons that were engaged in adding b-roll imagery, texts, and sound.[12] In all cases, the goal of these additions was to enhance or contextualize comment on the message of the delivered sermon.

An example of how the use of b-roll imagery could enhance the delivered sermon can be found in the previously mentioned All Saint's sermon. The spokesperson and the strategist negotiated that the sermon was to be recorded in the modern church, and the painting from the medieval church would be added during editing. When asked about this, the spokesperson thought the editing facilitated the visibility of the painting. Onsite, in the church, the picture was difficult to spot since it was located near the roof at the entrance of the church, and was thus impossible to see if you were seated in the pews. Online, the picture was easier for the viewer to see since the editing included a closeup where the picture's colors and outlines were enhanced. The effect enhancing the painting was that the preacher's words also were enhanced. As the preacher named and explained the saint's particular attributes, the relevant details were highlighted.

The team in Järfälla also frequently added pictures and clips of artifacts, art, surroundings, and other meditational means in the editing process. The spokespersons (technicians) in charge of editing reported that they had an extra hard drive with such material. When asked about how they selected what to include and where to place it, the spokespersons said that they would usually get inspiration after listening to the sermon. They were extremely positive about being able to contribute in this way: "Wow, here we can help and contribute to what they are trying to say through imagery". They gave an example of a pastor who, during Advent, preached on the theme "make way for the Lord," and brought his son's tiny toy car as "prop". The strategist's sermon related to the movie *Cars*, and how the main character, the racing car Lightning McQueen, was sentenced to repair the road he had accidentally destroyed. At first, he tried to do it quickly and sloppily, but then he learned that it was better to do it diligently and slowly. Taking it slow also allowed for detours where Lightning McQueen got to know others including the judge in the town (whom the strategist interpreted as a God figure). The preacher concluded by asking what would be the best way of preparing our hearts for Christmas: fast and expensive, or to take small, slow steps and allow for detours?

To the spokespersons, it had been natural to add a stop-motion animation in the end with the toy car, showing how it drove by slowly, taking a couple of turns. In this way, they wanted to enhance and comment on an element of the sermon that they thought was important.

The spokespersons in Järfälla also stated that they tended to work more with imagery when the preacher had structured their sermon in relation to a metaphor or "prop" of some kind. In addition, according to them, this practice of bringing in mediational means had increased dramatically among the preachers in the digitally mediated preaching events. In the subsequent focus group conversation, the spokespersons and strategists discussed the reasons for this and concluded that the digital format encouraged the use of mediational means. Interestingly, the reason for this was not just because it was easier to preach from an artifact or art when you were sure that the listeners would actually see it (for example, a tiny toy car would be very difficult to spot from the pews). The strategists also testified that it made them feel that they were less "lonely" in the delivery of the sermon. They saw it as another "body" with which to share the camera's attention.

The spokesperson in Täby worked in similar ways when editing. He added pictures from a variety of shots including imagery that he thought would suit the delivered sermon. Interestingly, in the conversation about this practice, the musician mentioned that she worked in similar ways with her choice of music, for example during funerals. According to her, it happened quite often that she had planned to play certain music during the funeral service, but after hearing the funeral sermon, she changed to something that she thought would enhance or even comment on the message. Both the musician and the pastor in the team commented that they appreciated the communications director's work on imagery, and that they thought it enhanced or even brought new dimensions to the message of the sermon. The pastor, especially, thought it was very interesting "to hear how he thinks in pictures, and how he thinks they [words and pictures] are theologically connected".

Of course, more than pictures could be added during editing. Sound or text could also be added. For instance, in Täby, the music from the hymns could be added to the opening and/or closure of the sermon, which functioned in similar ways as the musician's choice of music during the funeral service: as a contextualization of or enhancement of what the communications director thought was an important message in the sermon. In Järfälla, the communications director captioned the sermons, interpreting the spoken language of the preacher into textual language.

In sum: the digital spokespersons engaged by adding visual, aural, and textual enhancement or contextualization of what the they thought were important parts of the digital strategists' sermon message. The strategists engaged by adapting to the increased visual dimension of the sermon and the spokespersons' directions. Notably, the collaboration between these particular strategists and the spokespersons was characterized by negotiation and trust. While there were no instances when, for example, the choice of b-roll imagery obscured or contradicted the strategists words, it could potentially have occurred since the strategists did not review the spokespersons' choice of additions before publication in digital media. The spokespersons' interpretation and idea about what messages are important to enhance or convey is even clearer in the publication part of the second phase of verbalization and visualization.

4.3 RDC Engagement in the Second Phase of the Verbalization and Visualization Process: Publishing

When publishing the delivered, edited sermon, the spokespersons (communications directors) followed the rules of engagement in social media: they chose a thumbnail, a small image representation of the content of the recording of the worship service. They also wrote a short accompanying text—often a summary of the theme or content of the sermon—to encourage those who encountered the sermon on the church's website or social media channels to watch the video. In this way, yet another layer of interpretation and production was added to the process. Notably, the core messages presented in social media were not always the same as the preachers' core message in the sermon itself. Take, for instance, the All Saint's sermon which was previously mentioned.

As discussed, the spokesperson wanted to pay attention to the practice of lightning candles on graves and in churches during the All Saint's feast. The strategist adapted her sermon to accommodate that wish, and the sermon was recorded with the preacher standing next to the candleholder in the back of the church. This was mirrored in the publication phase. The main part of the sermon was the strategist's original sermon where she spoke about the saint as an example of how having Jesus as a light in your life, and how living your life with a firm hope of paradise, can affect your whole life. However, the sermon's framing in social media did not mention that at all. Instead, it included a thumbnail picture of the preacher next to the globe of light, with a text that read: "During the All Saint's weekend we remember those who have passed away. On [link to website] you can light a digital candle for someone you miss and watch it burn alongside candles lighted by other people. You are not alone in your grief".

A second example can be found in the Järfälla church. In this case, the sermon was on John Chapter 4. The strategist started by asking if the listener had heard about "the woman at the well who met Jesus," and painted a picture of a woman who was cast out and living in shame. However, when she met Jesus she became a "living advertisement poster" for Jesus. It was not an advertisement as in trying to sell a product, but:

She advertises because she is deeply touched by what he has said. He tells her about her life and it is true. She responds in honesty, bares herself. She dares to stand there with her shame and meets the man who will totally change her life. She receives the living water and wants to pass it on to others. The story is about us. We get to be living advertisement posters, here and now, with a message about love. A message that goes beyond what we can think and imagine, where there is no room for shame and self-loathing, and we are surrounded by love, grace, and mercy, where we can live in love, here and now, and pass it on to the people we meet, just like that woman went to others and told them about the meeting with the man who had told her everything.

In social media, the communications director wrote: "Maybe shame can't get a hold on someone who has been seen for who they truly are? Reflect together with [pastor] who tells the story about the woman at the well in the first digital worship service of the year. From St Luke's church".

The message about passing love on and our calling to preach a message of love in our everyday life was omitted. Instead, the spokesperson chose to emphasize the part about shame and being seen. In this case, there is a shift in content. Instead of the strategist's message about how Jesus changed the woman's life and wiped away her shame (sin) with grace and mercy, the spokesperson's message was that it is difficult for shame to even get a hold of someone who is seen for who they really are. A smaller but important difference: the description of the woman had changed from "the woman at the well who met Jesus," as the pastor wrote, to "the story about the woman at the well".

When asked about this practice in the first interview, the communications director in Järfälla smiled and said: "Oh, you caught on to me!" She continued to acknowledge that in a way she was doing the short summary as a translation to non-theologians in relation to her own experience of being interested in spirituality and theology, but "would probably not qualify as Christian, believing Christian, like pastors and people like that". Yet, she thought that Christian faith had been important to her, and that it could be important to others, if they are not excluded or turned away by a "churchy" language. In the final interview, she stated:

> What is my goal? It is to do a short summary, make accessible what [the sermon] is about, if possible in an unchurchy way [...] and I just try to formulate it without thinking too long or too deeply. In the beginning it just made me come into biblical formulations, and I thought that this will sound nice to the pastors, and to the people who do not read the Bible it is going to sound like gibberish. [laughs] And I thought about it: what am I trying to do? [...] If we are trying to meet as wide target audience as possible, then it is worth trying to not exclude the people who do not read the Bible.

Here we may note several interesting things. First, the spokesperson talks about her authority as role-based. According to her, she merely "packs" or "translates" the message. This is in line with the digital spokespersons described by Campbell, who emphasized that their work was not about theological interpretation but about making the message of the church accessible. However, as shown in the example above, the reality is that the adaptation to a format and style that suits her understanding of contemporary secular culture and digital platforms is a theological interpretation in its own right. Furthermore, since this interpretation contextualizes the sermon to the listener, it contributes to the listener's own "auredit".

It is also important to note that her colleagues do not view her framing as mere translation but as collaboration and interpretation. When the rest of the team was asked about the digital spokesperson's work, they were very appreciative. For example, the other spokespersons (technicians) in Järfälla thought that "she writes amazing texts about the content of the worship service, that really encourages people to watch".

In sum: the spokespersons engaged in the preaching event through the framing of the delivered and edited sermon in social media. As shown above, they engage in many other ways including through editing, directing, altering of the sermon manuscript, enhancing, and contextualizing. The strategists' engagement is characterized by relational authority—authority as created and negotiated between different parties through communicative interaction in an interdependent relationship. The spokespersons' engagement is often characterized by relational authority. While their way of expressing themselves points to their being accustomed to wielding role-based authority, in practice they are often wielding a relational authority. How, then, might this engagement be understood?

5. How Can These Effects of RDC Engagement in the Preaching Event Be Understood?

5.1 It Can Be Understood as Co-Preaching

In relation to the homiletical discourse on polyphonic preaching, in which preaching is seen as a "dialogical, polyphonic co-authorship" that is created through various voices that supplement each other, I propose that the engagement of RDCs in the preaching event can be understood as co-preaching.

The engagement of the RDCs in the preaching event differs from the engagement in the roundtable conversations described by John McClure (1995), for example, where the preacher listens to others but ultimately serves as a curator of what should go into the sermon or not. In the conversational approach, the preacher is still very much in control.

In these two cases, however, the preacher/strategist no longer serves as a curator. The digital spokespersons have agency and authority in their own right, and it would be very difficult for the preacher/strategist to silence their voices if she wanted. This could explain why the strategists frequently mention the experience of loss of control. Notably, the loss of control is only mentioned as a problem in relation to the listeners who might misunderstand or scrutinize, not in relation to the spokespersons. On the contrary, they are regarded as gatekeepers who through their engagement described here will decrease the risk of misunderstandings (Mannerfelt and Roitto 2022b, pp. 74–75). The relational authority they practice and describe in their interviews also points towards something more than a regular conversational approach. This is mutual collaboration, a co-preachership.

Since the material for this case study was assembled within the framework of an action research project, the practitioners were introduced to the concept of RDCs and co-preaching and asked what they thought about this theory as an interpretation of their work. They all confirmed it, although one of the spokespersons, the communications director in Järfälla, was a bit reluctant at first. She again emphasized her role as translator who is only concerned with the form of the message, not the message itself. However, in the next interview two months later, she stated: "I think it was very interesting how we found out that what I'm writing— well, I feel that I have snuck into a preaching niche". The other RDCs confirmed that they indeed functioned as co-preachers; however the spokespersons' feelings about this were a bit ambiguous. They stated that it was empowering, but at the same time they recognized the stakes involved in this statement. As one of the spokespeople in the Järfälla team put it, half jokingly: the tack of co-preaching "is a great responsibility to put on three "morons". [like herself and her colleagues] Isn't that fatal?"

Though this digital form of co-preaching is new, co-preaching as practice is nothing new in the history of the Christian church. During late Antiquity and the Middle Ages, it was common for distinguished preachers to engage scribes who wrote down their sermons. The scribes also interpreted and edited the sermons, thus contributing to the content. Bernard of Clairvaux and Nicholas of Montiéramey are, together, an example of such "co-preaching" (de Gussem 2017, pp. 190–225). In some churches, it is an established practice to interrupt the preacher if the Holy Spirit encourages you to say something. The practice of call and response could also be called co-preaching (Crawford 1995; Richards-Greaves

2016; Thomas 2016). When it comes to the practice of framing the sermon, this also occurs in some communities, for example when the preacher is introduced or when the worship leader is praying for the preacher and/or the sermon before or afterwards. Sometimes the worship leader gives a summary of the sermon afterwards (Halldorf 2018, pp. 144–53).[13] Singing could also be seen as a practice of co-preaching, as is very evident in the revival movements.[14] As I noted above, the musician in Täby also made this parallel.

Furthermore, there might be others involved in a digitally mediated preaching event who could be considered co-preachers. As I have discussed elsewhere, people who comment on and share sermons in social media could be understood as co-preachers (Mannerfelt 2020, p. 209).

No matter who the co-preachers are, a consequence of co-preachership is that it may facilitate polyphony.

5.2 It Can Be Understood as Enabling Polyphony

The polyphonic preaching approach also aids in understanding how the co-preaching in these two cases, enabled as it is through digital media, effectively makes the preaching event more polyphonic. More voices contribute, including those of persons and mediational means. In these cases, it is not as with Rystad's preachers who started out with polyphony but fell into old patterns of "one single harmonized voice". The dialogical polyphony held up all the way, for better... or worse.

Indeed, it is worth asking what happens when the voices in the polyphony belong to people without formal theological education and who have not been ordained—or as the practitioners in Järfälla very pejoratively put it: "morons"—have such a large influence on the preaching event. Is there not a risk that the message of the gospel becomes contorted? As mentioned earlier, this is discussed by Sigmon (2017, pp. 178–80, 185–87), who in her homilecclesiological vision underlines the importance of preachers building up laypeople for the task of interpreting and communicating God's words and actions. The preachers' own preaching must model how the sacred texts and traditioned dogmas can be interpreted and communicated, while also helping them both to acknowledge their own authority and to discern when they are subordinated to unjust authority by others. Sigmon's proposition points to the importance of a concept like co-preaching, which reveals that spokespersons (and perhaps other types of RDCs) are actively partaking in the interpretation of the message of the church.

Finally, while the digitally mediated preaching events could be said to enable polyphonic preaching through the engagement of co-preachers, there are certain limitations to the polyphony, limitations that are caused by the very same digital mediation. In a discussion on liturgy in digital spaces, art historian Johannes Stückelberger points to the fact that the choice of camera angles and visual content affects how the words of the preacher are interpreted. This means that the pictures included in a digitally mediated worship service are not just contributing to an atmosphere, they are liturgical elements that create a dialogue with the sermon. However, at the same time as digital mediation enables new constellations of visualization and verbalization that would otherwise be impossible in the onsite church, it also delimits the listener's choice of which visual element will contribute to the interpretation. The listeners cannot let their gaze wander around the church and choose something else, for the camera and editor are directing it (Stückelberger 2021).

6. Summary

This case study of six digitally mediated preaching events in two Church of Sweden (CoS) Stockholm-area congregations aimed to describe and discuss what happens when the use of digital technology introduces new human actors into the preaching event. These actors were identified as "Religious digital creatives" (RDCs), a concept coined by Heidi Campbell in her study of religious authority and new media. The case study involved RDCs from the categories "digital strategist" (pastors and musicians) and "digital spokesperson" (technicians and communications directors).

The research questions that guided the study were "When and how do the RDCs engage in the preaching event?" and "How can these effects of RDC engagement in the preaching event be understood?" The source material consisted of observations, individual and focus group interviews, recordings of the services, and screen shots of how the recordings were presented when they were published on the congregations' websites and social media platforms. This material was analyzed with regard to their practices, how they understood those practices, and what kind of authority that emerged in those doings and sayings.

I found that the RDCs in this case study engaged in the preaching event in the verbalization phase, turning it into a phase of both verbalization *and* visualization. In addition, their engagement introduced a second phase of verbalization and visualization. More specifically, the RDCs engaged through editing direction, altering the sermon manuscript, enhancing, commenting, and framing. The RDCs' engagement was characterized by relational authority, that is authority created in negotiation through communicative interaction in a mutual and interdependent relationship.

The results was discussed in the light of the concept polyphonic preaching, that draws on the communication theory of Michail Bakhtin to describe preaching as dialogical and listeners as co-authors or even the primary authors of the sermon. In line with this, the RDCs were understood as co-preachers. The perspective of polyphonic preaching also shed light on how the practice of co-preaching increased and upheld the polyphony of voices that contributes to the dialogical character of the sermon.

Funding: This research received no external funding.

Institutional Review Board Statement: The study was approved by the Swedish ethical review authority and conducted in accordance with their guidelines.

Informed Consent Statement: Informed consent was obtained from all subjects involved in the study.

Data Availability Statement: The data are not publicly available due to privacy.

Conflicts of Interest: The author declares no conflict of interest.

Notes

[1] "Preaching event" is a concept that has become increasingly common in homiletical discourse. But just like the term "practice of preaching" (Rystad 2020, p. 19), it is not always clear what is meant by "preaching event," since the term has been used in a variety of ways over time. John Claypool (1980), one of the first to invoke the term, understands a preaching event as the event when the human utterances of the preacher become God's living words to the listeners. To other homileticians, it designates the situation (oral event) when the preacher is speaking to the listeners (Bruce 2013; Maddock 2017). The concept preaching event could also be understood as the event that occurs in performative situations where the preacher, listeners and message interact (Fahlgren 2006, pp. 43–47). Finally, the concept could also be employed like Wilfrid Engemann, who argues that since it is not entirely clear when the sermon actually becomes a sermon, it is important to keep all the parts of the process together in the analysis. The concept "preaching event" is therefore used to designate everything from the preparation phase to the moment the audience listens (Engemann 2019, pp. xix–xx). In this article, I draw on Engemann's broad understanding of the concept. As Linn Sæbø Rystad has argued, there are several benefits to conceiving of preaching as an event. It allows for understanding preaching as a practice, which in turn sheds light on how preaching is both "processual, performative and emerging" and radically relational. The term also highlights the importance of material entities like architecture, art, artifacts, and other visual aids for the meaning-making process (Rystad 2020, pp. 122–23).

[2] In this article, I use the concept actor in the same sense as it is used Bruno Latour (1999, pp. 120–23) in his Actor-Network Theory: an actor is something that acts or to which activity is granted by others.

[3] Church in Digital Space was a collaboration between the CoS diocese of Stockholm and University College Stockholm. It involved five researchers and seven congregations, and it was led by professor of practical theology Jonas Ideström and the bishop's theological advisor, Sara Garpe. The project took place between January 2021–September 2022 (Garpe et al. 2022). The research project was inspired by Theological action research (TAR) (see for example Watkins 2020), as well as the methods and concepts developed by Jonas Ideström (2015) and the bishop of the CoS diocese of Stockholm, Andreas Holmberg (2019). There are very few action research projects that focuses on homiletics, Boyd (2018) being an exception.

[4] As stated in the introduction to the research report, the starting point of action research consists of two ideas: (1) Research can contribute to solving actual problems and develop knowledge and skills; (2) Participants possess knowledge that could significantly contribute to the research process. Research is therefore carried out in collaboration between researchers and practitioners, who come together in a process of interpretation and reflection. Practitioners contribute with their experience and knowledge, while researchers contribute resources like methods, theories, and research from other contexts (Garpe et al. 2022, pp. 13–16).

[5] For a detailed description of how the source material was created, see (Mannerfelt and Roitto 2022a).

[6] Although not its primary purpose, the article does contribute to confirming Campbell's hypothesis by giving concrete examples of how religious institutions are, in fact, changed by their adoption of new media.

[7] In the following, I will refer to them with professional title and congregation, for example "pastor in Täby" or "technician in Järfälla".

[8] Before Lorensen, there are other Scandinavian theologians who have used Bakhtin in their homiletical reflection. See for Karlsson (2008), and Bjerg and Lynglund (2010). In addition, it is not just Scandinavian homileticians who have drawn on Bakhtin. See Harris (2004).

[9] Homileticians suggest various reasons for this. It could be a matter of hermeneutics—for example historical-critical Bible studies who challenged the idea of the Biblical text as a source of absolute truth and authority—or general societal developments like secularization, pluralism, or postmodernism (Mervin 1983; Brueggemann 1990; Tornfelt 2004; Davies 2007). Interestingly, digitalization is never mentioned as a reason for changes in the understanding of authority.

[10] Here we may notice that Engemann's model is an example of the phenomenon I discussed in the introduction. While he does acknowledge that materiality plays a role in the interpretation as part of the particular context, it tends to tread into the background as part of the overall context. The main foci in his homiletical discussion are the Bible text, the preacher and the listener, and consequently the phase is conceived as centered on words.

[11] This is briefly discussed also in the Evangelical Lutheran Danish Church (ELDC) research report on worship services during the COVID-19 pandemic. The choice of location in the local church space has theological significance. It also enables perspectives that would not normally be possible for the participant, like being face-to-face with a preacher who stands in the pulpit, or a bird's-eye view from the church ceiling. (*Når Folkekirken Skal Spille efter Reglerne—Men Uden for Banen Folkekirkens Håndtering af Coronaperioden i Foråret 2020* 2020, pp. 177–85).

[12] "B-roll" is a term used in film production that designates supplemental or alternative footage that intercut with the main shot.

[13] It is interesting to see that these kinds of introductions and summaries to elements of the services are practices that congregations tend to cut out in digital worship services (See Mannerfelt 2021, p. 100).

[14] One of the first and most well-known examples of a preacher-singer collaboration where the singer act as a sort of co-preacher is Dwight L. Moody and Ira D. Sankey. In the Swedish context there are several examples, like Nelly Hall and Ida Nihlén (Gunner 2003) and Lewi Pethrus and Einar Ekberg (Halldorf 2017, p. 216).

References

Bjerg, Svend, and Sten Lynglund. 2010. Den karnevalesque praediken: En anderledes homiletisk model. *Praesteforeningens Bla*d 100: 943–46.

Boyd, Jason. 2018. *The Naked Preacher: Action Research and a Practice of Preaching.* London: SCM Press.

Bruce, Sarah Katherine. 2013. The Vital Importance of the Imagination in the Contemporary Preaching Event. Ph.D. thesis, Durham University, Durham, UK.

Brueggemann, Walter. 1990. The Preacher, the Text, and the People. *Theology Today* 47: 237–47.

Campbell, Heidi. 2021. *Religious Creatives and the Rethinking of Religious Authority.* London and New York: Routledge.

Campbell, Heidi, and Ruth Tsuria, eds. 2021. Introduction to the Study of Digital Religion. In *Digital Religion: Understanding Religion in a Digital Age,* 2nd ed. London and New York: Routledge.

Campbell, Heidi, and Sophia Osteen. 2021. When Pastors put on the "Tech Hat": How Churches Digitized during COVID-19. The Network for New Media, Religion & Digital Culture Studies. Available online: https://oaktrust.library.tamu.edu/handle/1969.1/194959 (accessed on 1 August 2022).

Claypool, John. 1980. *The Preaching Event.* New York: Church Publishing Inc.

Crawford, Evans E. 1995. *The Hum: Call and Response in African-American Preaching.* Nashville: Abingdon Press.

Davies, Andrew. 2007. A New Teaching without Authority: Preaching the Bible in Postmodernity. *The Journal of the European Pentecostal Theological Association* 27: 161–72.

de Gussem, Jeroen. 2017. Bernard of Clairvaux and Nicholas of Montiéramey: Tracing the Secretarial Trail with Computational Stylistics. *Speculum* 92: 190–225.

Digital Economy and Society Index (DESI). 2022. Available online: https://digital-strategy.ec.europa.eu/en/policies/desi-sweden (accessed on 1 August 2022).

Engemann, Wilfrid. 2019. *Homiletics: Principles and Patterns of Reasoning.* Berlin: Walter de Gruyter.

Fahlgren, Sune. 2006. *Predikantskap och Församling: Sex Fallstudier av en Ecclesial Baspraktik Inom Svensk Frikyrklighet Fram Till 1960-Talet.* Örebro: ÖTH rapport.

Gaarden, Marianne, and Marlene Ringgaard Lorensen. 2013. Listeners as Authors in Preaching: Empirical and Theoretical Perspectives. *Homiletic* 38: 28–45.

Garpe, Sara, Jonas Ideström, and Frida Mannerfelt. 2022. Inledning. In *Kyrka i Digitala Rum: Ett Aktionsforskningsprojekt om Församlingsliv Online*. Edited by Sara Garpe and Jonas Ideström. Uppsala: Enheten för Forskning Och Analys.

Gunner, Gunilla. 2003. *Nelly Hall: Uppburen och Ifrågasatt*. Uppsala: Swedish Institute of Mission Research.

Halldorf, Joel. 2017. *Biskop Lewi Pethrus: Biografi Över Ett Ledarskap—Religion och Mångfald i det Svenska Folkhemmet*. Skellefteå: Artos.

Halldorf, Joel. 2018. Mötet i frikyrklighet och väckelse. In *Kristen Gudstjänst—En Introduktion*. Edited by Stina Fallberg Sundmark. Skellefteå: Artos.

Harris, James Henry. 2004. *The Word Made Plain: The Power and Promise of Preaching*. Minneapolis: Fortress Press.

Holmberg, Andreas. 2019. *Kyrka i Nytt Landskap: En Studie av Levd Ecklesiologi i Svenska Kyrkan*. Skellefteå: Artos Academic.

Ideström, Jonas. 2015. Implicit Ecclesiology and Local Church Identity. Dealing With Dilemmas of Empirical Ecclesiology. In *Ecclesiology in the Trenches: Theory and Method under Construction*. Edited by Sune Fahlgren and Jonas Ideström. Eugene: Pickwick Publications, pp. 121–38.

Karlsson, Jonny. 2008. *Predikans Samtal: En Studie av Lyssnarens Roll i Predikan hos Gustaf Wingren Utifrån Michail Bachtins Teori om Dialogicitet*. Skellefteå: Artos.

Kaufman, Tone Stangeland, and Hallvard Olavsson Mosdøl. 2018. More than Words: A Multimodal and Socio-material Approach to Understanding the Preaching Event. In *Preaching Promises within the Paradoxes of Life*. Stellenbosch: African Sun Media, pp. 123–32.

Latour, Bruno. 1999. Technology is Society Made Durable. In *Sociology of Monsters: Essays on Power, Technology and Domination*. Edited by John Law. London and New York: Routledge.

Lorensen, Marlene Ringgaard. 2011. Carnivalized Preaching—In dialogue with Bakhtin and Other-Wise homiletics. *Homiletic* 36: 26–45.

Lorensen, Marlene Ringgaard. 2014. *Dialogical Preaching: Bakhtin, Otherness and Homiletics*. Göttingen: Vandenhoeck & Ruprecht.

Lorensen, Marlene Ringgaard, and Gitte Buch-Hansen. 2018. Listening to the voices: Refugees as co-authors of practical theology. *Practical Theology* 11: 29–41.

Maddock, Ian. 2017. "Like One of the Old Apostles": The Acts of the Apostles and George Whitefiel's Criteria for Describing Preaching Events. *Colloquium* 49: 55–65.

Mannerfelt, Frida. 2020. Back to the Roots or Growing New Branches: Preaching, Orality and Mission in a Digital Age. In *Missio Dei in A Digital Age*. Edited by Jonas Kurlberg and Pete Phillips. London: SCM Press.

Mannerfelt, Frida. 2021. Old and New Habits: The Transition to Digitally-Mediated Worship in Four Swedish Free Church Denominations during COVID-19. In *Svensk frikyrklighet i pandemin: En studie av församlingen i corona och corona i församlingen*. Edited by Ulrik Josefsson and Magnus Wahlström. Örebro: Forskningsrapporter från Institutet för pentekostala studier Nr. 9.

Mannerfelt, Frida, and Rikard Roitto. 2022a. Mellan rit och reklam del 1. In *Kyrka i digitala rem: Ett aktionsforskningsprojekt om församlingsliv online i Svenska kyrkan*. Edited by Sara Garpe and Jonas Ideström. Uppsala: Enheten för forskning och analys.

Mannerfelt, Frida, and Rikard Roitto. 2022b. Mellan rit och reklam del 2. In *Kyrka i digitala rem: Ett aktionsforskningsprojekt om församlingsliv online i Svenska kyrkan.* Edited by Sara Garpe and Jonas Ideström. Uppsala: Enheten för forskning och analys.

McClure, John. 1995. *The Roundtable Pulpit: Where Leadership and Preaching Meets.* Nashville: Abingdon Press.

McClure, John. 2001. *Other-Wise Preaching: A Postmodern Ethic for Homiletics.* St Louis: Chalice Press.

Mervin, Dick. 1983. Preaching with Authority. *Direction* 12: 14–22.

Når Folkekirken Skal Spille efter Reglerne—Men Uden for Banen Folkekirkens Håndtering af Coronaperioden i Foråret 2020. 2020. Folkekirkens Ud-dannelse-och videncenter. Available online: https://www.fkuv.dk/undersoegelser-og-viden/udgivelser-og-rapporter/nar-folkekirken-skal-spille-ef-ter-reglerne-men-uden-for-banen (accessed on 27 September 2022).

Promey, Sally M., and Shira Brisman. 2010. Sensory Cultures: Material and Visual Religion Reconsidered. In *The Blackwell Companion to Religion in America.* Edited by Philip Goff. Oxford: Blackwell.

Richards-Greaves, Gillian R. 2016. "Say Hallelujah, Somebody" and "I will Call upon the Lord": An Examination of Call-and-Response in the Black Church. *Western Journal of Black Studies* 40: 192–204.

Rystad, Linn Sæbø. 2020. Overestimated and underestimated: A Case Study of the practice of Preaching for Children with an Emphasis on Children's Role as Listeners. Ph.D. thesis, MF Norwegian School of Theology, Olso, Norway.

Schatzki, Theodore. 2019. *Social Change in a Material World.* London and New York: Routledge.

Sigmon, Casey Thornburgh. 2017. Engaging the Gadfly: A Process Homilecclesiology for a Digital Age. Ph.D. thesis, Vanderbilt University, Nashville, TN, USA.

Stückelberger, Johannes. 2021. Liturgie in Virtuellen Räumen: Der Raum in Online-Gottesdiensten. Available online: https://www.liturgik.unibe.ch/unibe/portal/fak_theologie/kompz_lit/content/e359272/e973272/e973422/e973425/Stuckelberger_Raumin Onlinegottesdiensten_ger.pdf (accessed on 26 August 2022).

Sundberg, Carina. 2008. Här är rymlig plats: Predikoteologier i en komplex verklighet. Ph.D. thesis, Karlstad University, Karlstad, Sweden.

Thomas, Frank A. 2016. *Introduction to the Practice of African American Preaching.* Nashville: Abingdon Press.

Tornfelt, John V. 2004. Preaching with Authority When You Don't Have It. *The Journal of the Evangelical Homiletics Society* 4: 23–50.

Watkins, Clare. 2020. Disclosing Church: An Ecclesiology Learned from Conversations in Practice. London and New York: Routledge.

Dissertationes Theologicae Holmienses

1. Eurell, John-Christian. *Peter's Legacy in Early Christianity: The Appropriation and Use of Peter's Authority in the First Three Centuries.* DTH 1. Stockholm: Enskilda Högskolan Stockholm, 2021.
2. Mannerfelt, Frida. *Co-preaching: The Practice of Preaching in Digital Culture and Spaces.* DTH 2. Stockholm: Enskilda Högskolan Stockholm, 2023.